Charles Francis Sheridan

A History of the Late Revolution in Sweden

Containing an Account of the Transactions of the three last Diets in that Country

Charles Francis Sheridan

A History of the Late Revolution in Sweden
Containing an Account of the Transactions of the three last Diets in that Country

ISBN/EAN: 9783337233587

Printed in Europe, USA, Canada, Australia, Japan

Cover: Foto ©ninafisch / pixelio.de

More available books at **www.hansebooks.com**

A HISTORY OF THE LATE REVOLUTION IN SWEDEN:

CONTAINING

An Account of the Transactions of the Three last DIETS in that Country;

PRECEDED BY

A short Abstract of the SWEDISH HISTORY,

So far as was necessary to lay open the true Causes of that remarkable Event.

BY

CHARLES FRANCIS SHERIDAN, Esq;

OF LINCOLN'S-INN,

And Secretary to the British Envoy in Sweden, at the Time of the late Revolution.

LONDON:

Printed for EDWARD and CHARLES DILLY, in the Poultry

M.DCC.LXXVIII.

ERRATA.

	For	Read
P. 43, l. 27,	*considerable,*	*inconsiderable,*
P. 147, note l. 2,	*Ambo*	*Abo.*
P. 176, note l. 1,	*Buddenbrog*	*Buddenbroke.*
P. 189 } 190 } 191 }	*Brake*	*Brabe*
P. 225, l. 9,	*produced by the labours of the English minister,*	*by the joint labours of the English and Russian ministers.*

There are two instances of false Paging; one, where 256 is followed by 259 instead of 257; and the other, where 322 is followed by 321; but the matter is right in both.

For *Christierne,* read *Christian, passim.*

Some other slight errors there may be, on account of the author's absence in another kingdom during the printing of this work.

INTRODUCTION.

THE prefent almoſt general ſubverſion of public liberty throughout Europe, furniſhes but too ſtriking and melancholy a proof, of the numerous, and as it ſhould ſeem irreſiſtible cauſes, which conduct men into a ſtate of political ſlavery.

Hitherto however theſe cauſes have been gradual in their operation; and the introduction of deſpotiſm among a free people, has, till now, been a work of time, as well as the reſult of an artful and inſidious policy.

Influenced by this conſideration, a free people may often have been lulled into a falſe ſecurity, with reſpect to their liberties, the loſs of which they may have conceived to be an event too remote to diſturb their preſent quiet; however the fate of other nations may have given them reaſon, at ſome period, to expect it.

They may have flattered themſelves, they could be in no immediate danger, till occurrences ſhould happen of a ſimilar nature, and the ſame ſyſtem of policy be purſued among them, which had in other countries been productive of the loſs of freedom.

Forgetful by what very different means the fa[r] ends may be accomplished, they might have be[-]held with the indifference of unconcerned spectators, measures in reality of the most dangerous tendency, yet whose object they either mistook, or would not be at the pains of discovering; and, deceived by an apparent respect paid to the forms of their constitution, they might have remitted that jealous attention, with which such a people should ever watch over their rights and privileges, till they had suffered the spirit of it to have been so far lost, as to awaken from their lethargy, perhaps to lament their folly, but too late to correct their error.

Nor is it surprising, that the bulk of a people should not be much alarmed at minute invasions of their constitution, made at separate and probably distant periods of time. Encroachments on their political, as long as their civil liberties remain untouched, do not come sufficiently home to individuals, to awaken their resentment, and rouse that spirit of opposition, so necessary to stop the farther progress of the usurpations of power; while a judicious prince will not attempt any fresh innovations, till the nation is become reconciled to those already introduced. Thus, together with the alterations in the government, change also the dispositions of the people: the designs of the governors, and inclinations of the governed, go hand in hand; and tyranny may steal as it were imperceptibly upon them, before they are aware of their danger.

But

But the late revolution in Sweden, which in one day produced a change as total, as it was sudden and unexpected: which in one day converted a government, supposed to be the most free of any in Europe, into an absolute monarchy: which was attended with a degree of facility in the execution, to be equalled only by the expedition with which it was accomplished: yet accomplished by means, in appearance so inadequate to the importance of the undertaking—This is an event, which, while it destroys the grounds on which a free people may hitherto have rested their security with respect to their liberties, must, at the same time, prevent for the future their any longer considering the loss of them as an object so remote as to admit of the smallest relaxation of that vigilance, with which they should ever attend to their preservation.

An attention the more necessary, as liberty, like honour, when once lost, is, for the most part, irrecoverably so.

If we look into the History of Europe, many are the instances which occur of free states submitting, by degrees, to the yoke of despotism: but we seldom, if ever, meet with an instance of a nation once completely enslaved, having recovered their liberties. So that the commonly-received axiom in politics, that all governments contain within themselves the principle of their destruction, seems unfortunately to hold good only with respect to those of a popular nature; while such as establish arbitrary power, appear, in a manner, exempt from the fluctuation generally incident to human institutions; and to be no otherwise affected by time, than to acquire stability in proportion to their duration.

The reason of this is so obvious, as scarce to need its being pointed out. A free government should be the just medium between the two extremes of despotism and licentiousness; and should equally avoid the oppression of the one, and the tumult and disorders attendant on the other. But as there is an almost natural tendency in the human mind to run into extremes, it will be found as difficult to obtain this just medium, as to preserve it when obtained: as such a government forms a system composed of a variety of parts, which ought to be duly fitted and proportioned to each other, the maintaining of an equilibrium among these parts, is a point as essential to its existence, as it is difficult to compass. For this purpose, a free people should understand as well as love their constitution; should know in what true liberty consists, as well as possess spirit to defend her when attacked; and have their minds sufficiently enlightened to direct and moderate that zeal and ardour, which should animate their breasts in the cause of freedom; but which, if unrestrained, by carrying them too great lengths, might rather endanger the loss, than secure to them the possession of it.

On the other hand, despotism, more simple in its nature, more uniform in its operations, is not liable to those internal disorders, to which free govern-

governments so often owe their ruin. *To obey*, sums up the whole duty of those who are bound to live under it. Whilst fear, ignorance, and prejudice, qualities by no means rare among mankind, are, perhaps, as well calculated to render them good subjects of such a government, as the contrary qualities of public spirit, resolution, liberality of mind, and freedom of sentiment, are found to be necessary in those, who are happy enough to possess a constitution, the object of which is political liberty.

It is not, therefore, to the complicated nature of a free, or simplicity of a despotic government, that we are alone to ascribe the precarious duration of the former, or stability of the latter; but likewise to the number of qualities requisite in the subjects of the one, in order to enable them to preserve it; whilst the other species of government will maintain its ground, whether those who are subject to it are possessed of such qualities or not.

But, at the same time that these reasons may serve to account for the revolutions to which free states have ever been so peculiarly liable; they might also teach us to expect, that liberty would flourish in proportion as the minds of men become enlightened: that in an age, in which the principles of society itself, have been considered as a science; the nature of government analyzed, ascertained, and reduced in some measure to a system: when, consequently, in proportion to the progress made in this science, and to the general increase

increase and diffusion of political knowledge among mankind, the benefits resulting from freedom, must not only be more universally known, but likewise the means of acquiring or preserving it, better understood: in such an age, it might have been expected, that liberty would have had some altars erected to her, where she had been forgotten or unknown before; and that she would have become doubly secure among those, who, already possessed of her, were well acquainted with her value. On the contrary, we need only give a glance over the present state of Europe, to perceive, that the very reverse of this has been the case. We shall find that liberty has been chased from some of the few asylums she had left; and that in most of the countries where monarchy was established, the regal power has, ever since the commencement of the fifteenth century, been constantly verging towards that despotism which at present prevails so universally throughout Europe. So that arbitrary power seems to have rivetted her chains the more strongly on the major part of the inhabitants of Europe, in proportion as they became more sensible of the advantages of freedom. And they must now content themselves with admiring the few monuments of public liberty yet extant; while they must patiently submit to that government, which the folly or ignorance of their ancestors, had suffered to establish itself too firmly, to render the destruction of it, at present, in any shape practicable.

Italy,

Italy, once filled with populous and independent cities, the seats of commerce, of riches, and of liberty, is, in general, governed by the hand of despotism. In the few states that still retain the name of Republics, the bulk of the people, in general, suffer a severer degree of oppression, than those are exposed to who acknowledge but one master.

The Swifs have indeed hitherto been indebted for their freedom, to their mountains, their poverty, and their bravery.

The ineffectual struggles for liberty of the Cortes in Spain, at the commencement of the reign of Charles the Fifth, answered no other purpose, than to give that monarch an opportunity of laying the foundation of the absolute power which his successors have since acquired.

Portugal has shared the same fate with Spain. The last revolution that happened in that kingdom, only gave the Portugueze a new master, but produced no change in favour of liberty.

In France, the ablest and most enterprizing of her ministers, under one of the weakest and most timid of her monarchs, unfortunately made the destruction of the small remnant of the liberties of that kingdom, which had escaped the artful and insidious policy of Louis the XIth, one of the chief objects of a long administration. He succeeded but too well; and whatever was left undone in this respect by Richelieu, was afterwards effectually compleated by Colbert.

To consider the little ceremony with which the French monarchs, at this day, treat their parliaments, and the real insignificancy of those bodies; which are become rather the instruments of the power of the sovereign, than the guardians of the rights of the people; one could hardly conceive, that those very parliaments were once the representatives of the states-general of the kingdom, in whom the supreme power was lodged, and who possessed an authority nearly similar to that once enjoyed by the states themselves.

The prodigious superiority of the houses of Austria and Brandenburg over every other power in the empire, certainly places the liberties of Germany, or rather the independence of the German princes, on the most precarious footing. The emperor, absolute in his hereditary dominions, (the generous spirit of the Hungarians having been long since subdued) seems to have no other barriers to the increase of his authority in the empire, than what his own moderation may lay down. It is certain, should their Imperial and Prussian majesties think proper to unite, for the purpose of carrying any particular point, the combined forces of the remainder of the Germanic body, would be scarcely capable of resisting them.

The maintaining of a balance of power among the different states of Europe, once considered as an object of such importance by them, seems, if we may judge from the partition of Poland, no longer to be held in the same light: the apprehension

prehension of the interference of any foreign power, would consequently prove no obstacle to the views of the above-mentioned monarchs, whenever ambition shall prompt them, or may hereafter their successors, to divide the spoils of the numerous petty princes of the empire.

The fate of Dantzick may likewise prove a lesson to the free cities, and teach them what they are one day to expect.

In Holland the government, it is true, nearly retains its form; but, since the office of stadholder has been rendered hereditary, it seems, in a great measure, to have lost its spirit. Attentive only to their mercantile interests, relying for their safety more on the divisions of their neighbours than on their own strength, the Dutch appear no longer to possess that martial and independent spirit which distinguished their ancestors; their attachment to liberty, which men feel strongest when she is most persecuted, must have abated in a proportional degree; so that the authority of the stadholder bids fair to equal that of any sovereign in Europe.

Poland, the nobility of which, at least, were the freest in the world, has fallen into the hands of two of the most absolute princes now existing, and into those of a third, who may become so whenever he pleases.

Denmark, a century since, made a voluntary surrender of its liberties into the hands of its monarch. The dreadful despotism of Russia is well known.

And

And now we behold a country, generally supposed to have possessed one of the most free governments that ever was established among any people, which has in one day been deprived of that government, and compelled to receive an absolute monarchy in its room. Thus arbitrary power seems, like a plague, to have spread itself over almost the whole face of Europe, from the coasts of the Mediterranean to the shores of the frozen ocean; whilst in these islands, liberty still finds a sanctuary, as if the sea had proved a barrier to stop the progress of the contagion.

Such is the present state of Europe, and such the progress made by despotism among its inhabitants, hitherto, indeed, with a slow yet steady and persevering step; but in this last instance with a sudden stride; notwithstanding there seems to prevail, in the present age, a knowledge of the nature of government, a freedom of sentiment, and a liberality of mind, not to be met with in any former period.

On the other hand, it was in an age of darkness and ignorance, compared to the present, that political liberty was most universally diffused throughout Europe; an age in which men, more accustomed to act than to reflect, possessed more spirit to defend their freedom, than judgment to lead them to the true means of preserving it: in which they had never considered government as a science; were ignorant of the nature and principles of power and liberty; and uninstructed by the fate of other nations,

nations, who, from having been free, had passed under the yoke of slavery, they could not foresee such consequences to themselves, and therefore could have had no idea of guarding against them.

The period I allude to is from the beginning of the thirteenth to the close of the fifteenth century *. To consider the forms of government at that time established in all the kingdoms of Europe; when the Spaniards told their sovereign in swearing allegiance to him: "We, who are "each of us as good, and all together more "powerful than you, promise obedience to your "government, if you maintain our rights and "privileges: if not, we do not."

When a king of France, in the prelude to one of his ordinances, expresses himself thus, "That "as all men were by nature *free born*, and as "their kingdom was called the kingdom of the "Franks, he determined it should be so in reality "as well as in name ‡." To consider, I say, the

---

* Montesquieu, in speaking of the origin of the Gothic government, says, " At first it was mixt with aristocracy and " monarchy; a mixture attended with this inconveniency, " that the common people were bondmen. The custom af- " terwards succeeded of granting letters of infranchisements, " and was soon followed by so perfect a harmony between " the civil liberty of the people, the privileges of the nobi- " lity and clergy, and the prince's prerogative, that I really " think there never was in the world a government so well " tempered as that of each part of Europe, so long as it " lasted." Vol. 1, book 11, chap. 8.

‡ Louis 10th Ordon. tom. 1. p. 583.

forms of government then established throughout Europe, and which lasted for the space of more than two centuries, it must afford matter of astonishment, how it was possible that nations once possessed of the most independent spirit, and the most enthusiastic love of liberty, should afterwards have degenerated into the tame subjects of arbitrary power.

I shall beg leave to hazard a few reflections to account for this; which I hope will not be deemed foreign to the main design of the present work, as they will serve to illustrate what I shall have to say hereafter, relative to the government of Sweden, and the various revolutions it has undergone.

Had the different sovereigns of Europe, acquired absolute authority over their respective subjects, during the course of the eleventh or twelfth centuries, there are many reasons which, upon a superficial view, would seem very naturally to account for it.

At those periods, and for a considerable time previous to them, the feudal system of government, almost universally established throughout Europe, had degenerated into a multiplied tyranny, and consequently the most insupportable of any. The usurpations of the feudal barons, had stripped their sovereigns of almost every prerogative, and reduced them to a state, in which they could neither protect a people groaning beneath the yoke of servitude, nor punish the petty tyrants who lorded it over them with as much
rigour

rigour as authority*. It would not have appeared in the least extraordinary, had the lower orders of a nation so circumstanced, united to transfer this authority from their respective masters to their common sovereign, and to have afforded him all the assistance necessary to enforce obedience to it. By this means they would have delivered themselves from the immediate oppression of their feudal lords (as tyranny is ever the more intolerable, the nearer we are placed to its centre) and would have had a secret satisfaction, inspired by revenge, in reducing their oppressors to a situation somewhat similar to their own. However, when the human mind becomes debased to a certain degree, by the depression of servitude, men are rendered not only incapable of executing any plan to rescue themselves from so miserable a state, but even of conceiving a remedy to the evils they labour under. Happily for the generations who immediately succeeded them, and perhaps too, for those few nations still possessed of freedom, the expedient above-mentioned did not occur to the oppressed people of those times; and it was owing to other causes, none of which originated with them, that they, at length, emerged from that wretched state of insignificance and obscurity, in which they had so long been plunged.

Among these, as set forth by a most elegant and judicious historian ‖, the forming of cities into

---

* As in Denmark, in the middle of the last century.
‖ Robertson: in his view of the State of Europe.

communities, corporations, or bodies politic, and granting them the privileges of municipal jurisdiction, was one of the principal.

The inhabitants of cities, whether artificers or merchants, would naturally, from the circumstances of their situation, be more independent of their lords than the peasants in the country, who cultivated the fields. Possessed of the means of acquiring riches, and united together, as it were, in one body, their strength and consequence must have increased with their commerce; and the feudal monarchs could not fail to perceive, that they might, in time, be made very instrumental in curbing the licentious spirit of the barons.

It was with this view, that Frederick Barbarossa, in Germany; Louis Legros, in France; and Henry the second, in England, adopted the plan of conferring certain privileges on the inhabitants of cities in their respective jurisdictions. These, under succeeding monarchs, acquired, in the persons of their deputies, a seat in the council of the nation, and consequently a share in the legislature of their country.

Here then a third power arose in the state, which at its commencement would naturally contribute to confer on the feudal monarchs, a sufficient degree of consequence and authority, to render the regal power a check upon the violence and oppression before exercised by the barons; but to which, this point being compassed, the latter

might

might in their turn have recourse, in order to stop the too great encroachments of their sovereigns. Thus, as in England, Henry the second raised the people in order to depress the aristocracy of the nobles, so under Henry the third the barons who rebelled called in the assistance of the people, to insure their success against the monarch.

Here then were three powers in the state, that, by being alternately opposed to each other, formed a species of balance; from which, during the space of upwards of two centuries, most of the nations in Europe derived and enjoyed no inconsiderable degree of liberty.

But as chance had a greater share than design in forming this balance; as the object of the sovereigns in taking those measures to which it owed its birth, had been only to increase their own power, not to establish liberty among their subjects; so it was maintained rather by the mutual jealousies that subsisted among the different orders of the state, than from any conviction in the minds of the people, of its utility and importance.

Instead of co-operating to form one system for the common benefit of the whole community, these three powers acted more as rivals; whose chief object seemed to be rather to encroach upon the rights and privileges of each other, than attend to the preservation of their own. As these were not ascertained with exactness, neither could they be known with precision; consequently, as that due proportion which should subsist between the constituent parts of a free state, must have

been

been wanting; the balance of power, on which the very existence of such states depends, could not be of long duration.

From the very nature of one of these three powers, it had obviously many advantages over the other two; I mean that of the monarch; which, with some other concurring circumstances, operated by degrees to raise it so far above, as finally in some manner to annihilate them, and establish itself in their room.

1st. The first and most obvious difference between the power of the monarch, and that of the nobles and the people, was the unity of the former; that is, its being possessed by *one*.

The clashing of interests and difference of opinion among the individuals of an assembly, (unacquainted with the true principles of government, as in those days popular assemblies must have been) although vested with an authority equal to that of the sovereign, might have rendered abortive the wisest schemes, and defeated the best-concerted measures: the prince had only to conceive and to execute; he had but one end in view, that of increasing his power: and, however the hands which held the reins of government might change, the same spirit would always conduct them, though with various success, according to the different abilities of the monarchs.

A variety of circumstances were, on the contrary, necessary, in order to give vigour and effect to the operations of the other two orders of the state. Men, who had been so lately galled

by

by the yoke of servitude, could not but preserve a secret enmity towards their former tyrants; and they would naturally more easily unite with their sovereign, to whom they were indebted for the new importance they had acquired, in order to depress the nobles, than join with these to check the encroachments of the prince.

Yet, though it was to the superiority they had contributed to give to their sovereign over the barons, that the people were first indebted for their liberty; in order to secure the preservation of that liberty, it was likewise necessary to prevent the too great depression of the nobles, which would have been the consequence of the too considerable increase of power in the prince.

There was a point, at which, they should have ceased to augment the authority of the latter, at the expence of the privileges of the former. At which, they should even have assisted the barons against their sovereign, in case he carried his pretensions too far.

But independent of the difficulty of ascertaining this point, which required, perhaps, greater skill, and more knowledge of the nature of government, than the people could, at that time, have been possessed of; in order to render such opposition of any efficacy, it was requisite there should be a union of two very different orders of men, between whom, there must have subsisted no small share of hatred and jealousy on one side, and an equal degree of contempt on the other. It would have been unreasonable to have expected unani-

C mity

mity in an assembly so composed; and unanimity alone could render them powerful. The measures, therefore, of the nobles and of the people were necessarily fluctuating, their object uncertain, and pursued with caution and distrust.

On the other hand, there were no such obstacles to prevent the monarch's uniting with either of the other two powers, as best suited his views or convenience.

His measures were not only fixed, ever tending to one end, but he was likewise possessed of a greater variety of means, to prosecute them with ease and certainty. To preserve an internal ballance of power, with the nature of which they were but little acquainted, should have been the object of the nobles and people; to overturn it, was that of the monarch: It is not hard to determine which of these two was the most difficult task.

2dly. Though one of the consequences of the establishment of the christian religion in Europe, was the enfranchisement of the peasants, who had before been slaves, fixed to the soil to which they belonged; yet the corruption of that religion *,

from

---

* When the christian religion, says Montesquieu, two centuries ago, became unhappily divided into Catholic and Protestant, the people of the North embraced the Protestant, and those of the South adhered still to the Catholic: the reason is plain, the people of the North have, and will for ever have, a spirit of liberty and independence, which the people of the South have not; and therefore a religion which

has

from the abuses of Popery, contributed, probably more than any other circumstance, to facilitate the execution of the designs formed by the European monarchs to acquire absolute power. "The "notion" (according to Lord Bolingbroke's observation) "concerning the divine institution and "right of kings, as well as the absolute power "belonging to their office, have no foundation in "fact or reason, but have arisen from an old al- "liance between ecclesiastical and civil policy."

This alliance sprung from the very nature of the Catholic religion: a religion, which claimed and obtained the most absolute empire over the consciences of mankind, could not but be an excellent instrument in the hands of a monarch, to establish his authority by governing through the ministers of it. These, on the other hand, must have perceived that their best security for preserving their dignities, wealth, and power, was their giving the prince the same authority over the persons of their subjects, that they had usurped over their minds.

In return for the immunities, privileges, and riches, conferred by their sovereigns on the clergy, these preached the doctrines of passive obe-

---

has no visible head, is more agreeable to the independency of the climate, than that which has one. Vol. II. Book 24th. Chap. 4.

The reason given by Montesquieu, why the Protestant religion is more favourable to liberty than the Catholic, is not the only one, though, perhaps, the only one he could venture to assign.

dience, non-resistance, &c. to the subjects of their benefactor; to whom they attributed a divine right to govern without controul.

The priests had likewise, perhaps, another motive for this conduct: that spirit of enquiry and freedom of sentiment, which must ever, in some degree, prevail among a people possessed of civil liberty, might have extended themselves, from political to religious matters; and this they apprehended would have sapped the foundation of a system, built upon ignorance, and supported by superstition.

The monarchs and priests playing thus into each other's hands, were enabled to dupe the rest of mankind out of what should seem their unalienable rights: and had not the reformation taken place, and had those princes in Europe who promoted it, known, how much it was their interest to prevent the introduction of the new doctrine into their respective realms, it is probable, there would not be at this day, a single state in Europe, possessed of the smallest share of political liberty. Henry the VIIIth in England, and Gustavus Vasa in Sweden, did not perceive, that by encouraging the reformation, they deprived their successors of one of the chief engines with which they were to acquire and maintain that absolute power, the foundations of which, they themselves had taken such pains to lay. Charles the Ist would never have made so tragical an exit, nor Sigismond of Sweden have lost his crown, nor the

States

States of Holland have shaken off the Spanish yoke, if the Catholic religion had continued to maintain its empire over the minds of men, with the same authority as it had done for many centuries previous to those events.

The violent persecutions the protestants underwent from some of the European monarchs, and the frequent attempts of these totally to exterminate them, did not, perhaps, proceed so much from fanaticism, and a blind attachment to the Catholic religion, as from foreseeing that the new doctrine, by making men acquainted with religious, might likewise give them a taste for civil liberty: in the same manner as the priests might have apprehended, that the destruction of prejudices in politics, would probably be the forerunner of that of superstition in religion.

Accordingly, we find that it was for the most part in those kingdoms where the monarchs had acquired the greatest share of power, that the reformation met with the most violent opposition: on the contrary, where the authority of the prince was limited, it made its way with a proportional degree of facility.

3dly. The introduction of standing armies throughout Europe, finally fixed the authority of the sovereigns on so firm a basis, as to render any resistance to it from the nobles and people, altogether ineffectual.

The luxury and love of ease, consequent upon the introduction of commerce and the arts and sciences among the European nations, must necessarily have greatly diminished that martial spirit for which they had been before distinguished, and which made them disdain any other occupation than that of war. Men who had tasted the sweets of peace, learned the use of riches, and acquired a relish for the enjoyments they procure, would naturally lose in a great degree their ardour for military expeditions: but, as from the feudal institutions, they were bound to attend their sovereign whenever he thought proper to summon them; this probably gave rise to the expedient of paying him certain sums, in order to raise a mercenary army, that they might be exempt from personal service.

The feudal monarchs could not be averse to a scheme, which, not only by rendering their troops more obedient and more immediately dependent on themselves, enabled them to act with greater vigour against their enemies abroad; but which likewise placed a force in their hands, that they could render subservient to the maintenance of their dignity, and augmentation of their authority at home.

Thus I have endeavoured to point out the natural steps by which the regal power has hitherto increased in most of the kingdoms of Europe. It is obvious from this view of them, that the ignorance of the true principles and nature of liberty, which prevailed among the inhabitants of Europe at the time when their respective sovereigns first laid the foundation of that absolute power, which

their

their fucceffors now enjoy; did not a little contribute to enable thofe princes to carry their defigns into execution. And had the minds of men been equally enlightened at that period, as, from the fpreading of literature, they are fince become; had they then turned their thoughts to the principles of fociety, and underftood the true nature of a free government; it is probable, that for the happinefs of mankind, the genial influence of liberty, would now have been felt over the whole face of Europe, inftead of being confined to a few, a very few, and, comparatively fpeaking, inconfiderable parts of it: but unfortunately, this knowledge has come too late for the major part of its inhabitants to derive any advantage from it. Arbitrary power was already eftablifhed among them on a foundation too firm to be eafily fhaken, and too well protected to be attacked with impunity. To them, therefore, it has, perhaps, anfwered no other end, than to make them fee the defects of a government, to which they are, notwithftanding, compelled to fubmit.

But the cafe is far otherwife with a people ftill poffeffed of freedom. To thefe a thorough knowledge of the true nature of a free government, and of the principles of liberty, is not only ufeful, but neceffary, in order to enable them to forefee and guard againft the dangers to which a free conftitution muft be continually expofed.

This knowledge is to be acquired only from a minute obfervation of the facts with which hiftory makes

makes us acquainted; an accurate examination of the various forms of government, which have flourished at different periods, in different parts of the globe, and of the various fate that has attended them. A multitude of these facts is to serve as the basis on which to build a system, that will reduce the science of laws and government to some fixed principles. Every political event, therefore, which tends to throw a new light on that science; which points out a new source of dangers to a free government; and consequently, at the same time, indicates the precautions necessary to be taken, in order to guard against them, certainly merits from a people possessed of such a constitution, the utmost degree of attention: and more real instruction is to be derived from an event of this nature, than from all the theories of their most able politicians: for whatever these may apprehend to be the probable effects of particular causes, or future consequences of particular measures, their conjectures must ever be attended with uncertainty: on the contrary, when the event has taken place, it is easy to trace effects back to their causes, and their dependence upon each other becomes as obvious then, as it was before difficult to be discerned.

The late revolution in Sweden is undoubtedly to be considered in this light. A change so important in its object, produced by means so inconsiderable; an attempt of such apparent difficulty in theory, yet attended with such facility in the execution;

cution; presenting us so bold an usurpation on the one hand, and a submission so tame upon the other, is not, perhaps, to be paralelled in any history either ancient or modern †.

Where the object of a revolution has been a change of the sovereign only, not of the constitution, it has, like this, sometimes been accomplished without difficulty or opposition. The deposition of one prince and advancement of another to the throne, can in general, materially affect those only who immediately surround their persons. To the bulk of the nation it is a matter of small importance, whether an Alphonso or a Pedro, a Peter or a Catherine, wear the crown.

But where the object of the change is to overturn the constitution itself, and establish a government

† Denmark, indeed, furnishes an instance of a revolution somewhat similar to this, both with respect to the object of the change, and to the ease and expedition with which it was accomplished; but in other points it was widely different. There the measure originating with the people, was proposed and carried into execution by the majority of the nation. Here it originated with the prince, and his subjects were compelled to acquiesce, whether it was agreeable to their inclinations or not.—In the first instance, the only object of wonder is, that the greater part of what was supposed to be a free people, could possibly be induced to form so extraordinary a resolution, as that of making a voluntary surrender of their liberties; but this resolution once formed, the ease and expedition with which it was carried into execution, followed of course. In the second, it was as natural to have expected that such an attempt would have met with opposition, as in the first case, it was morally impossible there could have been any.

of an opposite nature in its room; the question no longer relates to the partial interests of a few individuals.

The welfare of a nation is at stake, the state becomes convulsed from the center to the remotest parts of it, and the whole society receives a shock, which reaches from the greatest, to the most insignificant of its members:—a thousand obstacles seem to present themselves to an enterprize, so important in its consequences, so extensive in its effects; the power of opinion, the force of habit, that predilection so prevalent among mankind for what they have been long accustomed to, might incline a people, even under the worst of governments, to oppose any attempt to produce a change in that, which from their childhood they had been taught to respect, and were attached to, because it was their's ‡.

But that predilection for the established form of government, which, among those who are subject to despotic power, must proceed from prejudice, and be maintained by ignorance; among the more enlightened inhabitants of a free state is founded on principle, and preserved, from the conviction of the superior excellence of their govern-

‡ When Schwiskoi was elected by the Boyers (or nobles), Czar of Russia, he offered of his own motion, to take an oath by which he would bind himself, never to put any Boyer to death without the consent of his peers. Upon this the whole body of the Boyers threw themselves at his feet, and supplicated him not to deprive the imperial crown of its just rights.

ment

ment over any other. Their attachment then to the conſtitution is frequently blended with a zeal for its ſafety; and their love of liberty, with a degree of enthuſiaſm, of which the tame breaſts of thoſe ſubject to arbitrary power, are not, nor cannot be ſuſceptible.

If, therefore, the ſudden change of any form of government to one of a contrary nature, is in itſelf an enterprize of ſo difficult a nature, that it might be expected it would meet with oppoſition even from the ſubjects of an arbitrary ſtate, who could not but be benefited by ſuch a change—How are the difficulties multiplied, when the object of the revolution is to deprive a people of what it is to be preſumed their intereſts, their inclinations, their reaſon, and their paſſions, at once ſtimulate them to defend? An enterprize, one would imagine, to be attempted only by a force ſuperior to the united ſtrength of the nation, whoſe liberties were to be attacked, and to be accompliſhed only by ſlaughter and devaſtation.

In one day, therefore, to complete ſuch a change; in one day to deſtroy the eſtabliſhed conſtitution of a country, and erect its oppoſite in its room; a conſtitution that appeared to be the moſt guarded againſt the poſſibility of ſuch an event; at a time that the popular branches of the legiſlature were in the fulleſt poſſeſſion of their powers; at a time that the hand which ſtruck the blow, was moſt limited, deprived by the conſtitution of riches to corrupt, of authority to awe, or of the diſpoſal of employments

ments to influence: this is an event, which, previous to its arrival, would scarcely have been considered as possible. Yet we now behold a young prince of six and twenty, at the head only of two companies of guards, undertake to overturn the constitution and liberties of his country; we behold him accomplish this design, and establish in the room of the constitution he had destroyed, that very government, against the introduction of which, his subjects had laid down every barrier that human wisdom could devise, and had taken every precaution that human foresight could judge effectual. And this brought about by means, in appearance, so inadequate to the magnitude of the object, by a force so insignificant, compared to the opposition, it might have been presumed, the undertaking would have met with; that we should be lost in admiration at the boldness of the attempt, and the address manifested in the execution on the one side; did we not find much more ample subject for wonder in the tame submission exhibited on the other.

Though the royal authority in Sweden, had certainly been, originally, too much limited by the form of government established there in 1720; yet, from a striking defect, in that form, the king was not possessed of any constitutional means of preserving the small share of authority that had been allotted him.

Accordingly, from the many alterations and innovations afterwards introduced, the power of the king of Sweden was almost reduced to nothing.

One

One would have been tempted to imagine, the Swedes had designed to revenge themselves on the royal dignity, for the insult offered them by Charles the XIIth, who had threatened to send one of his boots to govern them; they, in return, seem to have been determined to render their monarch of pretty nearly as much consequence, as the mock governor that Charles said he would impose upon them.

Without money, power, or influence, the empty honours paid to his Swedish majesty, by giving him an apparent consequence at one time, served only to render his real insignificance the more mortifying at another.

A crown that conferred no authority: the title of king, with hardly the privileges of a subject: in appearance, the first in the council of the nation; yet the last whose inclinations were consulted: exposed to all the mockery of an insolent obsequiousness, dictated to upon bended knees, and compelled to obey the most humble requests: possessed of all the ensigns of royalty; surrounded by every external mark of power; yet suffering all the mortifications the real want of it could expose him to: the first could not but awaken ambition in a mind susceptible of it; whilst the latter could not fail to produce the most ardent desire to shake off restraints of so humiliating a nature.

Such was the state of the king of Sweden: every circumstance of his situation was an incentive to an undertaking, from the failure of which he could lose only an empty title; but whose success cefs infured him the higheſt reward an ambitious mind is capable of receiving.

It was not therefore the richneſs of the prize before him, or the luſt of power, ſo prevalent among the generality of princes, which alone excited him to undertake ſo arduous a taſk; no, it was to emancipate himſelf from a ſtate of thraldom, to which even a ſubject in a free country, would ſcarcely have ſubmitted. It was to ſhake off the moſt mortifying ſhackles that ever the extreme of jealouſy could have incited ſubjects to impoſe; or to which the total impotency of the royal authority could alone have compelled a prince to ſubmit: ſhackles that at once deprived him of the power of doing right, or of the poſſibility of preventing wrong.

Thus ſtimulated by whatever could rouſe a generous or inflame an ambitious mind, that his Swediſh majeſty ſhould have made what muſt ſeem ſo bold an attempt, will ceaſe to appear extraordinary.

But that he ſhould have ſucceeded; that his ſubjects ſhould have ſo tamely acquieſced; ſurrendered without a ſhadow of oppoſition, what they muſt have been taught to conſider as the moſt invaluable of bleſſings: this, on a ſuperficial view, cannot but appear wholly unaccountable.

This event is not therefore to be conſidered merely as an object of curious ſpeculation: an inveſtigation of the cauſes which produced it; a developement of the ſecret ſources of the aſtoniſhing facility which attended the accompliſhment of it; and an examination of those defects in the late Swedish form of government, which contributed to its fall; the result of such an enquiry cannot fail to throw a new light on the science of government and true nature and principles of liberty: a science which should undoubtedly be the peculiar study of a free people. It may serve to rectify many mistakes which some politicians, who possess more zeal than judgment, are apt to fall into; and whilst we may learn from it whence real danger is to be apprehended, it may quiet the ill-grounded fears of such, who without being able to comprehend in one view the whole of a system, are alarmed at the partial defects of the small and separate portions of it which fall beneath their observation. And lastly, it will teach us, that however well calculated a form of government may originally have been, in order to produce the great ends of political and civil liberty, the wisest institutions will avail but little, unless the possessors have sense to preserve, and spirit to defend them.

THE

THE HISTORY OF THE

REVOLUTION that happened in *Sweden*, ON THE 19TH OF AUGUST, 1772.

PART I.

Containing a review of the History of Sweden, previous to the establishment of the late form of government in 1720, as far as relates to any changes in the constitution of that country.

AMONG the events with which history makes us acquainted, revolutions in government and manners, are at once the most interesting and the most instructive. The lives of princes, a catalogue of their reigns, or detail of their battles, victories, or defeats, are points rather of curiosity than utility to the reader: but to convert the study of history to a useful purpose, the philosopher and politician will carefully search into the nature of such great events, in the annals of different countries, as have been productive of any considerable change in their constitution, their customs, or their laws.

In proportion to the suddenness of such a change, the example becomes more striking, at the same time that the developing of the causes which gave rise to it, appears more difficult. The final destruction of a building which gradually decays, is foreseen; and when the ruin at length falls to the ground, it creates no surprize.

In the same manner, gradual alterations in the constitution of a country, scarcely attract our notice: in these, the progression of causes and effects is obvious, and the event expected; or we are led to it by such insensible degrees, that though the change may have become total in the end, it would sometimes perhaps be hard to determine the precise point at which it commenced. But the destruction of a government, accomplished with such expedition, that none of those steps preparatory to a change, and which give warning of the event, appeared to have been previously taken, is like the sudden fall of an edifice which was preceded by no visible symptom of decay. Unable at first sight, to perceive the true causes of so surprising a revolution, we are apt to conclude that it must have been altogether produced by the policy and designs of those who were the apparent authors of it; and to attribute to the abilities and deep-laid schemes of persons, what was in fact either the necessary consequence of a peculiar situation of things; or the natural result of latent causes, which, from being concealed, and frequently remote, did not operate the less powerfully.

Upon

Upon a nearer examination however, we shall find that it is impossible for the ablest politician to compass a change of this nature, unless assisted by a certain concurrence of circumstances, which indeed he may render subservient to his designs, but which he cannot create.

He may, it is true, hasten the operation of these, and bring forward effects which would not otherwise have so speedily taken place; but this is all he can do; and he is in general, nothing more than an actor in those scenes, of which he appears to be the author.

Had his present majesty of Sweden worn the crown during the first years of the establishment of the late form of government of that country, it is probable that neither his abilities, popularity, or eloquence, would have obtained him the success that has since attended him.

What has been observed here, does not in any shape derogate from the merit of those who, actuated by a noble love of freedom, have been the chief instruments of rescuing their country from slavery; or from the abilities of others, who prompted by an ungenerous ambition, and invited by opportunity, have accomplished the destruction of its liberties. Discernment to seize the moment best suited to the undertaking, and skill to render circumstances apparently unconnected with, subservient to the design; sagacity to guard against the obstacles it might meet with in the execution; and spirit to contemn the dangers with which it might be attended, are without doubt requisite to those, who take an active part in revolutions of this nature. It only serves to shew, that in order to discover the true causes of a sudden change of the government of a country, it is not sufficient to examine those measures by which it was immediately accomplished: it is likewise necessary to enquire into the nature, origin, principles, and defects of the government so destroyed; to know how far it was founded in the inclinations of the people who were possessed of it; how far supported by their opinions and prejudices; and lastly to become acquainted with the genius and national character of those who had so tamely suffered themselves to be deprived of it.

For these purposes we must go farther back into their history than might at first sight appear necessary in giving an account of so recent an event as the late revolution in Sweden; and take a retrospective view of those parts of it, which relate to any of the above-mentioned points.

The fate of that country has been most singularly various, both with respect to her revolutions at home, and the figure she has made at different periods abroad.

The government of the hardy inhabitants of this northern region has, like their climate, been ever in extremes; licentiously free, or bordering on despotism. Whilst at one time their love of liberty seems to be their distinguishing characteristic; at another, they appear no less remarkable for the obsequiousness and servility of their submission to their monarchs. Impatient of restraint,

ſtraint, jealous to exceſs of the regal authority, and equally tenacious of their own rights; we ſometimes behold them tumultuouſly riſe, and like a torrent bearing down all before them, they at once overthrow their ſovereign, and every barrier he had raiſed to protect the ſmall ſhare of power he had been ſuffered to poſſeſs.

At another, as if exhauſted by too violent exertions, every ſpark of patriotiſm has been extinguiſhed among them: they appear patiently to have ſubmitted to every ſpecies of oppreſſion, and to have been as reſigned to ſlavery as if they had never known the ſweets of freedom.

In ſhort, from ſuch an apparent contradiction in their national character, whoever contemplates their hiſtory, will be tempted to imagine that two diſtinct races of men had inhabited by turns the ſame country.

Nor is there a leſs ſtriking variety in the degrees of conſequence and conſideration, poſſeſſed by Sweden at different periods among foreign powers. Now burſting from obſcurity, we behold her preſcribing laws to the firſt potentates: we perceive her armies, in imitation of the Goths their anceſtors, over-running kingdoms and empires, depoſing monarchs and beſtowing crowns. We next view her ſunk into oblivion, if not contempt: her conqueſts reſtored, her forces withdrawn, we find the conſequence ſhe had acquired as momentary, as her progreſs had before been rapid.

The superior genius of some of her monarchs, the bravery, the hardiness, and above all the discipline of her soldiery, on many occasions insured a degree of success to her arms, of which there are few examples in the histories of other countries. Her efforts, whenever she exerted herself, were violent, and often irresistible; but as they were disproportioned to her resources, they served rather to exhaust her strength at home, than increase her dominion abroad.

From the most brilliant victories she reaped little but honour; and after the most important conquests, she was frequently obliged in the end to content herself with her native rocks.

The Swedish history may be divided into three periods.

The first, to conclude at the revolution, which placed Gustavus Vasa on the throne 1523.

The second reaches from that event to the death of Charles XII. in 1718; the third from that period to the late revolution in 1773.

SECTION I.

Containing a review of the government, customs, and manners of the Swedes, during the first of these periods.

AT the time that most of the governments in Europe had begun to acquire a certain degree of stability, that of Sweden still continued in the most fluctuating state. The kingdom was torn by civil dissentions, wasted by internal wars, and successively a prey to the usurpations of foreigners, the ambition of its nobles, and the tyranny of its sovereigns.

In other countries the abuses of the feudal system had been corrected or removed. The rise and progress of commerce had in these, given to the bulk of the people, a consequence and consideration that enabled them in a great degree to shake off the yoke of the feudal barons, and to acquire that rank in society of which they had been so long and so unjustly deprived. In proportion as the rights of the people were ascertained, the royal authority became fixed on a more permanent foundation: from elective, the crown was rendered hereditary; and as the minds of men grew more enlightened, ideas of public good, a sense of justice, and the love of order began to prevail.

But these great changes in the policy and manners of most of the European nations, begun among them at the commencement of the twelfth century, did not take place in Sweden till towards the middle of the sixteenth: so that even so late as at that period, she presented to the rest of Europe a striking picture of the disorders, confusion, and anarchy, to which all its inhabitants had been formerly exposed.

The whole history therefore of the period under review, furnishes only a detail of intestine commotions, rebellions, and revolutions, accompanied by all the calamities which these necessarily carry in their train.

Though perhaps it will not prove a grateful task, to look back and contemplate scenes of so disagreeable a nature, yet it is amidst the confusion and disorders there exhibited, that we are to search for the origin of the late Swedish form of government. It is there we shall discover the genius and national character of the Swedes, and in them the true sources of the revolutions to which their country has ever been so subject. It is there too we shall find, however remote they may appear, some of the causes of the astonishing facility with which the last was accomplished.

When we take a view of the Swedish form of government, during the period we are treating of, we should at first sight be apt to give it the preference over any other at that time known.

Instead of the rigour of an oppressive aristocracy, conspicuous wherever the feudal system prevailed,

vailed, we perceive a conftitution in which the body of the people poffeffed a fhare fo confiderable as to render them in a great degree independent of their fuperiors.

We perceive the fupreme power neither lodged in the hands of one, nor divided between the fovereign and a few haughty barons, whilft an abject dependence was the portion of the reft of the nation; but placed, where it ought to be, in the States General of the kingdom.

Into thefe all ranks of men were admitted; and the meaneft peafant, through his reprefentative, as well as the proudeft noble, bore a part in the legiflature of his country. The ftates were compofed of four orders; thofe of the nobility, the clergy, the burghers, and the peafants. While they were affembled, the power of the fovereign was in a manner fufpended, or appeared loft in theirs; and after their feparation, a fenate, in whom great authority was vefted, ftill continued to act as the guardians of public liberty.

Such were the outlines of this conftitution, which, when viewed at a diftance, like a palace the walls of which only are finifhed, forms a fine object, but upon a nearer infpection, we find it anfwers none of the purpofes we were taught to expect from its appearance. Accordingly the internal government of Sweden was, as I have already obferved, more turbulent, more expofed to diforder, anarchy, and confufion, than that of any other country in Europe.

Many

Many circumstances concurred to produce these effects in Sweden, and to prevent that civilisation of manners from taking place there, which must necessarily precede any improvement in government. 1st. Previous to the establishment of the communication which commerce opens between the most distant countries, Sweden was, from her northern situation, in a great degree shut out from the rest of the world: and if the Swedes were, on this account, exempted from taking any part in those quarrels, in which the rest of Europe was continually involved; they were likewise deprived of the advantages they might have reaped from an intercourse with nations, which had so considerably got the start of them in the progress they had made towards refinement. The Russians certainly could not, on the one hand, contribute to civilize them, whilst their constant wars with the Danes, a people as barbarous as themselves, served only, on the other, to increase their natural ferocity. 2dly, The nature of their country, as well as that of their climate, are likewise very obvious causes of the wild licentious spirit which distinguished these people.

Where the climate is temperate, and the soil fertile, they invite to agriculture, by rendering the life of a husbandman both pleasant and profitable. Agriculture contributes greatly to soften the manners of those who apply themselves to it, and has a natural tendency to promote the love of order and tranquillity among mankind: it disposes them

them to peace, as without it, he who cultivates his land, cannot hope to reap the fruits of his labour. For the same reason, it introduces among men, all those ideas concerning the security of private property and the rights of individuals, which form the basis of civil societies. Where therefore the climate is rigorous and the soil barren, as in Sweden, the progress of the inhabitants towards civilisation will be proportionably slow.

The Swedes were however by these circumstances inured to hardships, which rendered their minds daring, and their bodies vigorous.

The first inspired them with a love of independence, which the latter enabled them to preserve. Discouraged by the nature of the climate, they neglected agriculture; and the immense woods which cover the face of their country, abounding with game, afforded them a means of subsistence by hunting, more suitable to their genius than the milder occupations of husbandry.

It is obvious how much such a mode of life must have contributed to maintain them in their native state of barbarism. That love of change and restlesness of disposition which are the natural consequences of it, are conspicuous in the conduct of the Swedes, through all the early periods of their history; and were no considerable sources of the convulsions which so often shook the state.

It is true indeed, that the more southern provinces of Sweden, were neither unfertile nor altogether uncltivated. But as these were continually changing their masters, sometimes belonging to
the

the Swedes, sometimes to the Danes, they were a constant subject of contention between the two nations, and as constantly the seat of war. This circumstance must therefore have in a great measure counteracted, among the inhabitants of these provinces, the tendency which their applying themselves to agriculture would otherwise have had towards softening their manners. Such an effect could hardly be expected to have become either general, or of long continuance, in a country where every peasant was a soldier, and obliged to use the sword more frequently than the plough.

3dly. From what has been said in the preceding article, it is evident, the peasants of Sweden must have been possessed of the utmost degree of independency.

If we take a comparative view of the state of society in Europe previous to the thirteenth and fourteenth centuries, we shall perceive the condition of the Swedish peasantry was totally different from that of the same order of men, in other European countries. In these they were reduced to the most abject state of servitude, and were not only destitute of any weight or influence in the government, but were, for the most part, deprived of the natural rights of mankind.

In Sweden, on the contrary, the peasantry did not content themselves with having preserved their independency, and with possessing the peculiar privilege of sending deputies of their own body to the States General of the kingdom; but they likewise frequently assumed to themselves the direction

rection of public affairs; took the lead in every revolution; and seemed to act on all occasions as a distinct body, which had views and interests of its own, separate from those of the other members of the state.

It might naturally be expected the greatest advantages would have resulted to liberty, and consequently to society, from the bulk of the people's being possessed of so much weight and influence: but the same causes to which they owed their importance, not only rendered them incapable of making a right, but for the most part prompted them to make a wrong use of it.

To their mode of life they were indebted for that spirit, with which they opposed every invasion of their rights. And if the Swedish monarchs appear seldom to have been awed into a respect for privileges, which the fierce disposition of their subjects rendered it so dangerous to attack; at least, it was on this account that their attempts to invade them, seldom proved successful in the end. But this mode of life, at the same time, communicated to the people an impatience of control, and fierceness of manners, that were incompatible with any regular government*, and

equally

---

* The ancient law in Sweden, which ordained that a part, or the whole, of the house of any one who had injured another should be pulled down, and burned, in proportion to the injury sustained by the party aggrieved; furnishes a striking proof of the unsettled state of the government, which was obliged to have recourse to such an expedient. This law
has

equally repugnant to every principle of real freedom. If at one time, it infpired them with a fpirit of refiftance, calculated to preferve their liberty; at another, by plunging them into anarchy, it expofed them to the lofs of it. When they delivered themfelves from the oppreffion of the few, they became expofed to the licentioufnefs of the many: and continually fluctuating between thefe two extremes, they never once ftopped at any intermediate point, where a balance might have been eftablifhed between their rights and the prerogative of their fovereign. Ignorant of the true nature of liberty, as well as of that of government, they neither perceived the neceffity of fuch a ballance, nor did they poffefs fkill to have formed one if they had. Incapable of forefight, and roufed only by what they felt, they oppofed the monarch, but knew not how to limit the regal authority: and in all their ftruggles, there feemed rather to be a perfonal quarrel between the king and the people, than a contention between the popular branches of the legiflature and the crown.

Union to concert, defign to form, or judgment to execute any effectual meafures, to prevent or

has been confidered only as a mark of the fimplicity and ignorance of the age in which it was enacted ; but it may with more juftice be attributed to the difficulty of feizing *the perfon* of an offender, among a people fo little accuftomed to order and fubordination. It was, therefore, in that part of his *property* only which it was eafy to come at, that there could be found a means of punifhing him.

oppofe.

oppose the constant endeavours of their sovereigns to acquire absolute power, could not be expected from men like these.

When they sought redress of their grievances, their temporary efforts to obtain it, were distinguished by that rash zeal and blind impetuosity, which characterise the proceedings of all irregular and tumultuous assemblies of men; and which seldom fail to defeat the very ends they have in view: the oppressor, indeed, often fell a sacrifice to their resentment; but as they neglected to guard against the oppression, subsequent princes were almost sure to give them the same causes of complaint, and to compel them to have recourse to the same mode of redress.

A striking proof of the unsettled state of the government of the Swedes, and of the violence to which both king and people must frequently have had recourse, is to be found in an ancient custom of theirs; that whenever one of their monarchs had occasion to pass through a province, the inhabitants, before they would suffer him to enter it, compelled him to give hostages for the security of their privileges; and he in return received the same from them for the safety of his person †.

Whilst such mutual jealousies subsisted between a Swedish monarch and his people; whilst neither

---

† So tenacious were the Swedes of this custom, that Ragwald, who reigned about the beginning of the thirteenth century, lost his crown and life for not complying with it. BOTIN. p. 246.

his prerogatives, nor their rights were afcertained, and force alone decided their differences; it was not extraordinary that a fpirit of oppreffion fhould have marked the conduct of the one; or that a pronenefs to revolt fhould have diftinguifhed that of the other.

Here it may very naturally be afked, Whence arofe, during the period we are treating of, this ftriking fuperiority difcernible in the condition of the Swedifh peafantry, when compared to that of the great body of the people in other countries of Europe?

The nature of the foil and climate of Sweden, partly accounts for it: but this was neither the only, nor the principal fource of it.

After the deftruction of the Roman empire by the invafion of the northern barbarians, thefe having eftablifhed themfelves on its ruins, and taken poffeffion of the countries they had fubdued, did not exterminate, but affociated with fuch of the ancient inhabitants as remained after the conqueft, and even divided the lands with them in certain proportions†.

If, therefore, we take a view of the ftate of Europe at that time, we fhall perceive the Goths or Vandals, Huns or Saxons, &c. fpread over the whole face of it.

But then the native countries of thefe barbarians, which were thofe fituated to the North, were inhabited only by themfelves, without any

‡ Efprit de Loix. liv. 30. 7 and 8.

intermixture of another people; whereas the Southern parts of Europe, which had before been under the dominion of the Romans, were in the joint poffeffion of the Barbarous nations, and of their own ancient inhabitants. Thus, in the latter, we difcover two diftinct people, viz. the conquerors, and the conquered, occupying at once the fame country. In the former, on the contrary, we meet only with the remaining part of thofe fierce inhabitants, who, perhaps, lefs enterprizing than their countrymen, inftead of fallying forth in queft of new fettlements, had continued at home contented with their native forefts.

Here then a very important diftinction has been made, which I think will ferve fufficiently to explain, why the bulk of the people in Sweden continued free, at the fame time that all the lower claffes of men in other countries, funk into fervitude.

Such parts of the Northern nations as had remained at home, it is to be prefumed, preferved their ancient cuftoms and government: but thofe who had acquired new poffeffions, in which the former inhabitants ftill continued to refide, were under the neceffity of devifing fome expedient, which would enable them to guard againft furprize, and fecure them from the fudden attacks, to which fuch a fituation muft naturally have expofed them.

This it was that gave rife to the feudal fyftem, which we find eftablifhed by thefe bold invaders, wherever they fettled.

E   A fyftem

A system so peculiarly adapted to the circumstances in which they then found themselves, to those circumstances obviously owed its birth: nor is it at all probable, that the feudal system was known to any of these people, previous to their emigrations from their several countries §.

Though this system did not immediately reduce the vanquished inhabitants of the countries seized upon by the northern intruders, to that wretched state of slavery into which the great body of the people shortly sunk, wherever it was introduced; yet it had an almost unavoidable tendency to produce that effect.

As its principles were founded in conquest, so the object of all its regulations, was the preservation of that conquest. It would, therefore, have been highly impolitic in the new proprietors of countries, the ancient inhabitants of which were still, perhaps, more numerous than themselves, to

---

§ There is no trace of any institution in Sweden similar to the feudal, till the year 824, when Brant Anund caused some lands to be cleared of the woods and cultivated, which he gave to his subjects, on condition they should serve him in the wars on horseback, or pay a certain tribute. Hence the peasants in Sweden were bound immediately to the king, and the nobles had consequently no vassals, till some of these Fiefs, as they may not improperly be called, in course of time were alienated from the crown and fell into their hands. But this was near three centuries after the destruction of the Roman empire, and, consequently, a considerable time after the feudal system had been established in other countries.

have suffered these to be in a condition to disturb them. If the vanquished people were allowed to cultivate the lands that had been allotted to them, it was all they could expect; and as the use of arms would certainly have been denied them, agriculture would have become their only occupation.

When we consider, therefore, the encroaching spirit which ever attends those who are possessed of power; that here there was, on the one hand, a body of men necessarily defenceless, whilst their fierce conquerors were, on the other, always armed and prepared for action: when we reflect too on the contempt, in which, during those martial ages, every man was held who was not a soldier; that among the ancient Germans, who disdained every occupation but that of war, agriculture was left entirely to their slaves[*]; it will not, I think, appear extraordinary, if they soon considered, and treated as such, all those who applied themselves to it.

Even if any of their own people were, contrary to the ideas which generally prevailed among them, induced by the fertility of their newly-acquired possessions, to apply themselves to husbandry; and, instead of holding their lands by military service, to return certain quantities of corn or cattle to their superior lord, they were soon reduced to a state little different from that of slavery[†].

[*] *Tac. de. mor. Ger.*
[†] *Dalrymple on feudal property*, c. 2. p. 28.

Thus in France, towards the commencement of the first race of kings, there was an infinite number of freemen, both among the Franks and the Romans; yet the state of villanage increased to that degree, that at the beginning of the third race, not only all the husbandmen were become bondmen ‡, but we find also, that at the same period, almost all the inhabitants of towns likewise were in the same state: as these were for the most part Romans, this too is a proof, that though the vanquished were not immediately reduced by their conquerors to a state of slavery, yet from the nature of their situation, they insensibly sunk into it afterwards.

Now as in Sweden, neither the soil nor the climate were favourable to agriculture; as its inhabitants were composed but of one nation, among whom there were neither conquerors nor conquered; so those causes which in other countries had contributed to reduce the major part of their inhabitants to the subjection of the rest, did not exist among them.

It is true that the northern nations had their slaves, previous to the invasion of the Roman empire; but they were few in number, and composed of such of their own people as had forfeited their liberty by various means; of such as had been made prisoners in battle, or had committed certain crimes, or had sold themselves; a practice not uncommon among these barbarians.

‡ *Esprit des Loix*, b. 30. c. 11.

Hence they did not, properly speaking, form a distinct race of men, as must happen when one nation becomes enslaved by another; and consequently, as the line drawn between them and their masters was not so distinct as in the other case, neither was it so difficult for them to recover their freedom. Besides, as they were chiefly employed in the cultivation of the land, it follows, that where the soil was least favourable to agriculture, such slaves were least wanted. Accordingly they were enfranchised in Sweden earlier perhaps than in any other part of Europe *. Towards the middle of the thirteenth century, Birgis Jarl rendered it unlawful for any Swede to sell himself; and in the year 1335 the state of slavery was altogether abolished there by an ordinance of Magnus Ladulas.

4th, The want of great cities in Sweden was likewise no inconsiderable source of the disorder and confusion which reigned so long in that kingdom.

Commerce is a great means of softening the manners of a martial people, and of correcting the fierceness of that military ardour which renders them equally fond of arms, and averse to every other occupation. Commerce presents new objects to the inclinations and passions of mankind. By placing the productions of various climates and

---

* In Denmark, Poland, parts of Germany, and some other countries, where agriculture was more followed, the slaves have never been enfranchised, which is the reason the peasants of those countries are all *Bondmen*.

§ *Botin. p.* 334.

countries within their reach, they acquire a relish for what they had no conception of before: with that relish they acquire too a taste for arts formerly unknown to them; and as they apply themselves to these, their attachment to their ancient mode of life must likewise decrease. But there is a still more important consequence attendant on commerce: as it necessarily assembles mankind together, it becomes the principal cause of the rise and growth of cities; and consequently the chief means of introducing among them a regular form of government. Without this it is impossible for any numbers of men to live together; and therefore where such numbers are assembled it is, that a sense of justice, the love of order, and desire of public tranquillity, first begin to prevail. It is obvious therefore how much the want of great cities in Sweden must have retarded the progress of improvements in any of those points. This want, owing to that of trade, may be placed among the many disadvantages resulting to Sweden from her northern situation, and the nature of her soil and climate. As commerce was first introduced into Europe through Italy, it was of course diffused among the other European countries, in proportion to their vicinity to the source from whence it flowed. But this was not all; those countries situated in the temperate parts of Europe, were likewise the best calculated from the nature of their productions, for the establishment and cultivation of commerce among them. The rigour of the climate and barrenness of the soil of Sweden, were,

on

on the contrary, by no means favourable to the progress of trade.

The produce of their mines indeed, furnished the Swedes with materials for it: but this branch of commerce, the only one to which they applied themselves, is perhaps too the only one that has no direct tendency to produce those good effects, which may in general be ascribed to the cultivation of commerce; I mean the improvement of manners and of government. The life of a miner is not calculated, like the occupations pursued in towns, to promote this end: trades and manufactures make men resort to cities; but they are in general necessarily kept at a distance from them when employed in the working of mines; and they consequently remain unacquainted with that subordination and order, which in cities must in some degree always prevail. Accordingly we find the miners of Sweden were the most restless part of the nation, the most ungovernable, and ever among the foremost to revolt. So ignorant were the Swedes of every species of manufacture, that till towards the end of the sixteenth century, they did not even know how to work their own iron; but the ore was carried to Dantzick and other parts of Prussia, to be there forged into bars. And at what a low ebb the trade of Sweden must in general have been, may be seen from the exorbitant privileges granted by Gustavus Vasa to the Lubechers*,

I have

* That they should pay no customs for the commodities they should bring into Sweden; that *they alone* should have *all the trade*

I have already had occasion to take notice of the beneficial effects which have resulted to government from the representatives of cities gaining a place in the legislature. But though the Swedish cities had early the privilege of sending members to the Diets, yet the number of these was very inconsiderable, and their influence there proportionably small. And as the little trade carried on in Sweden, was for the most part in the hands of foreigners *, they were neither so deeply interested in what related to the government of that country as natives would have been, nor could it be expected they would pay similar attention to points in which they were not equally concerned.

The representatives of the peasants being possessed of a seat at the Diets, was by no means an equivalent for the want of a sufficient number of the members sent by cities, nor productive of the like effects.

When citizens acquired a voice in the councils of the nation, they must have retained in their new capacity of legislators, the same ideas which prevailed in the communities to which they belonged.

These must have been of the most pacific nature, as merchants are more interested in the

---

trade of that kingdom: and lastly, that they might trade at Stockholm, Suderkoping, Calmar, and Aboo; not only with the citizens but with the peasants.

* In the thirteenth century the inhabitants of the Swedish cities were mostly Germans: and even among the magistrates one half were allowed to be foreigners. *Bosin. p.* 319.

preservation

prefervation of public tranquillity than any other order of men; and, accuftomed to the fubordination and regular government which take place in cities, they muft have communicated to the legiflature, in which they bore a part, a fpirit fomewhat fimilar to that of which they were themfelves poffeffed.

On the contrary, the greater importance and power the Swedifh peafants obtained in the ftate, the more turbulent and diforderly they rendered the government. For that impatience of reftraint and fpirit of independence, by which they were diftinguifhed on all other occafions, muft have had an equal influence on their conduct in their legiflative capacity.

5th, The Swedifh nobles were by no means fo formidable to the kings of Sweden, as in other countries the feudal barons were to their monarchs.

The former poffeffed neither the territories, wealth, nor exorbitant privileges, which enabled the latter to give law to their princes. The genius of the feudal fyftem naturally led to an ariftocracy: it had accuftomed men to behold extenfive domains, great riches, and confiderable authority, in the poffeffion of a few: and as previous to the corruption of this fyftem, no vaffal could legally diminifh the value of a fief, which at his death was to return to the fuperior lord; fo it happened here, as in many cafes where cuftoms have been obferved to continue long after the caufes which gave them birth have ceafed, that after fiefs

became

became hereditary, the same ideas of preserving them intire still prevailed.

Hence proceeded the device of entails; a contrivance which put it out of the power of the posterity of those who were possessed of such fiefs, to alienate any part of what was considered by them as necessary to support the dignity of a feudal chieftain.

In Sweden, on the contrary, as titles were unknown there till the middle of the sixteenth century, when Eric, the son of Gustavus Vasa, first created counts and barons: so were the Swedes alike ignorant of entails; among them it had ever been the custom to make equal divisions of the property of the father among the children*: the eldest son was not on account of primogeniture entitled to more than the others; nor indeed did there appear any reason why a difference should be made in his favour, since the title enjoyed by the father descended to all his children alike. This principle was carried so far as to be extended even to the crown; and the kingdom became frequently divided among the sons of the last king; which contributed not a little to increase the disorder and confusion into which it was at all times but too apt to be plunged.

It is evident, the above-mentioned custom necessarily prevented great riches from accumulating, or large estates from continuing long in the same

---

* That is, the sons all shared alike, as did the daughters, but the former had double the portion of the latter.

hands,

hands. It certainly occasioned a more equal distribution of property among the whole order of the nobles; but as it rendered the power of individuals of that order very inconsiderable, it may be reckoned a principal source of the instability of the government of Sweden.

In other countries the same power which rendered a baron the little tyrant of his own domain, served likewise to controul the authority of his sovereign. Three or four feudal barons, at the head of their respective vassals and retainers, were able to defeat any army he could bring into the field. And as it was the interest of these potent chiefs to make common cause against the crown, any attack of the latter upon the privileges of the former, was sure to meet with the most immediate and most powerful opposition. Hence the feudal monarchs were compelled to rest, if not satisfied, at least apparently content with the degree of power vested in them by the constitution; or, where they made the augmentation of their authority their object, they had recourse to an indirect and concealed policy, which would not alarm the jealousy of their barons, nor consequently excite commotions.

But the case was far otherwise with the Swedish monarchs: when these were disposed to infringe the rights of their subjects, no immediate obstacle presented itself to their designs. There was no power in the state ready formed, and as it were on the watch, as well as prepared to oppose them, like that of the feudal barons in other countries.
A general

A general spirit of liberty indeed existed in the nation, but the difficulty lay in directing this spirit. The peasantry, for the most part independent of the nobles, were not, like the vassals of a chieftain, compelled to follow a standard that was to lead them against their sovereign. Among the nobles *, the power and influence of each individual were, from causes I have already mentioned, so inconsiderable, that a union of numbers of them, could alone enable them to defend their rights against the encroachments of the crown. But it must have been a point of great difficulty to have formed a well-compacted confederacy, where so great a number of members were necessary, and these so little accustomed to order and subordination. Besides, from the nature of their country, covered with rocks, and consequently thinly inhabited, they were obliged to live at so considerable a distance from each other, that it would have been impossible for them to assemble on any sudden emergency when immediate exertion was necessary.

But this was not all; the Swedish nobles were not, nor indeed could they be, so deeply interested

* The power of the Swedish nobles seems to have been at its greatest heighth towards the end of the fifteenth century. According to an act of assurance of Christian Ist, in 1476, every noble was to be king over his own peasants, or tenants, *(vara konung öfver sina egna landt bönder) Botin. p.* 572. But when we consider the temper of the Swedish peasantry, and the independence to which they had always been accustomed, we cannot suppose they became very obedient subjects.

in the permanency of their government as the feudal barons, whose possessions were so considerable, must have been in the preservation of that constitution by virtue of which they enjoyed them.

The poverty of the former made them perhaps as fond of changes in which they might reap some advantage, as the wealth and privileges of the latter must have rendered them averse to any such changes. Hence the endeavours of the Swedish monarchs to acquire a more absolute power, did not in the beginning meet with that resistance which was sure to attend similar endeavours of the feudal kings. For this purpose it was necessary that the spirit of the whole nation should be roused; which seldom happened till their monarchs had persisted some time in the same conduct. Besides, the almost constant wars between Sweden and Denmark, placed their kings as constantly at the head of an army; and this not an army like that of a feudal monarch, which was composed of soldiers who were the vassals of their respective chiefs, to whom only they thought themselves bound to pay obedience; but of men who acknowledged no superior lord but their king, and who consequently were the more likely to be at his devotion.

Hence the Swedish monarchs not only never desisted from their attempts to acquire arbitrary power, but also carried them on without disguise; attempts from which no example could deter, no danger intimidate them. Not even the fate of their immediate predecessors, who had perhaps

forfeited

forfeited their crown, if not their lives, for having pursued a similar conduct. From the commencement of the history of Sweden to the elevation of Gustavus Vasa to the throne, the first object of almost all their princes seems to have been to increase their power at the expence of the liberties of the people; and to augment their revenues by arbitrary taxes, imposed in direct violation of the laws of the realm. And though sooner or later they almost all fell a sacrifice to their ambition, yet as many of them enjoyed their usurpations a considerable time, before the people were sufficiently roused to shake off by force of arms the yoke that had been imposed on them; each allured by the temporary advantages resulting to his predecessors on these occasions, was apt to overlook the fate which had afterwards attended them; and to flatter himself either that he should be more fortunate, or, that possessed of superior abilities, he should be able to succeed where they had failed.

But if many circumstances seemed to tempt every Swedish monarch, on his obtaining the crown, to attack those privileges of his subjects, which circumscribed its authority within such narrow limits; there were likewise many causes which prevented such attacks from being long successful.

Among these, that of Sweden's continuing an elective kingdom, during all the period I am speaking of, was one of the principal.

Where the crown is elective, it is impossible a regular system to increase its prerogatives and
humble

humble a turbulent nobility, can be purſued for any length of time.

One reign is hardly ſufficient to effect a change of this nature, where the body of the people is averſe to it. And the death of a prince, to whom no ſucceſſor has been before appointed, neceſſarily puts a ſtop to any meaſures however well concerted, that were calculated to eſtabliſh the authority of the ſovereign on a more ſolid foundation.

Every new king on his election, was obliged to ſubſcribe to articles, which undid, at once, all that his predeceſſor had, during, perhaps, the courſe of his life, been labouring to accompliſh; and which left him, in a manner, deſtitute of authority.

The jealouſy of the royal power among the Swedes, led them into an exceſs of precaution, which made them imagine they could never reſtrain it too much. A miſtaken policy which defeats its own ends; for when reſtrictions are carried beyond a certain point, they become inſupportable; and, therefore, frequently prompt thoſe whom they are meant to bind, to aim at the very objects, againſt their obtaining of which, theſe were deſigned to be the barriers.

The ſcantineſs of the revenues of the Swediſh monarchs likewiſe formed no inconſiderable check upon all their projects.

Unable to reward their adherents with the ordinary income of the crown, they, for that purpoſe, ſtripped it of almoſt all its patrimonial territories. When they had thus impoveriſhed it,

they

they were, in some measure, compelled to make use of extraordinary methods of levying money, in order to support their dignity, with any tolerable degree of splendor: at the same time, their favourites, who were rapacious in proportion to the uncertainty of the tenure by which they held their power, had no object in view but that of enriching themselves as expeditiously as they could.

These, therefore, encouraged their sovereign, in the pursuit of any measure, however unpopular or oppressive, provided it would enable him, for the present, to gratify their avarice or ambition. Whilst he, on the other hand, galled by the shackles, which the jealousy of his subjects had imposed upon him, was already but too well inclined to follow counsels, which flattered him with the hopes of shaking them off.

But the eagerness with which the Swedish monarchs pursued these objects, by betraying their designs too soon, rendered them abortive. The nation was alarmed in time, and consequently put upon its guard against attacks, to which a more cautious conduct and artful policy would have insured greater success. But to pursue such a conduct, required more time, than it could be expected an elective king, who naturally must be desirous to seize and make the most of the present moment, would devote to it. Where a monarch is certain his children are to succeed him, he probably will be content, should he be able to lay the foundation only of that power, which he expects

pects will be enjoyed by his posterity. Regard for his family will moderate his ambition, render him cautious in the carrying on of his designs, and, perhaps, inspire him with a means of accomplishing them, not the less sure for being indirect.

Unrestrained by this motive, the Kings of Sweden, excepting in one or two instances, pursued a contrary conduct. Scarcely were they seated on the throne before they began to act in direct violation of the laws. But their schemes were concerted without judgement, and conducted without address. They had recourse to violence, where artifice should have been employed; and they never failed to rouse that jealous spirit in the nation, which it was their business to have lulled to sleep.

Their success was answerable to the rashness of their measures. The liberties of the Swedes, during the early period of their histories, previous to the reign of Magnus Ladulas, though frequently endangered, could never be overturned by attacks, too open and direct not to render their tendency obvious; and too ill supported to overcome the spirit of opposition, which they were, for that reason, sure to create.

6thly. That order of men whose peculiar province it is to preach peace and concord to mankind, were in Sweden often the chief authors of insurrections, and the perpetual promoters of civil dissentions. During the early ages of christianity, the clergy had in all countries usurped an authority, and claimed powers very inconsistent with

F   their

their function. The ignorance and superstition of those times had rendered their persons sacred; and from the veneration in which they were held, as well as from their immense property, a property ever increasing, but incapable of being diminished, they were become in all the kingdoms of Europe the most potent body in the state. Great as their power must, from these causes, have every-where been, the same causes rendered it still more considerable in Sweden, than in other countries. In many of these, great part of the lands belonging to the laity, was, in consequence of being entailed, unalienable, as well as those in the possession of the clergy. Hence the bishops, although for the most part the temporal lords of their episcopal fees, were not, on that account, more powerful than many secular nobles; and a kind of balance subsisted between ecclesiastical, and temporal property.

In Sweden, on the contrary, the lands of the clergy were alone unalienable: such as were in the possession of the laity, were, as has been before observed, subject to be divided and subdivided into separate portions, as the families of those to whom they belonged, happened to be more or less numerous. It is obvious what a prodigious superiority the church must have derived from this single circumstance.

Accordingly the Swedish prelates affected the state of little sovereigns; they fortified their castles, and maintained garrisons in them; were ever attended by a numerous band of gentlemen and

and soldiers; were the abettors of every faction; and even forgot their character so far, as frequently to appear themselves at the head of their troops.

Here, indeed, was a power which might effectually have opposed any attempts of the Kings of Sweden upon the liberties of the nation. A power, not only considerable, but permanent; alike prepared to receive or make an attack; and which might have been alone a sufficient obstacle to every unconstitutional measure, or design to introduce an arbitrary government.

We behold, however, in the Swedish bishops, the strenuous protectors only of what they deemed the rights of the church; we frequently perceive in them, the promoters of tyranny; but never once find them the assertors of public liberty.

The popish clergy, from their profession of celibacy, form an order of men in the state, still more distinct and separate from the rest of the nation, than even that of the military: the latter may, by the ties of a family, be, in some measure, linked to the body of society, and have a general concern in the public welfare, independent of their partial interests as soldiers. But the case is otherwise with the former. Among them the citizen is lost in the priest; and the interests of the nation forgot in those of the order. When, therefore, the Swedish bishops opposed their sovereign, the good of the public was not even made use of as a pretext on the occasion.

Sometimes, it proceeded altogether from the licentious

licentious and turbulent spirit, by which all the Swediſh nobles were diſtinguiſhed, and which the wealth and power of theſe prelates furniſhed them more particularly with the means of gratifying: at others, it aroſe from an apprehenſion of a deſign in the crown, to recover the lands which properly belonged to it, and which they had uſurped. But as long as they imagined themſelves ſecure, and that the ſovereign had the policy to court their friendſhip, he might, undiſturbed by them, have purſued any ſchemes of oppreſſion towards the reſt of his ſubjects, that he had ability to conduct, or good fortune to render ſucceſsful.

Thus, to take in at one view, the whole ſtate of Sweden, during this period; we perceive a nation, all the orders of which openly aſpired at independence; who, by their fierce and intractable ſpirit, were rendered almoſt incapable of any political union; who, from a conſtitution, the great object of which was political liberty, derived none of the advantages, which alone can render ſuch a conſtitution valuable. The ſole end of political, being the ſecurity of civil liberty, the laws which give perſonal ſafety to individuals, and protect private property, ought to be the fruits of a free government; but theſe were unknown in Sweden. The monarchical, ariſtocratical, and popular branches of the conſtitution being ill adapted to each other, the limits of each undefined, and the rights of all unaſcertained, that concurrence of the whole, neceſſary to give effect to the reſolutions of a part, could ſeldom or never be obtained;

obtained; and consequently no provisions could be made for the interior order and tranquillity of society.

We find then kings ever violently grasping at a power, their obtaining of which was as constantly, and with equal violence, opposed by their subjects. A restless and turbulent nobility, too jealous of each other to suffer the title and dignity of King to be laid aside; too impatient of restraint to render the kingly office, when retained, of any use. A clergy, wealthy and potent, who were perpetually either the abettors of tyranny, or promoters of seditions and insurrections, as it suited their interest.—A fierce and independent peasantry; without union among themselves, and disdaining all subordination to superiors; obstinately bent to defend privileges and customs which were incompatible with any regular government; and the burghers, the only order of men inclined to promote public tranquillity, few in number, and held in little estimation. Such was for the most part, the state of Sweden, before, and at the commencement of the sixteenth century. With so many sources of disorder and confusion, it cannot appear extraordinary, that the kingdom should have been the constant seat of civil wars, and revolutions; of anarchy or oppression.

Miserable as the situation of this country must ever have been, it was rendered still more so by an event which took place there in the year 1385.

This was the famous treaty of Calmar; designed to establish a lasting union of the three Northern nations, but which, on the contrary, proved the fatal occasion of the moſt bloody wars, and tragical events to be found in the hiſtory of any people.

In order to comprehend what originally gave riſe to this treaty, it will be neceſſary to take a view of ſome of the tranſactions of the preceding reigns.

Magnus Ladulas, crowned in 1276, ſeems to have been the firſt king of Sweden who purſued a regular ſyſtem to increaſe his authority, and who had recourſe to policy, where violence had ſo often failed. That his predeceſſors had poſſeſſed ſo inconſiderable a ſhare of power, was as much owing to their poverty as to any other cauſe.

Magnus, therefore, made the augmentation of the revenues of the crown his firſt object. Motives of ambition would have been alone ſufficient to have prompted him to this; but he had likewiſe other inducements, perhaps, equally powerful.

He was poſſeſſed of a diſpoſition generous to an extreme; and a taſte for magnificence with which the Swediſh monarchs ſeemed to have been hitherto unacquainted. By theſe Magnus was hurried into expences which the royal income was by no means calculated to ſupport; but which it muſt have been highly mortifying to a prince of his temper to have been compelled to retrench. However, to accompliſh his point, he did not follow the example of former kings. The rock they had ever ſplit upon, was that of attempting to impoſe taxes without the conſent of their ſubjects, and to levy them by force. This certainly might have appeared

peared to them the most summary method of raising a temporary supply. It was likewise that which was best suited to the genius of princes; who, more accustomed to act than to think, were seldom capable of forming any of those schemes, which are the result of much art and deliberation. But, if it was the most speedy, it was at the same time the most dangerous method, and generally occasioned the ruin of those monarchs who had adopted it. Magnus, perhaps the ablest prince who had ever sat on the Swedish throne, could not fail to perceive this, and to regulate his conduct accordingly.

He knew the Swedes had at all times been peculiarly averse to taxes, and were equally apprehensive of that increase of the influence of the crown, which would be the necessary consequence of any augmentation of its income. To obviate the opposition to his designs which he had reason to expect on both these accounts, he resolved in the first place to find some expedient of raising a revenue without the imposition of taxes; and, in the next, to acquire so far the confidence of his people, that they should not be afraid of trusting him with a revenue so acquired.

Possessed of all the art and policy requisite to conduct with caution and secrecy the plan he had formed against their liberties, he was the more dangerous, from having, at the same time, a sufficient number of good qualities to conciliate their affections. If he gave occasion to awaken the jealousy of his subjects, he likewise won upon their hearts;

hearts; so that their judgment of his conduct became biassed by their attachment to his person.

Conscious of the influence of the clergy over the minds of the people, Magnus applied himself most assiduously to gain that body of men over to his interest. He paid his court to the monks, by founding a number of monasteries; and to the bishops, by affecting to place the greatest confidence in them, and by bestowing upon them the first offices of the state *.

When this artful monarch had by these means created in the nation a disposition which he judged favourable to his designs; having convened the States of Stockholm†, he represented to them the scantiness of the revenues of the crown, which he alledged were totally insufficient to support the dignity of a sovereign. And so great was his influence over the members who composed the states, that after three days deliberation, the whole convention voted him all the mines of Sweden and Gothland, the produce of the four great lakes ‡, to which they added the incomes of all the fiefs ||, alienated from the crown by former kings, when the leases in being expired §. Thus Magnus at one stroke rendered himself independent of his people; who, whilst they were so lavish of their

* *Botin.* p. 271. † A. D. 1282.
‡ The Meler, Veter, Vener, and Hillmer.
|| These were the farms, already taken notice of, which had been granted by Brant Amund, to those who cleared them of the woods.
§ Puffendorf.

grants

grants to the crown, forgot to have them accompanied by provisions for the security of their liberties. So that here was laid the foundation of a power, the weight of which was afterwards most severely felt by the Swedes, under subsequent monarchs.

But beside the augmenting of his revenue, in which we perceive Magnus succeeded so well, this prince had another object in view, of equal importance towards establishing his authority on a more solid foundation: this was, the humbling of his nobles.

He had observed that though the nomination to the dignity of a senator, and the disposal of the other great offices in the kingdom, were branches of the royal prerogative; yet they had added but little to the power of his predecessors. These offices approached too near to the royal dignity, where the authority of kings was so much limited as in Sweden, and rendered those who possessed them, the rivals rather than the subjects of their prince. The reason of this was, that though the king could make a senator, the states only could depose him. Whoever, therefore, became a member of the Senate, was immediately rendered independent of his sovereign. Hence, the very persons whom the king had raised to power and consequence, frequently employed them against himself. As they had nothing farther to hope or to fear from him, they could have no private interest in promoting, but would on the contrary, from the spirit of independence, and love of freedom

dom common to all the Swedes, oppose any designs he might entertain against the liberties of his country.

To remedy this, Magnus boldly hazarded a step, which a prince of less popularity durst not have ventured. He had married Hidwig, daughter of the Duke of Holstein, and was the first King of Sweden who formed alliances with foreign powers. Relying on the assistance he might receive from these, he resolved to bestow some of the great offices of the state upon foreigners. He even went so far, as to introduce many into the senate. As these had no weight or influence in the nation, but what they derived from their master, and possessed no interest separate from his, he was sure that the power with which he entrusted them would never be made use of to oppose his will. Such a conduct was a direct violation of the laws of the realm; and could not fail to excite the utmost degree of indignation and resentment among the Swedish nobles. But Magnus, secure of the affections of the body of his people, and likewise powerfully supported from abroad, paid little attention to the murmurs and discontents of his nobility.

Their haughty spirit could not, however, patiently submit to what they considered as the highest of indignities. Unfortunately this precipitated them into a measure, which only served to give the king a new and plausible pretext for pursuing the designs he had formed against them, with additional vigour. Nothing can exhibit a more

striking

striking picture of the savage temper of those times, than the methods taken by the Swedish nobles, upon this occasion, to seek redress for the grievance they complained of.

The queen going into Gothland to meet her father, was attended by many of the Holsteiners, who were the most obnoxious to the male-contents. This presented the latter with an opportunity they had long wished for. They resolved to way-lay her majesty on her journey, and to massacre all the foreigners that accompanied her. They spared only the life of the duke, father to the queen, who had herself the good fortune to make her escape.

From the reluctance with which all nations are apt to behold foreigners advanced among them to posts of honour and profit, it is probable that this action did not excite in the Swedes that indignation, which its barbarity might otherwise have raised. Magnus, however, was determined to punish with the utmost severity so atrocious an offence. But in this he was obliged to proceed with caution, and to employ his usual address.

Having, by the most artful conduct, lulled those nobles who were chiefly concerned in this transaction, into a false security, which entirely put them off their guard, he suddenly assembled the Diet; where accusing them of high-treason, he had influence sufficient to procure their condemnation. They were accordingly conveyed to Stockholm, where they were executed. This was the most fatal blow that the power and independence of the

Swedish nobles had ever received. So vigorous an exertion of the influence the king had been able to acquire, awed them into submission during the remainder of his reign; which concluded in the most perfect tranquillity.

But it ended too soon for the completion of all this prince's designs. He had, indeed, governed with far more authority than any of his predecessors; but he was indebted for this increase of power to his personal qualities, not to the throne he occupied. It was *Magnus*, not the *King*, who was respected and obeyed. To transfer, however, an authority so acquired, from the person of the monarch, to the crown itself, so as to render it part of the constitution, and enable him to transmit it to his children, was by no means an easy task. Had Magnus lived longer he might, perhaps, have effected it. But the death of this prince, in the prime of life, fortunately prevented the Swedes from carrying their complaisance towards a favourite sovereign too far; and the extreme youth of his successor prevented, in some measure, those immediate ill consequences to their liberties, of which the artful policy of Magnus might otherwise have been productive.

I have dwelt the longer upon the transactions of this reign, as, during the course of it, the grounds of the first material change in the Swedish constitution, from the time of its establishment, seem to have been laid.

So considerable an augmentation of the revenues

nues of the crown was neceffarily followed by a proportional increafe of the regal power; and whilft by the fteady and vigorous exertion of this power Magnus humbled the haughty fpirit of his nobles, and created in the reft of the nation a refpect for the royal dignity, with which they appear to have been before but little acquainted; he at the fame time, by employing them only for the public good, reconciled his fubjects to acts of authority, which in former monarchs they would have oppofed with the utmoft violence.

The character and conduct of this prince might in fome meafure have juftified their acquiefcence to his will; but they either did not forefee or did not guard againft the evil confequences of eftablifhing a precedent which opened a door for the admiffion of arbitrary power under future monarchs. Accordingly it is likewife in the tranfactions of this reign that thofe caufes originated, which afterwards gave birth to the treaty of Calmar.

The fucceffors of Magnus imitated his example only in aiming at the augmentation of the royal authority, but did not employ, like him, that authority for the good of the people.

It is the opinion of all the Swedifh hiftorians, that had the fucceffors of this prince been poffeffed of equal abilities, the free conftitution of Sweden would probably have been converted into an abfolute monarchy. But at the death of Magnus, his fon Birger was only eleven years old; and Terkel Canutfon, who was appointed regent during the minority of the young king, was not of a

difpofition

disposition to sacrifice the liberties of his country at the shrine of the royal authority.

Magnus had likewise committed the same error of which many of his predecessors had been guilty. He had given to his younger son separate portions of his dominions; so that though Birger had the title of king, his brothers Eric and Waldemar nearly equalled him in power and in the extent of their possessions.

This was productive of the same spirit of rivalship, the same jealousies, and the same civil dissentions, which had ever been the consequence of such a division of the Swedish territories.

One advantage indeed resulted from it: the king, engaged in continual contests with his brothers, could have neither leisure nor opportunity to pursue that artful policy practised by his father, which had threatened the total ruin of the Swedish liberties, even had he possessed abilities equal to the task.

The schemes of Magnus had been however too deeply laid not to be productive, after his death, of many of the consequences which this sagacious prince had foreseen.

By introducing a stile of magnificence into the Swedish court, which had been before unknown there, he not only indulged his natural disposition, but likewise forwarded by it his views of ambition. The pomp and splendour he displayed, at once gave new dignity to the crown, and in the opinion of the people, too apt to be governed by appearances, served in a great measure to diminish

the

the importance of the nobles. As the one gained, the other lost ground, with regard to the respect in which they were till then held by the nation. And Magnus, by inspiring his subjects with respect for the person, prepared them to submit to the authority of the king. In this his example was followed by his successors. They were indebted to him for the great augmentation of the revenue of the crown, which gave them the means of doing so; whilst from his conduct with respect to foreigners, they had been taught what advantages they might reap from foreign alliances, and how effectually they might be supported by these against their own subjects.

Hence it was that tho' many circumstances contributed to prolong the date of the Swedish liberties, yet from the reign of this prince we find the power of the crown gradually increasing, till at length under Albert of Meclenberg, liberty seems to have been totally subverted, and despotism established in its room.

From the same period too we may observe that a change in the temper and disposition of the Swedes began to take place; and that the eagerness of their monarchs to usurp authority, appears hardly to exceed the abject submission with which they were suffered to exercise it.

Not only Birger, but the two dukes his brothers, loaded the people with taxes; who bore the heaviest impositions, with a patience that had never been found in their ancestors on similar occasions. And when this at length produced some commotions,

they

they were quelled with unusual facility, and the princes persevered without obstacle in the same line of conduct. The riches they obtained or rather extorted from their subjects, not only enabled them to divide the nation into parties, but likewise to maintain bodies of foreign troops, which were the chief instruments of their power.

We find however that a revolution shortly takes place. Birger is dethroned, Mathas Kettlemunson declared protector, and Magnus, son of duke Eric, an infant only three years old, advanced to the throne. But we are not to attribute this revolution to the spirit of liberty, which had on former occasions produced changes of a similar nature. That spirit appears then to have been almost extinct among the Swedes; at least it had been so much enfeebled, that other motives seem to have been requisite to stimulate the nation to resistance. Hence, though Birger had been guilty of greater oppressions than those for which many of his predecessors had forfeited their crown, yet other causes were assigned for taking arms against him. Birger's two brothers Eric and Waldemar, had been put to death in the most treacherous and inhuman manner, by his order. His unnatural cruelty towards these princes, who perhaps deserved as little of the public as himself, was the ostensible reason for driving him from his throne and kingdom: so that this revolution is to be attributed rather to the power and number of the partizans of the murdered dukes, than to any remains of that spirit of resistance, which at former periods the love

of

of freedom had never failed to excite among the Swedes when they found themselves oppressed. We proceed but a few steps in the Swedish history before we meet with another revolution: Magnus, from the same infatuation which had possessed almost every monarch that had hitherto sat on the throne of Sweden, pursued the same conduct in encroaching on the liberties and trampling on the rights of his people. And though this prince possessed neither abilities to gain the respect, nor virtues to acquire the love of his subjects, he would probably have been suffered to continue his usurpations, had he not unfortunately for himself, employed the revenues appropriated to the pope, in an expedition against the Russians. Unable to reimburse his holiness, he was excommunicated. The consequence was, that superstition effected what the love of freedom, no longer powerful among the Swedes, could not have done. Magnus was dethroned, and the crown conferred on his son Eric.

Upon the death of Eric, who held the sceptre but a short time, his father, the deposed Magnus, having given the most solemn assurances that he would correct the errors of his former reign, was suffered again to ascend the Swedish throne. For this perhaps he was principally indebted to his being the only remaining prince of the blood royal. His conduct however answered but ill to his professions; and he made no other use of the authority to which he had been restored, than to gratify his resentments, and to satiate his revenge upon

G those

those who had before contributed to his deposition.

Wearied at length with his tyranny, the nobles who had most suffered, or had most to apprehend from him, resolved to shake off his yoke. But this was by no means an easy task. Since the reign of Magnus Ladulas, the power of the crown had increased in proportion as its revenues had been augmented.

The Swedish monarchs had of late been enabled to form to themselves so numerous a body of partisans, that nothing but a very general disaffection among their subjects could shake them from their seat. The spirit of liberty had so much decayed among the people as to have had little or no share in the two last revolutions. These had not been accomplished without difficulty and bloodshed, and would probably have never taken place but for some other circumstances, which bore no relation to those causes which on former occasions had been productive of similar events.

In the present instance no such circumstances existed. There was besides, as has been before observed, no prince of the royal race remaining to whom they could offer the crown; and any scheme of the nobles to elect a new king out of their own body would have been a point of the utmost difficulty. Not only their jealousy of each other was almost an insuperable obstacle to this measure, but had they been able to have overcome it, and to have chosen one from among themselves, their ability to support their choice was very dubious.

In

In this state of things they resolved upon an expedient, which was what first prepared the way for the accession of Margaret of Norway to the throne of Sweden; and which consequently immediately led to the famous treaty of Calmar. They resolved to offer their crown to some foreign prince, who from his connections and alliances, would be sufficiently powerful to make good the title they were willing to confer upon him. They imagined that such a prince, who should owe to them alone the scepter he bore, who could not, like a native monarch, have had any opportunity of forming to himself a body of partisans, dangerous to the liberties of their fellow subjects; and who, from the very circumstance of his being a foreigner, would be mistrusted by the people; would scarcely venture to invade the rights of men already on their guard against him.

Albert, second son of the duke of Meclenburg, was the prince made choice of on this occasion; He was at first proclaimed by the malecontents, and having seized upon Stockholm, was afterwards acknowledged sovereign by the whole nation.

Thus Magnus was a second time deposed, and so far the Swedes accomplished their wishes. But they soon found themselves severely disappointed in every other view which had induced them to place their crown on the head of a foreigner. One might have been tempted to think that the Swedish throne was itself infectious, and necessarily communicated the love of despotism, like a disease, to all who sat upon it. The same power which had enabled Albert to snatch the scepter out of the hands of Magnus, was afterwards employed to enslave his new subjects. Certain of support from the princes of Meclenburg, the earls of Holstein, and the Hanse towns, he resolved to carry his authority to the utmost extent. He bestowed all posts of consequence upon foreigners. These only possessed his confidence and shared his favours; he introduced a number of Germans into the senate, in direct violation of the laws of the realm; and maintained a standing army of foreign mercenaries, by means of the oppressive taxes which those military collectors enabled him to extort from his subjects.

Not content with having laid burdens on his people already beyond their ability to bear, Albert of a sudden demanded a third of all the revenues of the kingdom, ecclesiastical as well as civil. This the diet refused to consent to: but the king, who seems to have consulted them intirely for the sake of form, without intending to pay any regard to their determinations, immediately seized by force what he could not obtain by consent. So much was the spirit of the Swedish nobles at that time sunk, that had Albert contented himself with invading in this manner the property of the laity only, it is probable he might have enjoyed his usurpations undisturbed.

He betrayed however the utmost folly as well as rapacity, by this attack on the property of the church; which could not fail to render

der so powerful a body of men as that of the clergy, his mortal enemies.

The whole nation seems now to have been for once united, in order to free themselves from his tyranny. But if the deposition of Magnus had proved a point of no inconsiderable difficulty, the driving Albert from a seat in which he was so well fortified, must have been a much more arduous task.

The same difficulties must have occurred with respect to the choice of a successor, arising from the same cause, the want of a prince of the ancient blood royal, on whom they could bestow their crown without creating mutual jealousies among the nobles. But then Albert was infinitely more powerfully supported than Magnus had been; and the spirit of liberty, already on the decline among the Swedes under Magnus, had not certainly acquired fresh vigour during the despotic reign of Albert. An army of foreigners in the heart of Sweden; all the fortresses and strong holds of the kingdom in the possession of these; the chief part of the Swedish nobles in voluntary exile in Denmark, whither they had fled for protection; and the king, secure of receiving numerous bodies of troops from his allies abroad, the moment he should require them: these were all strong barriers in the way of any attempt to dethrone him. Thus circumstanced, the Swedes were either too weak to endeavour by themselves to shake off a yoke that was become intolerable, or perhaps wanted courage to exert the strength of which they might still have been possessed. Determined however no longer to submit to Albert, they rashly resolved to offer their crown to Margaret queen of Denmark and Norway. That sagacious princess, who had long beheld with a secret satisfaction the situation to which the Swedes were reduced, had too much ambition not to take advantage of it. She accepted of their offer, but upon her own terms. Terms which afterwards reduced Sweden to a more deplorable state of slavery than had ever yet been experienced in that country.

This measure was certainly as impolitic as it was extraordinary. From the national antipathy that had ever subsisted between the Swedes and the Danes, one would have imagined a Danish sovereign would have been the very last who could hope to ascend the Swedish throne. And with regard to the policy of it, the Swedes, without any great degree of penetration, might have perceived that a principal source of their grievances was the unconstitutional power which their monarchs had so frequently usurped. They might have observed, that from the great augmentation of the revenues of the crown, which had been insured to it to perpetuity, their kings had often been enabled to form at home a party sufficiently considerable to secure them in the possession of it, though against the sense of the rest of the nation: How much this security had been increased when a prince had likewise resources from abroad, they had but too well experienced in the person of Albert.

To

To bestow therefore their crown on the most potent sovereign of the north, who would not only necessarily succeed to all the authority possessed by preceding princes, but would likewise derive additional power from being already mistress of two kingdoms, seems to have been an expedient calculated only to increase the weight of those shackles, from which it was their object to free themselves. Little could they expect that so potent a princess as the sovereign of Denmark and Norway, would respect more their rights and privileges than their native monarchs had done; who, not being possessed of the same power, could not infringe them with equal safety. Yet such was the hatred the Swedes bore to Albert, and so precipitate were they in pursuing any steps which might rid them of that tyrant, that they not only acknowledged Margaret queen of Sweden, but, in order to cut off every hope the deposed king might entertain of ever remounting the Swedish throne, they waved one of those rights of which they had hitherto been most tenacious, that of electing their sovereign; and suffered Margaret, a short time after her accession, to nominate the prince who was to succeed her.

While the Swedes were thus industriously forging their own chains, Margaret meditated a stroke which had long been the object of her ambition. Not content with uniting the three Northern crowns in her own person, she aimed at rendering that union perpetual. The treaty of Calmar was designed to effect this purpose: a treaty to which her

her Swedish subjects were either so blind as to grant their assent, or, found themselves unable to refuse it. It was obvious they could never promise themselves any thing better from this measure, than to see their country become a province to Denmark; but the requests of their new sovereign carried with them the authority of commands; and as she possessed the power required to exact obedience to her will, she was of a temper too, that would not brook opposition. This event opens in the Swedish history a new scene of confusion, anarchy and distraction, arising from fresh causes, and exceeding, if possible, all the disorders which had before prevailed in Sweden, although the sources of these, were already sufficiently numerous.

The state of this country previous to the reign of Magnus Ladulas, has already been sufficiently laid open. But that reign furnishes an epocha, from which we may date a change both with respect to the government of the Swedes, and to that attachment to liberty, by which they were before distinguished. From that period[*] to the accession of Margaret, we perceive the power of the crown continually augmenting, at the same time that the spirit of the people seems proportionably to decline. Other motives than the love of freedom, visibly influenced their conduct, in the revolutions which then occurred. And if the frequency of these prove them on some occasions to have been

[*] 1394.

still possessed of their wonted restlessness of disposition, the patience with which they submitted, on others, to the severest oppression, sufficiently evinces that their passion for independence had considerably abated. But this alteration in their national character was not productive of any beneficial consequences to the tranquillity of the state. Of a temper too turbulent before to reap the advantages of any form of government, they then ran into the contrary extreme; and frequently betrayed a degree of submission, as inconsistent with their former character, as it was adverse to their liberties. The first not more repugnant to true, than the latter was subversive of all freedom.

The kings who reigned at this period, appear to have considered this change of disposition in their subjects towards obedience, as only a transient humour, of which they could not too speedily take advantage, for the purpose of augmenting their authority, and increasing their exactions. Accordingly we find the latter enormous, and the former almost unlimited. But we never see them pursuing measures of another kind, which such a change of disposition in the nation placed equally in their power; I mean measures that would have contributed to the happiness of society. We meet no improvement in their interior policy; no regulations to facilitate the administration of justice; to promote public order, render private property secure, or establish personal safety. None that tended to enlighten the understanding or soften the manners of the people;

ple; among whom we can as yet difcover, no knowledge of letters, no acquaintance with the arts and fciences, and few if any attempts towards the cultivation of commerce. If fuch was the ftate of Sweden previous to her having acceded to the treaty of Calmar, that treaty feems to have been but ill calculated to correct the diforders, which had fo long prevailed there. On the contrary, it at once opened an additional fource of oppreffion, and became a frefh caufe of new diffentions. Upon this were founded thofe claims of the kings of Denmark upon the crown of Sweden, which at different periods were purfued by thofe princes with various fuccefs; but which for upwards of a century plunged the two kingdoms into the moft bloody wars that ever brought ruin on a people. And it was this that divided the nation into two of the moft violent parties that were ever yet formed in it; the one, determined to affert the independence of their country; the other equally refolved to abide by the terms of the treaty; or under the pretext of abiding by them, to oppofe, from motives of jealoufy or ambition, the patriotic views of thofe, who refufed to admit the pretenfions of the Danifh monarchs.

It is true, that the Swedes, previous to their confenting to the union of the three Northern crowns, had taken every precaution againft the inconveniencies which might arife from it, that in their circumftances prudence could fuggeft. Among other articles, they particularly ftipulated, that they fhould retain their own laws, cuftoms,

and

and privileges of every kind; and that the subjects of Denmark and Norway should not be raised to posts of power or profit in Sweden.

Margaret, who had made no difficulty to consent to these conditions, used as little ceremony afterwards in totally disregarding them. Nor was there one article of the whole treaty of union adhered to by her successors. These having got into their hands all the fortresses of the kingdom, seemed to have no object in view but to depress the Swedish nobles, to remove them from all public affairs, and to reduce the people to such a state of servitude as must totally deprive them of the ability of redressing themselves. But it was otherwise with the clergy: to them was shewn every mark of favour and distinction. The Danish monarchs possessed policy sufficient to perceive, that without securing that body, they could never expect to tyrannize with safety over the rest of the nation. Accordingly monasteries were founded, churches endowed, and the power and privileges of the bishops augmented to the fullest gratification of their ambition.

Won by this conduct, the Swedish prelates were ever the most strenuous advocates for abiding by the treaty of Calmar; and consequently the most violent opposers of all who attempted to rescue their country from the shackles that treaty had imposed upon it. In consequence, therefore, of this fatal union of the northern crowns, the majority of the Swedes found themselves exposed to the worst of all oppressions, that which flows from subjection to foreign dominion; and what rendered their situation still more deplorable, was, that a confiderable number of their countrymen were interefted in promoting their oppreffion. Hence they became a prey to the rapacity of Danifh governors, whofe impofitions were exorbitant, in proportion as they were certain of plundering with impunity; and who, not content with feizing the property, often cruelly revenged themfelves on the perfons of this unfortunate people, for their inability to pay taxes that were impofed with as little judgment as feeling. And hence they fuffered no lefs from domeftic diffentions, than from the tyranny of foreigners. By every tranfient refpite from the latter, they became expofed to all the horrors of the former. When at any time enabled for a fhort-lived period to fhake off the Danifh yoke, which happened not unfrequently, the Swedes, diftracted by party rage, and ftimulated by all that bitternefs of rancour and violence of animofity which civil contefts ufually infpire, ftill continued, in their difputes with each other, to fhed frefh ftreams of that blood, with which even the fword of the Danes had been already glutted.

Soon after the death of Margaret*, we find Engelbrecht, and Erik Packe, rife to refcue their countrymen from the oppreffion of Erik her fucceffor. Animated by that enthufiaftic love of freedom, which once characterized the Swedifh

* A. D. 1415.

nation,

nation, their efforts were generous and bold. The senate renounce their allegiance to King Erik, and the administration of affairs is put into the hands of Charles Canutson, grand Mareshal of Sweden, his birth and rank obtaining what was in justice due to the services of Englebrecht and Packe. The murder of the first, and execution of the latter, who had taken arms to revenge the death of his friend, were the rewards they received at the hands of Canutson. Upon this the Swedes, as if they had already forgotten all they had suffered from the Danish government, appear desirous to recall Erik. The people, disgusted at the severity with which the Mareshal exercised his power; and the nobility, stimulated by jealousy at seeing an equal placed above them, determined to disappoint him in his views upon the crown, to which he now openly aspired. Erik having been deposed in Denmark and Norway, as well as in Sweden; they, in conjunction with those two countries, elect Christopher of Bavaria, who ascends the triple throne upon the same terms as Margaret and Erik. Christopher, uninstructed by the example of his predecessor, follows his steps; and would have met with a similar fate, had not death, by ridding them of a tyrant, spared the Swedes the bloodshed that must have attended another revolution. We now perceive, they have again recourse to the very man, whom they so shortly before judged unworthy to possess any authority.

On the death of Christopher, Charles Canutson

is

is elected King by a great majority. But he did not long enjoy his dignity. The intrigues of the bishops, and of the other partisans of Denmark, together with some tyrannical acts which the natural vehemence of his temper had made him commit, in a short time occasioned a universal revolt among his subjects; which ended in his deposition, a renewal of the treaty of Calmar, and the election of Christiern the Ist. It would be hard to determine, in this transaction, which we ought most to wonder at, the fickleness of the Swedes in so often changing their masters, or their absurdity in again consenting to that union, from which a dear-bought experience had most feelingly taught them they could expect nothing but the severest oppression. Christiern, indeed, soon gave them reason to repent of their folly; and we shortly find Canutson again seated on the Swedish throne. But it was only to renounce it as suddenly as he became possessed of it: and we next find him compelled to swear never more to aspire to the crown, which he bound himself not to accept, even were it proffered to him. Notwithstanding this, Charles again recovers the sceptre, for the third time; and his death, which happened soon after, we may presume spared him the mortification of seeing it once more wrested from his hands.

The conduct of this prince was certainly more extraordinary than even that of any of his predecessors; and furnishes a striking proof of the little attention

attention paid at that time among the Swedes to any ideas of order or principles of justice.

If the princes who preceded Charles pursued an arbitrary system of policy, and exacted supplies from their subjects with a rapacious severity, at least their power was previously established on a footing tolerably secure, and their authority undisputed. But that Charles should have proceeded upon the same maxims, that he should have been guilty of the same oppressions, he, upon whom the crown he wore had been bestowed by his countrymen, only with a view to deliver them from a tyrant; he, whose authority had ever been disputed by a considerable number of his own subjects, who had all the power of Denmark continually in arms against him, while the monarch of that country claimed a right to the Swedish throne, a right supported by a considerable party even in Sweden; that Charles, instead of conciliating the affections of his people, should in these circumstances have acted as tyrannically as any of his predecessors, we should be apt to attribute to madness alone, did not the general conduct of all the Swedes at this time testify, that the spirit of anarchy had taken possession of every breast, and that where all love for the constitution was lost among the subjects, an attention to their privileges could be but little expected from the sovereign.

From the time* that Charles first headed the troops raised by Englebrecht, to § the day of the death of this prince, containing a space of

* A. D. 1434.   § A. D. 1470.

thirty-

thirty-six years, nothing could be more dreadful than the state of Sweden. This indeed may easily be conceived from the summary view I have given of the history of this short period; a period in which there happened seven complete revolutions, besides innumerable insurrections and revolts, that were quelled before they had gained sufficient strength to produce others. And during which, the minds of men, continually agitated by a succession of reciprocal injuries, massacres, and all those outrages of which party rage, when under no controul, never fails to be productive, appear wound up to a pitch of fury bordering on madness.

So unaccountably inconsistent was the conduct of the Swedes at this time; so replete with the wildest absurdity; and so totally destitute of any apparent object but the destruction of each other; that in those days of superstition, an indifferent spectator might have been tempted to conclude, some dæmon, intent on the ruin of the country, had possessed its inhabitants.

Such were the fruits of the treaty of Calmar.

It were unnecessary to dwell longer upon scenes of so disagreeable a nature. It is sufficient to observe, that excepting a few intervals, these disorders continued to prevail in Sweden, till the horrid massacre of the nobility at Stockholm, under Christiern II*, filled the measures of the miseries of this country. This was a catastrophe well suited to the events which led to it; and all that seemed wanting to complete the desolation which

* A. D. 1520.

which those had already caused. It was however, in a great measure productive of the well-known revolution which soon after placed Gustavus Vasa on the throne. Before we proceed to a review of that transaction, it may not be improper to make a few cursory remarks upon the effects which the treaty of Calmar, and its consequences, must have had upon the manners and government of the Swedes, during a period of more than a century, in the course of which that treaty was occasionally adhered to. It is obvious no improvement could possibly have taken place in either, during times of such universal anarchy, such cruel civil dissentions, and so many bloody foreign wars. On the contrary, the restlessness of temper and fickleness of disposition which had ever been conspicuous in this people, must have been augmented in proportion as their government had become more unsettled. Previous to the union of the northern crowns, the vices of an elective monarchy had been in a great degree corrected, by the preference which in all their elections, the Swedes constantly gave to the line of their ancient kings. If disputes about the succession sometimes occurred between different branches of the royal family, at least all contention for the crown among the rest of the nobles, was by this means prevented. But the nation proceeded a step farther than merely to adhere to the royal line. Upon the death of the father, the son was generally sure to succeed, unless he had previously given some cause of disgust to those who were to elect him. Hence the Swedish kings seem to have possessed a double right to the crown they wore. The one, in virtue of their election; the other, on account of their birth. This last indeed was not nor could not, in an elective government, be vested in them by the constitution; but, which amounted to the same thing, it was founded in custom, and in the predilection of the people for the royal family.

This, to a nation so restless and turbulent as, before the reign of Magnus Laudulaus, the Swedes appear to have been, was productive of many advantages; whilst it cut off the source of those divisions, which in elective kingdoms seldom fail to ensue upon the death of a monarch; it gave to a Swedish sovereign a degree of security in the possession of the crown, which would not have been the case, had his subjects considered him in no other light than that of being the creature of their choice. Ever fond of change, as well as prone to sedition, they would, upon the slightest grounds for discontent, have used but little ceremony in unmaking kings, who were devoid of any other claim to the throne they occupied, than what they derived from their election.

Fluctuating therefore as the Swedish government was, this circumstance, without doubt, rendered it less so than it must otherwise have been. But when the treaty of Calmar took place, the ancient royal family of Sweden being then extinct, it is obvious that the Swedes, far from possessing any predilection for the princes, who in virtue of that treaty became their fovereigns, would, on the contrary, from the national enmity that had ever fubfifted between Sweden and Denmark, have naturally been difaffected towards them.

Thefe princes then were not only deftitute of what had formerly been the main prop of the authority of their predeceffors, but likewife found, in a national prejudice of their new fubjects, a frefh fource of difcontent among them, that was fure to augment that reftlefnefs of difpofition, which had already rendered it fo hard a tafk to govern them.

Accordingly, if we except Margaret, whofe fuperior abilities preferved the fcepter in her hands till fhe died; and Chriftopher, whofe death prevented a revolution: none of the Danifh fovereigns who fucceeded to the throne of Sweden, could ever maintain themfelves in it, although backed by all the power of Denmark and Norway. And notwithftanding that Charles Canutefon was a native monarch, yet as he poffeffed no right to the crown but what he derived from his election, he feems to have been rendered the fport of the caprice of his fubjects, from the number of times he was depofed and reinftated.

But the anarchy, confufion, and devaftation, which muft neceffarily have attended fuch frequent revolutions, were not the only evils refulting from the treaty of Calmar. Thefe indeed may have increafed the natural turbulence of the Swedes, and have revived that ferocity of manners among them, which had begun to abate during the reigns of Magnus Ladulaus and his immediate successors. Other consequences, still more fatal to liberty, ensued from that unfortunate measure. The question seemed no longer to be, how the nation ought to be governed, but who was to govern them. Whether a Dane or a Swede, a king chosen according to the terms of the treaty of Calmar, or in opposition to that treaty. This was the great object to which every other appears to have been subordinate.

Hence the love of freedom was in Sweden converted into the spirit of party; the generous enthusiasm of the one, sunk into the violence and rage of the other; and attachment to the constitution, lost in the devotion to persons. For the space of near a century and a half, during which this country was torn by intestine commotions, it was impossible that any attention could have been paid even to the forms of a free government;—and in such a government the forms are too intimately connected with the spirit of it, to admit of any suspension of the former, without risking the loss of the latter. Accordingly all sense of oppression in the partizans of either side of the question, seems to have yielded to the satisfaction which each in their turn experienced from having defeated their opponents; and both parties suffered themselves to be enslaved by the very persons whose cause they had supported at the expence of their blood. So that without having made one step towards the advancement of order and establishment of public tranquillity, the only benefits which can possibly arrive from the loss of liberty,

the

the Swedes found themselves at once deprived of freedom, and destitute of any of the few advantages which are supposed to belong to an absolute government. Such was their condition about the middle of the sixteenth century, and such were the causes of their being at this late period so far behind almost every European nation, in the improvement of their policy and civilisation of their manners.

SECTION II.

Containing a review of the history of Sweden, from the revolution effected by Gustavus Vasa, in the year 1520, to the death of Charles XII, in 1718.

AT no period of the Swedish history do we meet with a juncture so favourable to the establishment of an absolute monarchy, as that at which Gustavus Vasa ascended the throne. During those bloody contests for power, which had so long divided the nobles, harrassed the people, and desolated the country, we have seen that the nation had in a great measure lost sight of liberty; and that their attachment to rights and privileges, once so dear to every Swede, appeared to have decreased in proportion to the length of time they had been deprived of them.

Nor was it extraordinary, that all love for the constitution should have been extinguished among a people, who whatever might have been the case with their forefathers, never had themselves experienced

experienced any of those benefits which ought to have resulted from it.

In fact, for upwards of a century previous to the revolution brought about by Gustavus, the ancient Swedish form of government had existed only in idea; and consequently the ancient Swedish liberty could have little or no place in the recollection of those Swedes who were witnesses to that event. On the other hand, we find they had been long a prey to all the violences of party rage; they had been long accustomed to devote themselves blindly to those who headed the different factions which distracted the state, and whichever side prevailed, the people may be said to have been in some degree trained to submission by the despotism of those who directed the public affairs.

Thus circumstanced, thus prepared for slavery, their fate seems to have been suspended only because they could not agree among themselves in the choice of a master. There were so many competitors for power, that no one of these was ever permitted by the rest to establish his authority on a more permanent foundation; and hence the form of the government had not as yet been rendered absolute, although the temporary directors of the state acted with an authority purely arbitrary.

But Gustavus had none of these difficulties to contend with. On the first news of his revolt, Christiern gave orders to all the Danish officers in Sweden, to put to death indiscriminately every
Sweden-

Swedish gentleman within their reach, whether a friend or an enemy. This horrid action had been preceded by the massacre of the principal nobility at Stockholm. The Dane little imagined that the very measures by which he meant to secure himself on the Swedish throne, in reality, served only to prepare the way for the success of his enemy. They left Gustavus without rivals for the crown, and the people without leaders for faction.

Hence it gave to the one, the secure possession of the kingdom; and to the other, that unanimity without which they could never have shaken off the Danish yoke.

Thus from the blackest transactions which ever disgraced the annals of a monarch, the most beneficial consequences resulted to the very persons whom this tyrant had devoted to destruction.

Here then we perceive that whatever had prevented hitherto the establishment of an absolute monarchy in Sweden, was completely removed at the time Gustavus ascended the throne. But this was not all. The Swedes beheld in this prince, not only their sovereign, but likewise the deliverer of his country. They saw in Gustavus the man, who at the moment they were sinking beneath the weight of a foreign yoke, when they were reduced to a state of wretchedness too deplorable to allow them even to hope for relief, not only rescued them from that yoke, and all the miseries it had occasioned; but by the wisdom and lenity of his government prevented the return of those civil dissensions which had so often distracted the nation; and to whom therefore they were indebted for tranquillity and peace, as well as independence.

To such a prince, a grateful people, even supposing them possessed of the spirit of liberty, might notwithstanding have been too apt to consider the most unreserved submission on their part, as only a just return for the inestimable services rendered on his. The most implicit obedience in a people so circumstanced, however repugnant to the principles of their constitution, would wear the appearance of a virtue: it would seem the offspring of their gratitude for benefits which they knew not otherwise how to repay.

The same motives therefore, must, if possible, have operated still more powerfully on a people, who, as was just now observed, had been previously prepared for slavery. It was accordingly not at all surprising that the Swedes should have suffered Gustavus to lay the foundation of an absolute monarchy; particularly as the amiable qualities and conciliating manners of this prince, were as conspicuous after he was seated on the throne, as his courage and abilities had been in raising himself to it.

The situation of Denmark also, left Gustavus entirely at liberty to pursue his designs. Christiern had been driven from the throne of that country, but he was still alive, and had still a number of adherents.

His successor Frederick therefore, carefully avoided

avoided creating to himself a new, while he had any thing to apprehend from an old enemy. He assumed accordingly a very different conduct from that held by his predecessors ever since the date of the treaty of Calmar.

From that period the Danish monarchs had constantly laid claim to the crown of Sweden. A claim necessarily unjust, as it was solely derived from a treaty, to no one article of which they had themselves adhered. But Frederick, far from attempting to make good this pretended right, cultivated the friendship of Gustavus with the utmost assiduity; so that his Swedish majesty found an ally in that potentate, who had during the course of more than a century proved the most implacable enemy to his country.

Thus a number of circumstances conspired to give to this monarch a degree of power never possessed by any who had preceded him. How firmly that power was established, the change he brought about in the religion of his subjects, furnishes a most striking proof. The Swedish prelates, from their wealth, pride, and ambition, had certainly had no inconsiderable share in reducing their country to the deplorable state from which it had been rescued by Gustavus. To diminish the riches and curtail the power of these haughty priests, were consequently objects as desirable, as they were hard to be obtained. Hitherto, the smallest infringement of the rights of the clergy, had often cost a Swedish monarch his crown. To attack therefore the religion itself, in order to

humble

humble the ministers of it; to aim at extirpating the superstition of the Romish church, among a people so bigotted as the Swedes then were, was an attempt well suited indeed to the bold and enterprizing genius of Gustavus, but which only a prince of his abilities, and who possessed like him the love of his subjects, could have accomplished. He succeeded. The reformation was complete. They who had been the rivals of their sovereign, who had even given law to the crown, who had promoted sedition instead of preaching peace, and who with the most rapacious ambition, grasped at wealth as eagerly as they had done at power, sunk into their proper sphere; and were compelled to fulfil the long-neglected duties of their function.

Salutary as the consequences of this measure were, it was certainly rather a dangerous experiment, for an elective King, at the commencement too of his reign.

A less adventurous politician would probably have deemed it more prudent to have paid court to the clergy, and by gaining that body over to his interests, have secured his authority, with respect to the rest of his subjects. But Gustavus had other views. The chief opposition he had met with in his glorious enterprize had proceeded from the bishops. He, therefore, not only disdained dissembling with men, who must certainly have incurred his keenest indignation, but he foresaw that as long as these prelates possessed the

temporal

temporal power*, which their influence over the minds of the laity had enabled them to usurp; there could be no security for the duration of the public tranquillity, nor could the royal authority acquire any degree of permanency.

In order, therefore, to lessen a power which had been often exerted for the worst purposes, he judged it necessary to diminish too that influence, in which it originated; and this was only to be done by abolishing popery.

On his accession to the crown, Gustavus found the public revenues totally exhausted. The ruinous state of a country, all the inhabitants of which, excepting the clergy, had been long exposed to the unfeeling rapacity of foreign collectors under an insatiable tyrant, left Gustavus with but few resources to repair the finances of the kingdom. He thought the immense and superfluous wealth of the church, could not be more usefully employed than for this purpose; and we may add too, that the freedom and liberality of this prince's sentiments, must have made him behold with regret and indignation, the manner in which the Romish clergy then imposed upon the credulity of the people.

Yet still there was apparently so much hazard and danger in an undertaking of this nature, that, perhaps, these motives would not alone have been sufficient to have determined Gustavus to venture upon it. What he had already atchieved, proved, it is true, that he was not to be deterred by difficulties.

* I have shewn on a former occasion, together with the causes of it, that the power of the bishops was greater in Sweden than in any other country.

But

But then, previous to his enterprize against Christiern, his situation was such, that whatever he might gain, he at least risked nothing by his attempt, however wild and desperate it might at first sight have appeared. And the measures he used to surmount the many obstacles he had to contend with, were conceived with a prudence that demonstrated he judged on all occasions as coolly, as he executed with fire and vigour. That he, therefore, who was only an elective monarch, should involve himself in new troubles at the moment he had begun to reap the fruits of what he had already accomplished, agrees well enough with one part of his character, but does not by any means correspond with the other. The motives then, which on this occasion probably operated the most powerfully on the mind of Gustavus, was a design he meditated, of rendering the crown hereditary in his family; and consequently, he determined to give every possible security to a throne that was to be occupied by his posterity. In this design he likewise succeeded *. The Swedes surrendered in favour of his issue, the right of electing their sovereign; and by that means relinquished any chance they might otherwise have had, of being able, upon the death of Gustavus, to stipulate such conditions with his successor, as might have brought back the constitution to its pristine principles.

Such, however, were the moderation, justice,

* A. D. 1542.

and wisdom of this prince, and such had been the dreadful state of the kingdom during a long period previous to his reign, that the Swedes far from conceiving they had lost any thing by the changes introduced by Gustavus, must, on the contrary, have looked upon every alteration as an advantage. They did not foresee what their country was one day to suffer from the despotism of a Charles the XIth, or a Charles the XIIth. Instead of all the horrors of domestic broils and civil wars, superadded to the weight of a foreign yoke, they found the independence of the kingdom recovered, peace restored, order established, justice duly administered, commerce protected, and the arts and sciences encouraged. They found this, and they looked no farther.

It cannot, indeed, be said with propriety, that Gustavus either changed the government, or destroyed the liberty of his countrymen. In fact, when he ascended the throne, they had been for some time as destitute of the one, as they were ignorant, perhaps incapable, of the other. It is very possible for a people to have occasional masters, and to be, at the same time, without a government. This had been long the case in Sweden; where even the forms of the constitution had been neglected; the spirit of it lost; the laws fallen into disuse; and the sword rendered the sole arbiter in every dispute.

The being sooner or later subjected to an absolute power, must have been the doom of a nation so circumstanced. And when we consider how

palatable

palatable that power was rendered to them by Gustavus, it will appear nowise extraordinary that the Swedes, however in the early ages of their history they may have been attached to liberty, should have sunk by degrees, from the reign of this prince, into the state of slavery, in which we beheld them under Charles the XIIth.

It is to be observed, that Gustavus did not accomplish all his schemes, without opposition: but as this was produced by a spirit of superstition, not of liberty, it went no farther than to such of his plans as related to religious concerns.

But the most remarkable circumstance is, that none of his subjects opposed him in this point with so much violence, as the very men who had been his first and great support: these were the Dalecarlians. There is something so peculiar in the character of this people, that to take some notice of them before we conclude with the reign of Gustavus, will not I hope be deemed an unjustifiable digression.

They inhabit one of the most barren and mountainous parts of Sweden. Perpetual snows cover the tops of their hills, and long dreary winters whiten over their vallies too, for the greatest part of the year. Their inhospitable climate, so far from furnishing any of the comforts, does not even afford what the more Southern people of Europe deem the necessaries of life. For want of corn they make bread of the bark of certain trees, and of a piece with such nutriment, is their whole mode of living. Every Dalecarlian renders to himself

self all those offices, which it is the province of different trades to supply in other countries. He makes after his own rude fashion whatever is requisite for his cloathing; the homeliness of which corresponds with the poverty of his diet. Ignorant of all those inferior arts which administer to the conveniencies of life, and the nature of their soil prohibiting agriculture, these people chiefly follow the laborious occupation of miners. Thus inured from their infancy to hardships of every kind, the Dalecarlians form perhaps the most robust and hardy race of men in Sweden. If they are unacquainted with the refinements of more polished societies, who dwell in gentler climates, they are likewise ignorant of their vices. They have ever retained their primitive simplicity of manners. Humble, yet brave, they are patient of labour, but not of oppression: submissive, where they think submission due; intractable, where they conceive authority to be usurped. Generous and romantic in their untaught notions of honour, and possessed of that spirit of enterprize which commonly accompanies great courage, they have been perpetually volunteers in redressing grievances by which they were themselves but little or not at all affected. Secure in their mountains, they were left to the enjoyment of their own rude customs; and placed beyond the reach of tyranny, they felt not the yoke imposed, at different times, upon the other inhabitants of Sweden: but when these wanted spirit to oppose their tyrants, the Dalecarlians undertook the task for them. They
sallied

sallied from their rocks and forests; they followed the standard of an Englebrecht; they spilt their blood in defence of a Sture; they conquered under the banners of a Gustavus.

Such were the virtues of these people! but then their simplicity was attended by its general companion, credulity, as their ignorance was by superstition.

Hence a people possessed of a disposition that might have been directed to the best purposes, were often rendered the tools of designing men to answer the worst; and, therefore, the Dalecarlians appear to have been the most turbulent of all the Swedes; wrought upon, on one occasion, by an impostor, who personated the son of the late administrator; at others, by their priests, they rebelled no less than six times against Gustavus. Three of the conditions which upon the last of these insurrections, the Dalecarlians proposed to this prince, at once give a full idea of their spirit of independence, their superstition, and their simplicity. These were, that he should never pass the boundaries of their province, without giving them hostages for the security of their privileges; that whoever eat flesh on a fast-day should be burned; and that both the king and his courtiers should re-assume the old Swedish habit, and never afterwards borrow new dresses and fashions from strangers. The last article was that which they most insisted upon.

Gustavus treated this generous, though simple and credulous people, with all the tenderness that

was

was confiftent with the tranquillity of his kingdom, and fafety of his crown; fo that towards the clofe of this prince's reign, they, like their fellow-fubjects, had become reconciled to all his meafures.

Thus when Erick afcended the throne of his father, he found himfelf fovereign of a united and contented people. No prince ever came to the crown of Sweden with fuch advantages. He was the firft who had taken poffeffion of it in virtue of hereditary right. The long happy reign of a king, adored by his fubjects, fecured to the fon not only the obedience, but in fome meafure the attachment of the nation. Tired of faction, and bearing frefh in memory the horrors of civil diffentions, they were difpofed only to tranquillity, and fubmiffion. They had, during the reign of Guftavus, who was the patron of fcience and commerce, tafted the fweets and learned to cultivate the arts of peace. The reformation had totally cut off the fource of thofe difturbances, which the wealth, pride, and ambition of the popifh prelates, had formerly created in the ftate. Moft of that ancient nobility, whofe turbulence was wont to be productive of continual revolution, had been cut off either at the maffacre of Stockholm, or in the courfe of civil wars. The race of nobles who fucceeded them, had been brought up with new ideas, and with notions fafhioned to the times. The claims of the Kings of Denmark upon the crown of Sweden were annihilated, as the act which rendered that crown hereditary, had cancelled the treaty of Calmar. And finally, the royal revenues had for the first time, not only been rendered amply sufficient to maintain the dignity of a crowned head, but immense riches were lodged in the treasury, which had accrued to Gustavus from the suppression of monasteries, and other consequences of the reformation.

The tranquillity of Sweden appeared now to rest on a basis sufficiently firm. The boisterous scenes which she had long exhibited, had yielded to others of a more pleasing aspect; and a variety of circumstances seemed to promise that the continuance of these would have been lasting.

It was not, indeed, to be presumed, she could retain any part of her former liberty; the foundations of arbitrary power had been too deeply laid, and the superstructure was too far advanced: it might, however, have been expected, that freed from public troubles, she would have sunk peaceably at least, into the lap of despotism.

The event was, however, otherwise. In this country, fated to revolutions, not only fresh commotions shortly break out, but the spirit of liberty appears once more to awake among its inhabitants.

The insanity of Erick was the cause of the first; and the appearance of the latter originated in the reformation.

Erick by his first acts of authority gave great disgust to his nobles. But it seems to have been a matter of little importance how he treated men, whose abject servility surpassed the utmost turbulence of their ancestors. This unfortunate prince was not destitute of good qualities: but the disorder

order in his understanding frequently made him commit actions equally unjust and cruel. It is truly astonishing with what slavish submission the once fierce and spirited Swedes, bore with the frantic violence of a lunatic*. Violences which in his lucid intervals struck Erick himself with horror, were sure to obtain the sanction of the states, whose decrees never failed to be a justification of his conduct.

The King's brothers, however, the dukes John and Charles, were not so patient. The former had been condemned to death by Erick, and had with difficulty escaped. Both the dukes, therefore, were convinced there could be no safety for them, as long as Erick continued on the throne: they determined to depose him. Sweden was again plunged into a civil war, but it was not of long duration. The cause of the dukes was popular. Erick was in a short time abandoned, dethroned and imprisoned; and John assumed the sceptre that had been wrested from his brother's hands.

* Of this the two following instances are sufficient: Nilus Sture, of the family of the late Administrators, had been long an object of the jealousy and ill usage of Erick, although this prince had never had the smallest reason to be offended with him. The king, at length, went so far as to stab Sture with his own hand: Sture drew the poniard out of his side, kissed it, and presented it to Erick, who, notwithstanding, ordered his guards to put him to death.—The other instance is that of six and twenty nobles having been massacred at once, upon groundless suspicions, and the states after their death condemned those persons, whom it was impossible they could have tried.

We now once more behold tranquillity restored to Sweden. John succeeded to all those advantages already enumerated, of which Erick, at his accession to the crown, had been possessed. The source of all the disorders of the last reign no longer existed: and the patience exhibited by the people during the continuance of it, sufficiently evinced that neither the love of freedom, nor the spirit of faction, were any longer sufficiently powerful among them to be productive of fresh troubles.

It must have been a point of some difficulty to have devised any thing that could create new disorders in a country, where a prince so circumstanced, reigned over a people so disposed. But John shortly hit upon, perhaps, the only expedient, which had he wanted to plunge his subjects into confusion, would probably have been attended with success. This was an attack upon the religion which his father Gustavus had taken such pains to establish. It was this attack that once more gave the Swedes an opportunity of restoring their country to liberty. An opportunity they certainly did not improve as much as the circumstances of the times seemed to allow, but by the means of which the compleat introduction of despotism was for a short period retarded.

John had married Catherine daughter of Sigismond king of Poland. This princess, bigotted to the church of Rome, and possessed of great influence over her husband, appears to have directed that influence to no other object but the conversion

sion of the king, and the re-establishment of popery in his dominions.

In the first, she seems to have succeeded. In the latter, her endeavours served only to plunge the kingdom into confusion, and ultimately to deprive her son of the succession to the crown.

Duke Charles foresaw the consequences of the system pursued by the king at the instigation of Catherine; and regulated his conduct accordingly. Men who have once shaken off the papal yoke, have seldom been weak enough to resume it from motives of religion, however they might from those of interest; and since the reformation the Swedes had held the church of Rome in abhorrence. Charles therefore could not have rendered himself more popular, than by opposing every measure of his brother which tended to restore popery.

He accordingly did most vigorously oppose the king on this occasion, and with a success that laid the ground-work of his future elevation to the throne.

Sigismond, the son and successor of John, had, under the tuition of his mother, imbibed all her prejudices respecting religion. This prince, some time previous to the death of his father, had been elected king of Poland. Secure therefore at all events of one crown, he flattered himself he should be sufficiently powerful to effect in Sweden by force, what the late king had in vain endeavoured to accomplish by address. His attempts were however equally fruitless. The Swedes having tasted the sweets, knew too well the value of religious liberty; and Charles opposed his nephew on the same principles, and with the same spirit and success, by which he had counteracted the designs of his brother.

During the course of these contests it was, that a most favourable juncture presented itself for restoring the ancient constitution of Sweden. Charles, who had an eye upon the crown, perceived the conduct of Sigismond would infallibly place it soon within his reach. But it was necessary for him to hold in the mean time a very delicate and cautious conduct.

The catholic party in Sweden, however diminished, was not yet extinct. Sigismond had still no inconsiderable number of adherents there; and what rendered him most formidable, was an army of Poles, which he could at any time introduce into the heart of the kingdom.

The residence of Sigismond in Poland however gave Charles great advantages, which this wise prince did not fail to improve. It furnished him with an opportunity of paying his court to the states, and of flattering the pride of the senate. By the former, he was considered as the guardian of the protestant religion; and he wrought upon the latter, by making an agreement with them never to engage in any enterprize without having first consulted them and obtained their consent.

On the other hand, Sigismond, in order to defeat the schemes of his uncle, pursued, as nearly as his situation would permit, the same policy. He accordingly endeavoured to create a misunderstanding between the senate and the duke; and

having

having in some degree succeeded, he took the first opportunity to devolve the whole administration of affairs upon the former, totally excluding the latter from any share in it, although he had been appointed regent by the states. Sigismond rightly judged that the most effectual method to gain the senators, was to invest them with power. And however dangerous it might prove to his own authority to entrust too much of it in their hands, he was compelled to adopt this measure as the only one by which he could counteract with any prospect of success the intrigues of his uncle. It is obvious that this situation of things put it amply in the power of the Swedes to recover all their ancient rights and privileges. The states and senate, from having been reduced to a degree of insignificancy that rendered them little more than an echo to the royal will, found themselves on a sudden so circumstanced as to be able to make their own terms between two contending princes; either of which with their consent would be secure in the throne, whilst neither could be so without it. But we do not find that they made a proper use of an opportunity so favourable to the recovery of their liberties. Unfortunately the senate was too fond of power, and the states were too jealous of the senate, to admit of their uniting together for the purpose of maintaining their common freedom. Accordingly, when the bigotted Sigismond was dethroned, and the crown was at length placed on the head of Charles, though the Swedes had without doubt a right to impose what conditions they pleased upon a prince who was

raised

raised to the throne by their free choice, yet they by no means provided against further encroachments of the royal authority, as effectually as upon such an occasion they might have done.

Charles however had long been accustomed to make the sense of the nation the rule of his conduct; and more anxious perhaps to secure the crown to his son, than for his own sake, to extend the regal power beyond those limits within which he had himself endeavoured to confine it, during the reign of his immediate predecessors, he governed in a manner that left his subjects a greater share of liberty than they had had the prudence to provide for themselves.

This confirmed in the senate that relish for power, which the chief administration of affairs in the absence of the king during the late reign, must certainly have given them; and though they had not sufficiently guarded against an arbitrary conduct in their future monarchs, they were rendered by this less likely to submit to such a conduct.

The generous and noble nature of Gustavus Adolphus the son of Charles the IXth, secured to his subjects the full enjoyment of whatever rights and privileges they possessed on his coming to the crown. The great asserter of the liberties of Germany would scarcely have aimed at despotism at home. This excellent prince, who united every social virtue to all the more brilliant qualities which constitute the hero; whose passion for glory, great as it was, did not exceed his piety; whose judgment equalled his bravery; and who in both surpassed the generality of mankind, as much as as he exceeded them in rank: he, I say, only desirous to reign in the hearts of his people, was satisfied with the power he derived from their affections, and never once checked that returning spirit of freedom, which, previous to the deposition of Sigismond, had begun to make its appearance in Sweden.

The thirty years war however, consequent upon Gustavus' invasion of the empire, had a strong tendency to counteract the effects of this spirit. The passion for military fame, which animated their master, caught hold of the nation. This passion is certainly by no means favourable to liberty, when the bulk of a people are under its influence; but it becomes very much the reverse when a monarch is himself the leader of his troops. Men are too apt to lose sight of liberty in the subordination and discipline of an army. The despotism, which in all points respecting the duties of a soldier, must necessarily reign there, gives them a habit of paying that sort of obedience to persons, which free men think only due to the laws. Accustomed to follow implicitly the orders of the general, they are easily brought to pay the same deference to the commands of the king. To obey him in one capacity and not in another, is a distinction perhaps too nice for a soldier. It will readily be conceived then what effect so long a war as that commenced by Gustavus in Germany, and afterwards carried on by his successor, must have had upon those who had spent the major part of their lives in it. An effect which must have been very general, as the Swedish nobles at that time disdained

dained to follow any other profession than that of arms: and as they were all emulous of sharing the glory as well as dangers of such a general as Gustavus, it may be presumed that few of them remained idle spectators of the exploits of their sovereigns. The whole nation too, charmed and astonished at the success which attended this prince, and their pride highly gratified to find they had of a sudden burst from obscurity to hold a most distinguished rank in the eyes of Europe, were too much dazzled by the lustre of those victories which placed them in so elevated a point of view, to give that attention to the more solid advantage of establishing their constitution in the manner which the death of Gustavus and the infant age of his successor, afterwards afforded them an opportunity of doing. Oxenstierne indeed presented to the diet, assembled on that occasion, a form of government said to have been projected by Gustavus; which was approved of, accepted, and ratified by the states. But from the time the senate had acquired that consequence, which their acting as arbiters between Sigismond and Charles had procured them, the object of every effort nominally made in favour of liberty by the leading men in Sweden, was in fact to establish an aristocratic power, equally at the expence of the royal authority and of the rights of the states. Had Gustavus lived to carry into execution himself the above-mentioned form of government, he would probably have so framed it as that it should have curbed the aristocratic spirit of the nobles, by confining the power of the senate within such

limits

limits that it would no longer have given umbrage to the inferior orders of the state. But when the framing of this form of government by which the boundaries of the authority of the senate were to be ascertained, fell to the lot of the very persons who were themselves to possess that authority when ascertained, it was not to be expected that they should adopt a similar conduct.

Accordingly one article in this form of government, sufficiently evinced that the object of those who had planned it, was rather to secure power to themselves than give liberty to their country. The article alluded to, was that which deprived the states of the right of framing or proposing any law, or of debating upon any matter that was not first communicated to them in writing by the king or regency. Now this regulation effectually took those who had the administration of public affairs from under the controul of the states; which was perhaps the very design of it, since they who devised it were to be regents during a long minority.

The power of the senate created no discontent among the nobles, out of whose order the senators were chosen; but it was borne with some degree of impatience by the other orders of the state. Hence a foundation was laid for those jealousies and divisions between the nobility on the one hand, and the peasants and burghers on the other; which ultimately brought slavery upon all, and which enabled Christina to govern her ministers with as much authority, and to exact as
implicit

implicit an obedience from her people as if she had been the most absolute monarch in Europe.

We are to observe likewise, that in the course of the two last centuries, the temper and manners of the lower order of men among the Swedes, had undergone a total change. It has been shewn on a former occasion, that the reign of Magnus Ladulaus was the point of time in which this change was first discernible. From that period, if we except the Dalicarlians, we shall scarcely find among the Swedish peasantry, any traces of that spirit of independence and love of liberty by which they were once distinguished; and indeed from the period just mentioned, to the accession of Gustavus Vasa, every occurrence in the Swedish history was particularly calculated to debase the human mind, and depress every generous sentiment belonging to it. We shall find them therefore under Christina, as henceforward we ever shall find them, a very different race of men from their ancestors. Patient, laborious and submissive, they will appear possessed of every quality an arbitrary monarch could wish to meet with in his subjects, but destitute of those without which men neither can be free, nor desire to be so*.

A people

---

* Whitelock, who was ambassador in Sweden in the reign of Christina, (and whose account of the Swedes, I have been assured by many Swedish gentlemen well versed in the history of their country, is most perfectly just and accurate) gives as one of the reasons of the small number of law-suits which occurred there in his time " That the boors and burghers, and men of mean condition, are in so much slavery of
" their

A people like these could have seconded but ill any endeavours of their superiors to establish real freedom; much less could they be wrought upon to give their assistance to measures, which, without procuring one advantage to themselves, tended only to throw power into the hands of a few of those, who already lorded it over them with no small degree of insolence and pride.

Accordingly, when the vain and capricious Christina, by taking the whimsical resolution of abdicating the throne, gave the chief men in Sweden a fair opportunity for carrying their designs into execution, they were not able to succeed. It appears from the reply made by this princess to the states upon their endeavouring to dissuade her from quitting the crown, that she suspected there were some projects on foot for new modelling the government at her death. But the nomination of Charles Gustavus to succeed Christina, a measure taken some time before her abdication, put a total stop to these intrigues, and once more deprived the Swedes of an opportunity of guarding against future despotism.

Nothing occurs in the short reign of this prince with respect to any alteration in the constitution.

He exercised as much authority as his immediate predecessors had done, and received from his subjects the same obedience. But his object seemed to be rather to emulate the conduct of Gustavus

---

" their lords and great men, that they hardly dare contest
" with them upon a matter of right or title, but submit to
" their will."

by

by the boldness of his enterprizes and rapidity of his conquests abroad, than to endeavour to extend his prerogative at home. The death of this prince being followed by a minority which lasted near sixteen years, once more presented a most favourable juncture to the states for putting their government on a footing that might secure them from the yoke of arbitrary power. Nothing however can furnish a more striking proof how totally incapable of liberty the Swedes must have been, than their having had after the death of Gustavus Vasa, such frequent opportunities of recovering it without having once taken any effectual methods to succeed in the attempt.

At the death of Charles indeed, the states shewed some spirit in their conduct respecting the regency as settled in his will. They deprived duke Adolphus, brother to Charles, of the guardianship of his nephew the young king, assigning as a reason for so doing, that the will which had appointed him to that office, had been drawn up without their knowledge. And that such dispositions as related to the government of the kingdom were never valid unless they had received the approbation of the states.

Afterwards, when Charles XI. assumed the reins of government, they exacted an oath from him; which serves to shew in what manner the Swedes wish to be governed, however little they understood the means of limiting their monarch to the degree they desired; or however deficient they might have been in the spirit with which they should have opposed him, whenever he attempted

to

to exceed such limits. The oath was to the following purpose:

"—We shall equally hold and observe whatever the law of Sweden requires of us with regard to the states in general, and in particular, in the same manner as we shall conduct ourself towards all our subjects, as well as each individual, for their rights, privileges, and property duly acquired, being willing to give as far as depends upon us satisfaction to the kingdom— and in case it should be necessary to make any changes in what relates to the defence, safety, advancement, and wants of the kingdom; we will in these cases do nothing, nor suffer any thing to be done, without the advice of the senate, or without the knowledge and concurrence of the states."

One would hardly have imagined that within two years after Charles the XIth had given this assurance to his subjects, he should have become the most absolute prince that had ever swayed the Swedish sceptre.

Those jealousies and divisions which subsisted between the nobles and the other orders of the state, during the reign of Christina, having been fomented by that Princess, were in no shape decreased in the minority of Charles. The intrigues, perhaps the money of France, had prevailed with the regency to involve the kingdom in an expensive and fruitless war. The taxes which, in consequence of this, the king found it necessary to impose when he took the administration of affairs into his own hands, proved a source of disputes among his subjects; which were productive of an event nearly similar to that which happened in Denmark a few years before; when the clergy and burghers, out of hatred to the nobility, united to surrender into the hands of the king their own rights, in order that the nobles might be deprived of theirs.

The Swedish nobles bore little or no proportion of the weight of those burdens, which sat heavy on the burghers and peasants. The paying of no taxes they considered as one of the privileges annexed to their order. A distinction that exempted those from contributing towards the exigencies of the state, who were best enabled to do so, was in its own nature odious, as well as highly unjust; but more particularly so, when the burden of taxes became so heavy, that the rest of the nation could no longer support it.

According to the Swedish constitution, what had been resolved by three of the orders, was, excepting in some particular cases, binding to the fourth; however this last might have refused their assent to the measures so resolved upon, and had the force of an act of all the states. This put it in the power of any three of them, when they thought proper to combine for that purpose, to pass acts highly injurious to the interests of the dissenting state. It is true, that whatever was proposed relative to the rights and privileges of each particular order, required the consent of all before it could pass into a law. But it was easy to avoid any direct attack upon an order considered in their legislative capacity, and at the same time

time to give a fatal blow to their interests as members of society. Accordingly Charles procured a decree, that all the lands which had been dismembered from the crown, since the year 1609, should be re-annexed to it. This was a stroke altogether aimed at the nobles, in whose favour every grant of this nature had been made, and by which many of them were reduced to the utmost poverty and distress.

But the inferior orders did not stop here.

The umbrage they had conceived at the power which the senate had of late assumed, nearly equalled the impatience with which the king had borne it. They, therefore, contracted the authority of that body within such narrow limits, that it altogether ceased to be any check upon the crown. The resolution of the states upon this occasion was worded so ambiguously, that the king seems to have been left entirely at liberty, to govern either with or without the advice of the senate. It is not hard to judge which was the most agreeable to such a prince as Charles the XIth. And finally, as if wholly regardless of their own fate, provided they could gratify their animosity against the nobles, the inferior orders came to the following extraordinary decision:

* " The states have decided, that all the forms
" of government, with their additions, should no
" longer be considered as binding to the king;
" but that he ought to be at liberty to change
" them according to his good will and pleasure.

* A. D. 1680.

"And

"And that it will be found necessary for the well-being of the kingdom, that he should be bound by no form of government, but only by the laws and statutes of Sweden; and that if he governs his kingdom with the consent of his senate, it is to be interpreted only as depending upon his good and just discernment. So that his majesty, as a king vested with supreme power to govern his kingdom according to the laws and statutes, as his own inheritance which God has given him, is responsible for his actions to God alone."

What did not a nation deserve to suffer from tyranny, who were thus capable of forging their own chains, and of establishing despotism by law?

The two sovereigns of the north were now become, from having been the most limited, the most absolute monarchs in Europe. But the means by which they had arrived at their power, altho' productive of the same effects, were the very reverse of those which had served to augment the authority of princes in other countries. In each of these it was the monarchs who endeavoured to raise the people in order to balance the power of the nobles: in Sweden and Denmark it was the people who endeavoured to sink the nobles to a level with themselves. The consequence was, that in the former, the people as well as the crown, were benefited by what the nobles lost; whereas in the latter, the crown alone was a gainer and the situation of the people continued the same.

This accounts for a greater degree of despotism having prevailed at various times in the northern kingdoms, than in the more southern countries.

As

As in Sweden, the object of the burghers and peasants had been to lower the nobles, so that of Charles the XIth seemed to be to depress the whole nation.

Not content with being the absolute master of their liberties, he appears to have considered himself as possessed of the same power over their property. By his injustice and rapacity half the individuals in his kingdom were involved in ruin. He liquidated, indeed, the public debts, and at his death left a treasury well replenished to his successor; but it was by means equally repugnant to honour and humanity. Resistance on the part of his subjects, was however vain. The spirit of the nation was broke; despotism was firmly established; and Charles the XIIth succeeded to a crown in the possession of all that absolute power which was so consonant to his disposition.

The reign of this prince and the calamities he brought upon his country are well known. A prince, whose ambition was madness; whose courage was ferocity; and whose chief claim to the admiration in which mankind seemed to have held him, was derived from the singularity of his make, from his being totally destitute of all those feelings, which are the parents of every social virtue.

The Swedes had certainly little chance of recovering under this iron-hearted monarch, any of those rights and privileges of which they had made a voluntary sacrifice to his father. Neither would they probably have ever regained a shadow of freedom, had not, at a very particular juncture, a lucky ball freed them from the shackles in which they were held by this extraordinary man. This event took place at a time that the greatest discontent pervaded the nation; that all divisions among them were at an end; that faction had been silenced by that still greater evil despotism; that all orders of men, forgetting their jealousies and animosities, concurred in one wish, to see their country extricated from the miseries to which it had been for some time exposed; and, which was the most important point of all, at a juncture when there was no immediate heir to the crown, and consequently they were left at liberty to new model their government.

PART

PART II.

SECTION I.

Containing the state of Sweden at the death of Charles XII; and an account of the form of government established there soon after that event.

IN the two preceding sections I have endeavoured to give such a sketch of the Swedish history, and such a view of the national character, genius, and manners of the Swedes, as were requisite to enable the reader to judge how far they may hitherto have been justly denominated a free people, as well as how far they were in reality capable of being so.

I shall now proceed to give an account of the form of government established in Sweden upon the death of Charles the XIIth, by which the most absolute monarchy in Europe, was of a sudden rendered the most limited; as likewise to lay open the causes which facilitated the accomplishment of so great a change.

Nothing could be more deplorable than the state to which the wild ambition and inflexible temper of Charles the XIIth had reduced this country. She had lost her best provinces, those situated south of the Baltic, together with the major part of Finland. Her commerce had been annihilated, her armies and fleets destroyed, and equally

equally drained of men and money; she had been rendered incapable of maintaining the wars which Charles had obstinately persisted in renewing, unless such expedients were made use of, as only the fertile genius of a Goertz could have devised, or which the callous heart of a Charles the XIIth could alone have consented to employ. Every species of oppression, every kind of extortion that a cruel ingenuity could conceive, or despotic power carry into execution, were practised on the Swedes, to enable a mad man to pursue fantastic schemes, useless to his country should they succeed, but certain to entail destruction on it should they fail. It were endless to enter into a detail of these; it is sufficient to observe, that notwithstanding his subjects foolishly admired in Charles those very qualities which were the source of all their miseries, yet their patience was well nigh exhausted, when the death of this monarch left them no farther occasion to exercise it. The execution of the unfortunate Goertz, who paid the forfeit of his life only for having served his master too faithfully, sufficiently proves the latent resentment and discontents of the people during the preceding reign; although, awed into submission, they had been compelled to suppress them.

These discontents were not confined to any particular order of men in the state; they pervaded the whole nation. The nobles and clergy, burghers and peasants, had all suffered alike under one common tyrranny. Wearied out with foreign wars, and indeed hardly able to defend themselves at home, they now sought only security and peace,

peace. But as they owed their misfortunes to the unlimited power with which their two laſt monarchs had been inveſted; they were convinced, that to obtain either of theſe ends, they muſt no longer ſuffer ſuch a power to continue in the crown. They had experienced to their utmoſt height all the horrors of deſpotiſm, and had had full leiſure to lament their folly, in having impoſed upon themſelves that yoke by which they were afterwards ſo much galled.

The ſenate had been taught a leſſon of moderation. Deprived of all their authority by Charles the XIth, and by Charles the XIIth of the few privileges which had eſcaped the graſping policy of his father; they were perſuaded that their beſt ſecurity for the preſervation of their own rights, was, that the ſtates ſhould be maintained in the full poſſeſſion of theirs. The ſtates, on the other hand, cured of their jealouſies of the ſenate, perceived how much miſtaken they had been in humbling that body to ſuch a degree, as to have rendered it no longer a check upon the crown.

Thus circumſtanced, thus diſpoſed, the Swedes likewiſe found themſelves at liberty to recur to their ancient mode of electing their ſovereign. One advantage had reſulted to his ſubjects from the ſavage temper of Charles the XIIth: incapable of every tender ſentiment, this prince had never ſhewn any inclination to matrimony, and conſequently left no ſon behind him to inherit a deſpotiſm, which in that caſe, would probably have been rendered perpetual. Upon the death of Charles, the senate resolved to place his sister Ulrika Eleanora, consort to the prince of Hesse, upon the throne; but they likewise determined that it should only be in consequence of the free election of the states, and upon the conditions these should think proper to impose.

They seemed however to think it necessary previously to invalidate all claim to the crown, which this princess might conceive she possessed on the score of hereditary right. But they appear purposely to have gone out of their way in search of an objection to any such claim on her part, whilst the most obvious one that could be, naturally presented itself to them. Ulrika was the youngest of Charles's sisters; consequently the right of succeeding to the crown upon the demise of that prince, if lodged any where, must have been in his elder sister; or in case she had not survived him, in her offspring. The states however did not chuse to make use of an argument with regard to Ulrika's title to the crown, which would have been acknowledging a good title to it in another. They wisely judged, that a prince, in whom they should either admit, or who had himself any grounds to conceive he was possessed of an hereditary right to the crown, (as might probably have been the case with the duke of Holstein, son of the elder sister of Charles) would be too apt to imagine he had likewise an hereditary right to all the authority enjoyed by his predecessors. They were therefore determined that the grounds upon which they judged Ulrika devoid of any title of this sort, should no wise relate to the objection

that

that might be started against her, with regard to her being the youngest of the remaining branches of the royal family. They asserted that the laws relating to the hereditary right of females to succeed to the crown, expresly declare, that a princess, in order to be capable of so succeeding ought to be unmarried*, and therefore as Ulrika was married, she, on that account, had forfeited all pretensions to the succession.

Any title whatever to the crown being therefore denied her, Ulrika could have no pretext to object to the conditions upon which the Swedes might offer to elect her their sovereign. Accordingly, she implicitly followed in all things the advice of the senate, and consented to whatever changes in the constitution they thought proper to propose.

Before the diet could be assembled, she published a declaration, whereby she renounced in her own name and in that of her posterity, all absolute power, or what the Swedes call sovereignty; as well as every prerogative hitherto possessed by the crown, which was not consistent with the liberties of the nation.

On the meeting of the states, their first declaration was, that they had voluntarily assembled themselves to elect a successor to the vacant throne. And they even exacted a written assurance from Ulrika, by which she declared she was willing to hold the crown in virtue of a free election, and disclaimed all other title to it whatsoever. They then thanked her majesty, " For having testified " in her preceding declaration so just and reason-

---

* Reces des Etats.

able

"able an aversion towards an absolute or arbi-
"trary power; the consequences of which (ad-
"ded they) have greatly weakened and much
"injured the kingdom, to the almost irreparable
"ruin of us all in general. So that we, the coun-
"sellors and states of the kingdom assembled,
"having had this sad experience, have seriously
"and unanimously resolved to abolish entirely an
"arbitrary power which has proved so preju-
"dicial *.".

But however seriously and unanimously they might have come to the foregoing resolution, it was by no means an easy task that they had imposed upon themselves. To tie up the hands of a sovereign who was to receive the crown from them upon their own terms, appeared indeed no difficult undertaking; but in order entirely to abolish arbitrary power, simple conventions with the prince would scarcely have been found sufficient. It was requisite for this purpose that they should totally new model their government. It was necessary they should frame a constitution, the object of which was to be the immediate restoration of liberty to a people, who had been long accustomed to a slavish submission. Independent then of the difficulty of framing such a constitution, which must have required talents, experience, and a depth of knowledge in those, who on this occasion, took upon themselves the office of legislators, of which few men are possessed; it must also have been a point of no less

* Reces des Etats. 1719.

difficulty,

difficulty, to have established such a constitution, when framed, upon any solid foundation.

Liberty is not a plant of sudden growth; time only can give it vigour. It will not take root, but in a soil congenial to it; and, to be rendered flourishing or lasting, it must be cultivated with care, and defended with unremitting attention from the dangers which perpetually surround it. But how to defend, and how to cultivate it, are points which experience alone can teach mankind; and with which, they who have been accustomed to live under an absolute monarchy, can scarcely have had an opportunity of becoming acquainted.

In vain, therefore, shall a form of government calculated to give liberty to a people, be established among them, unless these are prepared to receive it. Emerging from slavery, they can hardly be possessed of the freedom of sentiment, liberality of mind, and manly spirit, which, perhaps, only a sense of independence can inspire, and which are all so requisite to produce that consonance between the genius of a people, and the nature of a free government, without which such a government cannot long subsist. Let us see then how far the Swedes were prepared for liberty, at the time their late form of government was established among them, as well as how far that government was in reality calculated to render them free.

It is to be remembered they had so frequently worn the yoke of despotism, that its effects upon their tempers, notions, and manners, must have been very considerable. If they had severely suffered

fered during the reigns of their two last princes; this might, indeed, have inspired them with a dread of arbitrary power; but it could not have communicated to them those qualities without which men are incapable of becoming free.

The Swedish peasantry no longer possessed that bold and independent spirit which distinguished their ancestors: and as these had been often turbulent and licentious in the highest degree, so their posterity, depressed by servitude, had now sunk into the contrary extreme of servility and submission.

The burghers, in the ruin of their commerce consequent upon the wars of Charles XIIth, had lost that influence and importance in the state, which it is so requisite in a free constitution, that this order of men should possess.

Many causes had contributed to render the nobles poor, and consequently dependent.

The custom of dividing the property of the father equally among the children, without any regard being paid to primogeniture; the frequent resumption of the crown lands; and the reduction of estates throughout the kingdom by Charles the XIth*; all these had concurred to reduce that body to a degree of poverty, which, together with their

---

* When Charles the XIth resumed those lands which were supposed to have formerly belonged to the crown, of which he himself was to be the judge, he suffered the possessor to retain to the value of about seventy pounds per annum, but at the next assembly of the states, even this small pittance was forced from the unfortunate proprietor and likewise annexed to the crown.

absurd

absurd pride, that made them disdain any other profession than that of arms, certainly rendered them fitter to be the tools of an absolute prince, than the legislators of a free country. Men trained only to a military life, will scarcely imbibe principles of liberty in a camp.

But the circumstances which must have proved on this occasion, as it ever had on all others, the chief obstacle to the establishment of true liberty among the Swedes, was the division of the nation into those distinct classes which were totally unconnected with each other, and never associated together. As in order to preserve a free constitution, a certain degree of opposition, to use the words of a most ingenious foreign writer[*], should on the one hand take place between the different views and interests of the several bodies that compose it; so likewise, on the other, it must, in a great degree, owe its safety to a conjunction of views and interests in the body of the nation at large.

As members of different branches of the legislature, each possessing distinct rights and privileges, those entrusted with power ought reciprocally to be a check and control upon each other.

As members of the same society, possessing, in fact, one common interest in the general welfare of their country, a people cannot be too much united among themselves[†].

But

---

[*] Mr. de Lolme, p. 201.

[†] This nowise relates to those party divisions which must ever take place among a free people; these arise from a difference

But nothing tends so much to prevent this union from taking place, as those distinct classes in society, which, without contributing to the good order of it, or the support of government, serve chiefly to inspire one class of men with pride and insolence, and another with jealousy and envy.

No unnecessary distinctions should therefore be admitted among a free people. Those only should be allowed, which are requisite to create a degree of opposition between the views and interests of the component parts of the legislature §.

None should be suffered to take place among them merely for the purpose of gratifying the pride of individuals.

England is the only country in Europe where the distinction, for instance of noble and not noble, is carried no farther than the nature of the government requires it should; because there the nobility do not, *as such*, form a distinct class from the rest of the nation.

rence of opinion, not of interests; and consequently there is among such a people but one common object, and the point in dispute is only how that object is to be obtained.

§ Thus if of two of the component parts of a free constitution, one is hereditary, and the other elective; this circumstance will naturally produce an opposition between their interests; were both elective, or both hereditary, they might unite for the purpose of augmenting their common power at the expence of the liberties of the nation; but in the other case the hereditary legislators will be too fond of that distinction to suffer the elective to usurp it, and for that reason, the latter will not join with the former, in order to acquire an unconstitutional power; which, at a certain period, the representative body know they shall be obliged to surrender, whilst the hereditary are to enjoy it to perpetuity.

As

As it is only the head of each noble family, who is there entitled to the honours and privileges of the peerage, it is not the man who can count a long train of titled anceſtors, but the hereditary legiſlator who is himſelf noble.

The younger branches of theſe families, as they have no ſhare in the legiſlature, are but little, if, by courteſy, at all diſtinguiſhed from their fellow-ſubjects; with whom they, and their deſcendants aſſimilate, and are ſoon, if I may ſo expreſs myſelf, melted down into the general maſs, of the people. Hence theſe become a ſort of link between the nobility and the commoners; a link that, connecting their intereſts, prevents all diviſion between theſe two orders in their capacity of members of the ſame ſociety, and which forms of that ſociety a continued chain, no part of which can be touched without affecting, by an almoſt electrical communication, all the reſt.

In other countries, where thoſe who have been once ennobled, tranſmit the honours, and privileges of nobility to all their poſterity alike, there is no link to connect the nobles to the reſt of the nation; on the contrary, a line is drawn between them to perpetuity; a line which cuts, as it were, the chain of ſociety in two, the ſevered ends, of which appear rather to repel than attract each other. There, conſequently, that conjunction of views and intereſts cannot take place in the nation at large, to which I have ſaid a free conſtitution muſt, in a great degree, owe its ſafety.

It muſt appear then pretty evident, from what has been now alledged, that the diviſion of the

Swediſh

Swedish nation, into those three distinct classes of nobles, burghers, and peasants, whose interests were perpetually clashing, was a circumstance by no means favourable to liberty.

But this will be placed in a more striking light, by taking a summary view of their late form of government, as it was established upon the death of Charles the XIIth.

This consisted of fifty-one articles, which the states presented to Ulrika Eleanora, for her approbation. Her majesty could not fail to approve of them, as the condition of her election was an entire acquiescence in whatever the diet thought fit to enact. I shall only take notice of such of them as were designed to be barriers to the royal authority, or bulwarks of the liberties of the nation.

The states were composed, as formerly, of the four orders of the nobles, clergy, burghers, and peasants.

These were to be assembled every three years in the middle of January, or oftener, if the king, or (in case of his absence, sickness, or decease) the senate found it necessary to convoke them.

But if the king or senate should neglect to assemble them, at the end of three years, as the law required; or even should they not convoke them on the very day the states had, the last time they were assembled, chosen to appoint for their next meeting, these should then have a right to assemble of themselves; and whatever the king or senate should have done in the mean time, was to be considered as void.

The

The time specified for the duration of the diet was three months; but as its members alone had the power of dissolving it, they consequently could continue sitting as long as they judged proper.

While the states were assembled, they were, in fact, possessed of the whole supreme power. The authority of the king and senate was then suspended: they became mere cyphers, having little or no share in the public transactions, but what consisted simply in affixing their seals and signatures, to whatever the Diet should think proper to resolve, whether agreeable to them or not. In short, the states were vested with the same powers, independent of the king and senate, that in England the two houses of parliament possess only in conjunction with the king.

The legislative power they reserved at all times wholly to themselves. The king and senate having no share whatever in it, did not even possess a negative on those resolutions of the Diet, which directly attacked the regal and senatorial rights. For the preservation of these, they were entirely to depend upon the moderation of a popular assembly. The following powers were likewise vested in the states alone. Those of declaring war, or making peace. That of altering the standard of the coin. Whenever a vacancy happened in the senate, that of presenting to the king three persons, one of whom his majesty was bound to make choice of to fill the vacant office ‖ : so

‖ We shall see in the sequel how even this privilege, inconsiderable as it was, became abridged.

that in case of the death of a senator in the interval between the Diets, no one could be appointed to succeed him till the next meeting of the states. And lastly, that of dismissing any member of the senate whose conduct they disapproved of, or of allowing him, when he demanded it, permission to retire.

The executive power during the sitting of the Diet, may be said to have been, in a great measure, lodged in a certain number of persons selected from the three orders of the nobles, clergy, and burghers, who constituted what was denominated the *secret committee* *. The reason is plain why it could not continue in the senate, since that body was accountable to the states for their administration during the interval of the diets, and was liable not only to be censured but deposed by them. So that admitting the executive power to have still resided in the senate, it would in that case have been compelled to destroy itself. With regard to the judicial power, the states assumed to themselves a right of exercising that also, whenever they thought proper, by taking at pleasure causes out of the ordinary courts of justice, to try them before a temporary tribunal, erected

---

* The standing secret committee was chosen the first of any, at the diet, and continued all the time this lasted.

The number of which this committee was to be composed, was left to the option of each assembly, provided it was so contrived, that there should be two nobles to one of each of the other orders.

by

by themselves, and composed of their own members ‡.

Nothing could be more formidable than the power of this court, or more subversive of liberty; as in reality it united within itself, at once, the legislative, judicial, and executive powers; and as it was to decide principally in cases of treason, what rendered this extraordinary jurisdiction most preposterous was, its being generally at the same time both judge and party ‖.

At the expiration of the diet, the executive power was divided between the king and the senate, in such a manner, that but a very small share of it fell to his majesty.

He was distinguished from the senators only in having two votes, with this privilege, that if after

---

‡ There are three high courts of justice in Sweden: one at Stockholm, one at Jonkoping, and one at Ambo. According to the original form of government, no person could be tried by any other courts than these, for matters which concerned his life or honour. But the states dispensed when they pleased with this article, not finding these courts fit instruments for party to make use of. They had therefore sometimes recourse to the erection of the temporary tribunal, abovementioned; in the same manner as in France, the ministers have at times appointed particular judges to try such men as they had resolved to ruin. No Asiatic despotism could exceed that which such a court might exercise.

‖ This court too took cognizance of all such publications as the ruling powers thought proper to deem libels upon the government, and awarded the punishment of the authors of these.

The liberty of the press could scarcely have subsisted, where the offended party was to judge the offence, and condemn the offender.

dividing upon a question, the numbers on both sides should prove equal, the opinion the king had embraced, was in that case to prevail.

The persons of the senators, as far as related to the duties of their functions, were held inviolable; so that it was no less a penalty than death, to any one who should reproach or charge a senator with any thing defamatory respecting the execution of his office, unless such person was able to make his charge good by legally proving it. (*Crim. Laws of Sweden. 5th Chap.* 2.) Or whoever said or wrote any thing against a senator in his public capacity, was to ask pardon in public for his offence, as well as to be condemned to pay a considerable fine.

The senate was likewise possessed of so considerable an influence with respect to the disposal of all employments beneath the rank of a senator, that they were in fact, in a great measure, enabled to appoint whom they pleased to every vacant office ‡; and finally, what rendered them almost wholly

---

‡ All employments, from a colonel to a field-marshal inclusively, and such as were of the same rank in civil departments, were disposed of in the following manner. The senators pitched upon three persons, whom they presented to the king, he being obliged to make choice of one of them, although all three might be equally obnoxious to him.

With regard to inferior employments, the different colleges (that being the name given to public offices in Sweden) to which they belonged, presented what they called a *proposition* to the king, in presence of two senators, which proposition contained the names of three persons, for his majesty to make choice of one of them, to fill any vacancy that should have happened in a civil department: but if the vacant employment

wholly independent of the king, was, that they could assemble themselves whenever they thought proper, without having received any orders for that purpose from his majesty; and even without his being present, they could proceed to transact the most important business of the nation.

They read, without consulting him, all dispatches from foreign ministers; in short, left him nothing to do but to sign orders given without his consent.

If such was the power of the states, and such the authority of the senate, it is obvious, no very considerable degree of either could have remained in the hands of the king.

In reality he could not be considered as a sovereign himself, but only the representative of the majesty of the states; and a representative too so limited by his constituents, as to possess no will of his own; or rather he appeared to be nothing more than a state-puppet, who upon some gaudy days, was decorated with the trappings of royalty to impose upon the people, and make them imagine they had a king.

We have seen that he was allowed no share in the legislature, not having a negative upon the propositions of the states. He was consequently

---

ment was in the military line, then the college of war, (War-office) presented only one person, and the senate another; one of which two the king was obliged to appoint to it. Some of the highest and most confidential employments of the state, were excepted from those regulations, and bestowed in the senate, according to the majority of votes.

destitute of any means of preserving entire, the few prerogatives he found annexed to his crown.

He could neither levy troops, equip fleets, or build fortresses without the consent of the diet. He therefore could neither make war or peace, form treaties or alliances of his own authority. He was dependent upon each assembly of the states, for the revenues necessary to support his ordinary expences; which were granted him with so sparing a hand, that there certainly was never any superfluity in his finances, to enable him to make up in influence what he wanted in power. The states had taken as effectual precautions against the crown's obtaining the one, as it had to prevent its possessing the other. We have seen that the king was not allowed the unrestrained disposal of even the most insignificant employments. Nay, the very servants of his houshold became independent of him; and at one time he could not discharge a domestick who should have offended him.

Thus was the power of that crown retrenched, which had been so lately worn by Charles the XIIth. The few prerogatives that remained to the king, were simply these:

1st, The office of king was hereditary, which was not the case with any other office in Sweden.

2dly, The attribute of sovereignty or pre-eminence, with the outward pomp and decorations of majesty.

3dly, His person was sacred, so that whoever spoke or wrote concerning the king, without due respect

respect for him, was liable to be punished with the loss of life.

4thly, He was to be the only visible source of honours; that is, he only could create counts and barons, or introduce new members into the house of nobles: but he was much restricted in the exercise of this right, by one of the articles of the form of government.

5thly, He only could pardon after sentence had been passed upon a criminal. The senate was however authorised, to dissuade the king from exercising this branch of his prerogative, when they judged it would be improper; and the being so authorised, amounted to their having a negative upon the resolutions of his majesty on such occasions.

6thly, and lastly, The king, as has been already observed, was allowed two voices in the senate.

Such was the form of government established in Sweden, when Ulrika Eleanora succeeded her brother Charles the XIIth, in the throne of that country.

It is obvious, that the grand object of those Swedes who framed it, was to guard against all possibility of their monarchs ever again becoming absolute.

The retrenching of the regal power seems alone to have occupied their thoughts; and blinded by what they had suffered from the despotism of the two last reigns, they not only did not perceive that liberty may be liable to dangers from other quarters, nearly equal to those she has to apprehend from the usurpations of the royal authority; but they forgot, that when a prince finds himself galled by the shackles imposed upon him, he may become desperate, and in order to free himself, have recourse to the most fatal extremities.

Having seen monarchy of late only under its most frightful aspect, that of despotism, they would probably have wholly abolished it, but that the bulk of the nation were still prejudiced in its favour. If for this reason they retained the kingly office, they seem to have treated it as men would some fierce and dangerous animal, which they did not wish to destroy; but were resolved to secure, by loading it with chains.

But was this form of government, from annihilating the regal power whilst it retained the office, the better calculated to give liberty to the nation? Was it in any respect suited to promote an end so desirable, and so hard to be obtained? Was it adapted to the genius, disposition and circumstances of the nation? Or were the Swedes capable, at any rate, of reducing it to practice?

These questions I believe must all be answered in the negative.

The reader cannot but have perceived there were defects interwoven in the very texture of this government, which indicated from the beginning, where it must fail. These, in a short time, infecting the whole mass of the constitution, before any political principles, consonant to the new situation in which they found themselves, could possibly have settled among the people, disclosed to the public

public view, such scenes of corruption, dissentions, confusion and anarchy, that the nation had scarcely tasted liberty, when they began to be exposed to all the disorders and tyranny, of which the violence of contending factions, is in general productive.

The principal and most glaring defect in this constitution, a defect, which alone must have brought on its destruction, was the total want of all balance of its parts. For the very existence of the executive power, depending upon the legislative, this could arrogate to itself what authority it pleased.

It consequently might unite in itself both powers, and to them add the judicial likewise. This we have seen it actually did in the case of erecting those temporary tribunals I have already taken notice of. For as the members of such tribunals were persons selected out of, and chosen by the legislative body, it amounted nearly to the same thing as if that whole body had formed itself into a court of judicature.

The king's being totally destitute of power was certainly another very considerable defect in this form of government.

Nothing could have been more absurd than the idea of preserving the kingly office in a free constitution, without endeavouring to render that office subservient to the purposes of freedom.

It was, however, very natural for those who had suffered so severely from despotism, to carry their precautions against the royal authority too far,

when

when they found themselves in a situation which enabled them to set bounds to it.

They were not sufficiently acquainted with the true principles of liberty, to know how to reconcile kingly power with national freedom; and they were so intent upon restraining the former, that they forgot, as has been before observed, to guard the latter from dangers arising from other quarters.

Thus they rendered it impossible for the crown either to influence or corrupt the states; but, as shall be shewn in the sequel, they left another door open for a corruption of a more fatal nature, more ruinous to the country, and more destructive of liberty.

The only design then of retaining the kingly office in the late Swedish form of government, was, as I have already hinted, to comply with the prejudices of the people, who were still attached to monarchy; and who, therefore, would not have been satisfied, unless some person in the state was allowed to bear at least the title of king. What other end it could have answered, one must be at a loss to conceive.

As that office made no part of, it could prove no check upon the legislative power: which, therefore, could assume to itself all the rights of the executive power. Where these powers are united, it is allowed that tyranny must ensue; and such a union is only to be prevented, by suffering the executive power to possess a share in the legislative, sufficient to enable it to defend its own prerogatives.

The

The great ufe of eftablifhing a chief magiftrate in a free government, is, that the executive power may then be placed in the hands of one. But the King of Sweden had only a very fmall fhare of this power, which, as has been already fhewn, was almoft wholly engroffed by the fenate. He therefore in no fhape whatfoever contributed to preferve a balance between the component parts of the conftitution. He could neither on the one hand, prevent the ariftocratical branches of it from fo far encroaching on the others, as to convert the government into an oligarchy; nor could he, on the other, check the progrefs of that licentioufnefs, which muft ever prevail in popular affemblies when under no control.

The confequence was, that the Swedes became alternately expofed to both thefe evils. While the ftates were affembled they experienced all thofe diforders, of which faction and party violence are productive; and during the intervals between the diets, the fenate in its turn, made them feel the rigour of that oppreffion which naturally flows from an oligarchy.

Thus without reaping one of the advantages which a free government may derive from the kingly office, when vefted with a due fhare of conftitutional power, the Swedes were expofed to all thofe dangers which muft have arifen to their liberties, from placing their prince in a fituation, in which every thing was calculated to mortify him on one hand, and on the other, to ftimulate his ambition, or to infpire him with that paffion, fhould he not naturally be under its influence.

Whilft

Whilst, from the habitual respect paid to the title of majesty, and the influence of outward pomp and decoration upon the minds of men, the people continued to look up to him with the same reverence, with which they had been accustomed to behold their former sovereigns: and thus he was necessarily possessed of a sure road to popularity, as no misconduct in public affairs, could ever be attributed to one who had so little share in directing them.

Next, when we consider of whom the states were composed; what were the situation and condition of those who were called upon to exercise the function of legislators, with a supreme and almost unlimited authority; innumerable defects will then appear in this form of government, which at first sight might escape observation.

We have seen that the states were composed of the nobles, clergy, burghers and peasants.

1st. With regard to the nobles: that body formed in Sweden, as in other countries on the continent, a class entirely distinct from the rest of the nation. The honours as well as property of each noble family descended alike to all its branches. Numerous therefore, proud, and needy, they were certainly but ill calculated to have a share in a legislature, which was designed to establish liberty. Their poverty necessarily rendered them dependent, whilst their pride as necessarily kept them poor; since they disdained by means of commerce to acquire that independency with respect to fortune, which ought to be annexed

nexed to the character of a legiflator. The lines of diftinction which divided them from the reft of their countrymen were too ftrongly marked to be overlooked, and too flattering to their pride to be difregarded by them.

They feldom affociated with thofe who did not belong to their order, in general kept at a moft abfurd diftance from them; and retained under a free government all that arrogance towards their inferiors, with which nobles under abfolute monarchies feem frequently to confole themfelves, for the confcioufnefs of their own infignificancy, with regard to their common mafter.

The head only of every family had a right to fit in the houfe of nobles; their body being too numerous to admit of the whole being affembled at once. But the perfon poffeffed of fo important a privilege, not being diftinguifhed from the reft of his family in point of property, muft frequently have been wholly deftitute of the means of exercifing it; infomuch that it is literally a fact, that a very confiderable number of thofe nobles, who had a right to affift at the diets, were fo poor, as to be abfolutely unable to pay the trifling expences attending their leaving their homes, to refide at Stockholm for the fhort time a diet was to laft.

It is equally true, that the heads of the major part of the moft ancient families in Sweden, of thofe who held the firft rank among the nobles, and were in the greateft confideration among the people, had *bona fide*, no vifible means of fubfiftence, but what they derived from the poffeffion of

pofts

posts and employments under government: even the members of the senate were frequently destitute of any other income but that annexed to their office; and as the senators in case of their being deposed, could never afterwards accept of an inferior employment, they were compelled, in a manner, to make use of every possible means of maintaining themselves in power. The constitution, by allowing nobles an hereditary share in the legislature, who were totally destitute of property, placed them in a situation in which they were equally exposed to be corrupted, and under the necessity of becoming so: while the senators were under the same necessity of making use of corruption, since their very existence depended upon the party they could form to themselves in the states.

Such of the nobles as had a seat at the diet, might, if they did not chuse, or could not afford to attend themselves, give full powers to any persons of their own order not possessing a seat, to act and vote for them.

The persons who received these *fullmaghts*, as they were called, became to all intents and purposes members of the diet, and were nowise accountable to their principals for their conduct there.

Considering the poverty of the Swedish nobles, it was not at all surprising if many of them were induced to part with these *fullmaghts*, upon pecuniary considerations. Neither did the purchase of a right amount to any thing considerable, which remaining in the hands of the owner, would,

would, from his inability to exercise it, have been useless to him*.

This (supposing foreign interference out of the question) would have furnished the senators with an opportunity of introducing into the house of nobles, as many of their dependents and creatures as were necessary to secure that body in their interests: and as the senate was in the possession of its power for three years, and during that period, had in a great measure the disposal of all the posts and employments in the state, whether civil or military, it could by these means establish an interest among the members that were to compose a future diet, not easily to be overturned in the short time this was assembled. It is obvious therefore, that, putting foreign influence out of the question, the genius of this government naturally tended to an oligarchy.

2dly, With regard to the clergy. How far that order of men should be admitted to a share in the legislature of a free country, it may not at present be necessary to enquire. I shall only observe, that from the nature of the church establishment in Sweden, it was not productive of so many evil consequences there as it might have been in other countries ‡.

3dly, As

---

* In a short time these fullmaghts became a species of merchandise to be sold to the highest bidder; it was necessary, however, that the purchaser should be rather cautious on these occasions, as instances might be produced where the same fullmaghts had been sold twice over, to the different agents of the opposite parties.

‡ The clergy in Sweden are perhaps the poorest in Europe,

3dly, As to the burghers: these were chosen by cities and corporate towns, nearly in the same manner as the members for cities and boroughs are in England; but then none but burghers, literally speaking, and by no means nobles or gentlemen were capable of being elected *.

This exclusive right in merchants and traders of representing cities and towns, seems well enough calculated to give them a certain rank and consequence in the state; but then it served to maintain and continue with the utmost precision, the distinction of noble and plebeian.

Had the younger branches of noble families, been rendered by the constitution eligible to a seat among the order of burghers, this would probably have induced many of them to turn their thoughts to commerce; and by that means they might have acquired a property that would have enabled them to become independent members of the legislature, instead of continuing in a character, in which their poverty rendered their titles and their pride equally ridiculous.

rope, so that the nobles or gentry hardly ever think of the church for their professions. But as the parishioners in each district elect their ministers, this prevents that servility in the clergy which a dependence on particular patrons may create among them in other countries.

* Burghers in Sweden does not at all convey the same idea as burgess does in England; it implies, literally speaking, persons who either are, or have been engaged in trade or commerce: it no wise includes persons of any other order, who may be free of a city.

4thly, What

4thly, What has been said here with regard to the order of burghers, is equally applicable to that of the peasants.

These too could elect their representatives only from their own order. Their deputies were, in the literal sense of the word, to be peasants themselves.

Nothing surely could be more absurd, than to allow men a seat in the legislature, and a voice in the most important affairs of the nation, who, from their situation in life, could not possibly have possessed the information requisite for functions of this kind; who must have been too ignorant either to devise measures themselves beneficial to the state, or to judge of their expediency when proposed by others: and lastly, who from the lowness of their condition, must have been greatly liable to corruption, as a bribe too insignificant to have tempted persons in a more elevated station to depart from their duty, might easily have prevailed upon peasants.

If there was apparently so much reason to object to the persons of whom the states were composed, there was equal reason to object to their mode of proceeding when assembled. The burghers and peasants did not, like the knights of shires and burgesses in England, sit together, when elected, in one house; but each assembled apart. The clergy and nobles had likewise their meetings separate from each other; so that the legislature was composed of four distinct houses of parliament, as they may be termed without impropriety.

The assent however of all the four was not necessary to give force to a law; that of three of them was, as has been remarked upon a former occasion, sufficient for this purpose. Hence each component part of the legislature, did not singly possess a negative upon the resolutions of the other three, but was obliged to acquiesce in what these should think proper to enact.

By this means questions might be passed in the states, although the sense of the majority of all the members, if taken collectively, was obviously against them. For instance, suppose one order should unanimously reject a measure, which in each of the other three had been carried only by a small majority. This majority might have consisted of no more than one or two persons in each order, and put all together might not amount to above half a dozen. In this case it is evident that the votes of these half dozen persons, would outweigh those of a whole order.

On this account too, it was in the power of a party formed in any three of the states, to come to resolutions, and to enact laws, highly detrimental to the interest of the remaining state, as well as to pass regulations, concerning points, in which the latter only was interested.

Thus the nobles who despised commerce, the clergy who had no concern with it, and the peasants who were totally ignorant of every thing relating to it, might pass acts which would materially

ally affect it, although the burghers should be unanimous in rejecting them. Nor was it extraordinary if the four orders when assembled, appear sometimes to have had little piques and resentments towards each other to gratify, when we reflect that they belonged to classes entirely distinct from each other; and, when the states were separated, seldom or never associating in private life.

Hitherto I have considered only some of the defects of the form of government itself, and of the objections which might with justice be started against the persons in whose hands it placed the legislature.

But the great error committed by the framers of this constitution, was, that while they paid so much attention to political liberty, that is, to the share the nation was to have in the government; they totally forgot that an equal attention was due to civil liberty, or the freedom of individuals considered in their private capacity.

It is the full enjoyment of the civil, which attaches a nation to their political liberties. The influence of the former, extends itself over the whole society, the meanest member of which partakes of the benefits it diffuses. The immediate advantages resulting from the latter, fall to the lot of, comparatively speaking, a very small portion of the nation.

We are not however to attribute it altogether to neglect, if the framers of the late Swedish constitution did not pay the same attention to the private rights of individuals, as to the political liberty of the nation. The latter had been established of a sudden, or at least the form of government was so established which was designed to introduce it. But those laws which have civil liberty, or personal safety and security of private property for their objects, cannot perhaps be devised and reduced to practice with equal expedition. These are in general the result of experience, and it is only after frequent trials that they have been brought to a sufficient degree of perfection to answer the purposes for which they were intended.

'The immediate introduction therefore of such laws, among a people not fitted to receive them, was perhaps a task which exceeded the abilities of those who had framed the new constitution of Sweden; or, content with what they had done towards establishing political liberty, they seem to have left private freedom to the care of their posterity. The consequence was, that the change in that government, produced little or none in the situation of the great body of the people. They still found themselves exposed to the same oppression as before, and could not therefore have any reason to be satisfied with an alteration in the one, which was productive of no improvement in the other.

Besides, their prejudices were all in favour of that government to which they had been accustomed. The number of great and able princes who had sate upon their throne, by attaching them to their monarch, insensibly attached them to their monarchy likewise. Their national vanity

vanity had been flattered by the great reputation many of their sovereigns had acquired; by the lustre these had given to the Swedish arms; and by the glory which they conceived the victories of these princes had reflected upon their country. The miseries they had suffered from the ambition or despotism of their kings, were in a few years forgotten. But their pride did not suffer the exploits of a Gustavus Adolphus, or of a Charles the XIIth, to sink into equal oblivion.

The memory of Charles is still rooted in the mind of every Swede. He is known among them only by the name of the great king: and those who recollect the having seen him in their childhood, still speak of him with tears in their eyes.

SECTION II.

Progress of corruption, and of the French influence in Sweden; change of system in the Diet of the year 1738; and some of the most remarkable transactions of that held in 1756.

WE may have observed in the preceding section, that the framers of the late Swedish constitution, had not only confined the power of the crown within the narrowest limits, but had likewise taken every precaution that a dear-bought experience could suggest to them, to guard against the influence it might acquire through corruption.

By placing their liberties beyond the reach of any attacks open or indirect on the part of their sovereigns, they imagined they had effectually secured them, and quite forgot they had left a door open for another species of corruption, one equally fatal to liberty, but in its consequences infinitely more ruinous to the country; I mean that proceeding from foreign powers.

Foreign corruption, while it is as fatal to the liberties of a free people, as that proceeding from their sovereign could be, is also more ruinous to the interests of the kingdom, and at the same time without a remedy. Who is to punish corruption in senators, or check the progress of it among them, if the executive is lodged in the senate? Who is to punish it in the members of the state, when the states themselves are corrupted? In a limited monarchy, on the contrary, when properly constituted, the prince not only is above being tempted by foreign bribes, but, however he may be inclined to make use of corruption himself, he certainly will not suffer foreign powers to acquire by that means an influence among such of his subjects, as are members of the legislature. But what was the case in Sweden? the king it is true was there deprived of the means of corrupting himself the members of the legislature, but he was likewise divested of all power which could enable him to prevent foreign corruption from spreading itself among them. While he was so streightened in his finances, as well as limited in his authority; while he had so little share in directing

recting the public measures, and a portion so small of the advantages which might result from the prosperity of the kingdom; there hardly seemed to be a single circumstance in his situation, which could serve to connect his interests with those of the nation. And at the same time, the poverty of those who were entrusted with a share in the government, was such, as naturally rendered them open to corruption, from whatever quarter it might come, and apologized for what they must otherwise have blushed to own.

This state of affairs in Sweden could not remain long unobserved by foreign potentates; who would naturally take all the advantages it afforded them, for acquiring such a degree of influence in that country, as suited their political views and interests.

Among these, France took the lead. The busy restless spirit of intrigue which characterizes the policy of the cabinet of Versailles, was no-where more conspicuous in its effects than in Sweden. Having lost that weight in the scale, and ascendency in the affairs of Europe of which she was once possessed, it seems to be now the object of France to acquire by artifice and corruption, that influence among the other European powers, which her real superiority over them had formerly given her.

Hence her emissaries at foreign courts are perpetually carrying on intrigues there, sometimes in order to effect internal revolutions; sometimes to promote dissentions between neighbouring powers, 'and by that means kindle a war; but always for the purpose of checking the prosperity of such, as are become the objects of her jealousy.

Never was a country more egregiously 'duped by another, than Sweden has been by France, from the time of their being first connected. I believe it would be scarcely possible to produce a single advantage which has resulted to the former, from her union with the latter; whilst the losses she has sustained in consequence of it, have been frequent and manifest. Neither is it easy to conceive why France should interest herself so much in the affairs of this northern kingdom, but upon the principle just now mentioned, in order to be able whenever she should think proper, to create an enemy to another northern potentate, whose rapid rise into power and consequence, she could not behold without envy.

But if Sweden has been duped by France, the latter country certainly has been no less mistaken, in her policy with regard to the very object of her alliance with the former.

The circumstances which might have once rendered a connection between these two countries advantageous to both, have long ceased to exist. Since that time the face of affairs in the northern part of Europe has undergone a total change; and consequently, in the political interests of the countries situated there, an equal alteration must have taken place.

It was in the reign of Gustavus Vasa, that the first treaty of alliance between Sweden and France

took

took place. I mention this, becaufe it is not at all improbable that the opinion of fo great and wife a prince as Guftavus, with refpect to the choice of an ally, may have been the groundwork of the preference afterwards given upon all occafions by his countrymen to France. But nothing could be more obvious than the reafons which induced that prince to form a French alliance, nor any thing more evident than that they were only of a temporary nature, and ought not confequently to have been productive of a connection that was to laft longer than thefe fhould fubfift. Charles the Vth, emperor of Germany, had conceived the defign of placing Frederic count Palatine upon the northern thrones; it was, therefore, very natural that Guftavus fhould connect himfelf with the Prince who was the declared enemy of Charles, and fuch a one he found in Francis the Ift. A union with England would certainly have ultimately proved more advantageous to his country, and Guftavus might probably have been of that opinion; but the ficklenefs of the temper of Henry the VIIIth rendered him an ally by no means to be confided in.

This monarch was befides clofely connected with the emperor, at the time Guftavus wanted to ftrengthen himfelf againft the attacks of the Imperial power: and confonant to his wild fyftem of politicks, Henry had actually purchafed Denmark, with which country Guftavus was then in clofe alliance, of the Hanfe towns, (though thefe only meditated the conqueft of it) and advanced

vanced 20,000 crowns of what he had stipulated to pay when delivery should be made. These reasons were therefore sufficient to determine Gustavus in his choice of the French alliance, which he conceived the situation of his affairs rendered it necessary he should form.

Sweden next entered into a subsidiary treaty with France, in the reign of Gustavus Adolphus.

The object of France was, at that time, to humble the house of Austria, and for this purpose she could not, as Europe was then circumstanced, have pitched upon a fitter instrument than the Swedish monarch.

When Gustavus invaded the empire, he was the most powerful sovereign of the north. Russia still continued in a state of barbarism, and consequently of insignificance; and the petty Electorate of Brandenburg, had not as yet started up into a potent kingdom. It was, therefore, perfectly consistent with the usual policy of Richlieu, to form an alliance with, perhaps, the only power then both willing and capable of abetting his designs against the emperor.

But as the preference given to France as an ally, by Gustavus Vasa, seems ever after to have biassed the Swedes in favour of that country, so the successors in office of Richlieu appear, with respect to the Swedish system to have followed the example of that great minister, and probably for no other reason than because this was a system that had been adopted by him. Both parties forgetting that different junctures and new arrangements

-ments of power required their pursuing a different policy; and that what was perfectly wise in one situation of things, might become as absurd in another.

Thus when Sweden had nothing to dread from Russia, and held the Electors of Brandenburg in contempt, she might have afforded to France the most powerful aid against the encroaching spirit of the House of Austria; and the Swedish monarchs, by means of French subsidies, might have indulged their passion for war at no great expence to their country. When this was the case, a union between Sweden and France was founded in the soundest policy.

But when afterwards the situation of the North of Europe had undergone a total change; when Sweden from being the first became one of the most insignificant of the northern powers; when the little electorate of Brandenburg, had become a great kingdom, alone sufficiently potent to bar the progress of the Swedes into Germany, beyond their own insignificant province of Pomerania; when an immense empire bordering upon Sweden, from which she had before little or nothing to apprehend, bursting from obscurity into power and consequence, by the most rapid progress from barbarism to civilization of which the history of mankind can furnish an example, became an adversary to Sweden far too formidable for her declining strength; an adversary, with whom it was impossible that Sweden could alone contend, while it was equally impossible she could for that purpose

purpose receive any effectual assistance from her French ally: surely under these circumstances, the connection between France and Sweden could not answer any of those ends, which either party might formerly have expected to obtain by it.

The idea which the cabinet of Versailles might have entertained of rendering Sweden a thorn in the side of Russia, was in itself a mistaken one; for the sowing of dissention between those two powers was, in fact, only giving the latter a pretext to make conquests upon the former, and therefore served but to augment the power of that potentate, to reduce whose strength and importance, could be the sole object of the immense sums privately spent by France in corrupting the Swedes; whilst the subsidies these publicly received, were both too insignificant, and too ill paid, to compensate for the losses the nation necessarily sustained from being at enmity with Russia *.

* Notwithstanding the predilection entertained by Christina for France, it was a maxim with that Princess, as well as with Charles the XIth, that Sweden should no more form an alliance with that country. In a letter written by Charles to the senators, during an illness from which he did not expect to recover, he expresses himself thus:—" As I am well in-
" formed that among the senators whom I have appointed
" guardians to my son the Prince Charles, as well as among
" the remainder of the senators, there are many who are en-
" tirely devoted to France, I cannot refrain from exhorting
" them to continue firmly attached to those alliances I have
" concluded: as I find them the surest and most advantage-
" ous for Sweden. France has deceived me once, and I
" would, therefore, never again have recourse to her."

Hence

Hence we may with juſtice affirm, that if a French alliance, proved on many occaſions, highly injurious to the intereſts of Sweden, France was in her turn equally miſtaken in the policy, which induced her to connect herſelf with that country. In this policy however ſhe ſtill perſiſted; and from the moment the late Swediſh form of government was eſtabliſhed, ſhe bent all her endeavours to create to herſelf ſuch a party in Sweden, as might enable her to govern that country with the ſame eaſe as ſhe did one of her own provinces.

When the framers of the late Swediſh conſtitution gave a new government to their country, they at the ſame time adopted a new ſyſtem with reſpect to foreign politicks. They had opened their eyes to the change wrought in the ſituation of ſome of the powers which ſurrounded them. The miſeries they had experienced from the recent wars of Charles the XIIth, rendered peace abſolutely neceſſary to the ſtate. They ſaw plainly that the armies of Ruſſia were no longer compoſed of thoſe ſoldiers, twenty thouſand of whom after the battle of Narva, had ſurrendered at diſcretion to no more than eight thouſand Swedes. They perceived the immenſe power that empire had ſuddenly acquired, to cultivate the friendſhip of which, they conſidered as the only means of obtaining ſecurity to themſelves. The power too of Pruſſia formed a new barrier againſt every attempt they ſhould make at recovering the loſſes Sweden had ſuſtained on the ſide of Germany. Thus circumſtanced, they apprehended an alliance with France could be of no farther ſervice to them,

them, but might, on the contrary, plunge them into fresh difficulties.

To maintain therefore a close correspondence with Russia, and to continue on good terms with all their neighbours, appeared to count Horn * and his coadjutors, not only as the wisest policy they could pursue, but as that which the distrest state of their country had rendered it absolutely necessary for them to adopt.

To this system Sweden continued firm till the year 1738: it was then that the fruits of the intrigues of France, began first to discover themselves, and that a total, and most certainly unfortunate change in the politicks of the Swedes took place.

Those defects in their form of government, of which I have already taken notice, gave to France but too favourable opportunities of employing corruption among them in the most effectual manner.

The consequence of this corruption was, that in the diet assembled in 1738, a most powerful party appeared in favour of French measures. The persons who composed it went under the denomination of Hats. The object they held out to the nation, was the recovery of some of the dominions yielded to Russia; and consequently the system they were to proceed upon, was to break with that power, and connect themselves with France.

The party directly opposite to them was headed

* Count Horn was the person principally concerned in the establishment of the late constitution.

by

by count Horn, and those who had contributed to establish the new form of government.

Their object was peace, and the promoting of the domestick welfare of the nation. The system therefore which they adopted, was to maintain a close correspondence with Russia, and to avoid all farther connection with France. These were stiled the Caps. There was besides a third party, called the Hunting Caps, composed of persons who were as yet undetermined to which of the other two they would join themselves.

In this diet, which, contrary to custom, continued sitting eleven months, the Hats soon appeared to have a very great majority; and the event was, that an end was put to the virtuous administration of count Horn and his colleagues; their pacific system was overturned, and the French party assumed the whole direction of the public affairs.

A war with Russia, as must have been expected, soon afterwards ensued. This, from the beginning, was attended by nothing but losses and misfortunes ‡.

The

‡ The time at which the ruling party in Sweden, in its wisdom, thought proper to commence hostilities against Russia, was when the latter power was in profound peace, and consequently at liberty to exert her whole strength to repel the impotent attacks of the former. In order to delude the nation into this war, it was said the senate transmitted to the Swedish minister at Petersburg, ready-made minutes of the reports he was to send back to Sweden; and these were such as were calculated to create among the Swedes a belief that the armies of Russia had been almost ruined by her late war with the Turks.

The Swedish army in Finland was totally destroyed, and the whole of that country lost. The unfortunate generals who commanded there, count Lewenhaupt and baron Buddenbrog paid the forfeit of their lives; not for their own misconduct, but for the madness and infatuation of those who promoted a war, to which Sweden was by no means equal; and which consequently in a short time, compelled the Swedes to sue for peace upon whatever terms the enemy should think proper to impose.

These were the first fruits of the French influence in the Swedish diets, after the establishment of the late form of government.

I shall now hasten to some of the principal transactions of the diet 1756, as they will serve to give the reader a full idea of the manner in which the Swedish constitution was administred, of the abuses that then crept into it, and of the encroachments by the Hats upon the royal authority; authority, which it has been already observed, was originally insufficient to answer any useful purpose to the government, but which, in this diet, was reduced almost to nothing.

After the states were assembled, one of the first subjects of dispute between them and the king, was of so curious a nature, in itself so trivial, yet considered by the diet as an affair of so much importance, that it merits a particular relation.

Turks. And baron Buddenbrog, who was sent into Finland to inspect the state of that country, it may be presumed, had instructions to make such representations of it as favoured the martial designs of the persons in power.

However

However a people may be desirous of limiting the authority of their sovereign, in those points which relate to the preservation of their liberties, there are others properly belonging to his private concerns, in which it were illiberal, if not indecent, for his subjects to interfere. But the Swedes seem to have thought otherwise, and they acted accordingly. From the time that the French party in 1738, had got possession of the reins of government, they appear to have considered it as no wise incumbent on them to keep any measures with the court. Not content with continually imposing fresh restraints upon the regal power, they resolved to reduce the situation of the king, to an absolute state of pupilage, in which he was to have neither will nor property of his own.

Early in the diet, the states presented a very singular address to his majesty. The purport of it was, That whereas by the thirteenth article of the ordinance of the year 1723, the states were to examine into the condition of the jewels and moveables belonging to the crown, as well such as were in the king's treasury, as those that were presented to the queen ‖ at Berlin, upon his majesty's marriage, for the use of his royal consort; they therefore begged to know when it would be convenient to her majesty, that the above-mentioned jewels should be visited by some deputies from their body, and compared with the inventories made of them.

‖ The late king married the princess Louisa Ulrika, sister to the present king of Prussia.

It is true by the article above alluded to, the states were vested with the power claimed by them upon this occasion; but it was a power which had never been exercised, and was probably never intended to be so, but in case of a minority or a vacancy of the throne, when it was proper such a power should be lodged somewhere, to prevent the embezzlement of the effects belonging to the crown. At any other time to claim the exercise of it surely betrayed the most illiberal suspicions on the part of the states, and placed the sovereign in the most humiliating point of view. But to examine into the state of those jewels which had been given to her majesty as a marriage-present from the king, was certainly a demand as much beneath the dignity of the states, as it must have been mortifying to the queen *.

Her majesty accordingly refused to submit to such a rewiew of the jewels, which, said she, in her answer to the request of the states, " seems to arise " from some distrust in the states of the kingdom;" but she added, " I shall let the two members of " the secret committee know my thoughts, that I " design to have the jewels in question separated " from my own, and so to deliver them up to the " states, because from that hour I account my- " self too good to wear them."

* The fact was with respect to these jewels, that Mr. Tessin, the Swedish ambassador at Berlin, had presented them to the queen only in the name of the king, and she consequently considered them as her own. It certainly never could have occurred to a foreign princess, that a marriage-gift was to be considered by the nation merely as a trust, of which she was upon demand to give an account.

This

This was productive of a most serious remonstrance on the part of the states, which I shall give here at full length, as it will serve to convey a perfect idea of their mode of proceeding, and of the situation of the king.

"The states cannot any longer conceal from your majesty, what they must unavoidably have observed, that the queen does not view them in the light in which they ought to be considered, as states in possession of power, as well as faithful subjects of your majesty; and as those very states that raised your majesty to so glorious a rank among kings, and who most willingly offer for your majesty's and the kingdom's *united good*, their lives and fortunes whenever occasions shall require.

"The queen's carriage towards the states has been accompanied likewise by a contempt for the senators and other officers of the kingdom*, most conspicuously shewn in a conduct founded on caprice, and which pays no respect to the dignity of persons; as if there were any

---

* This pretended contempt for the senators and other officers of the kingdom, was nothing more than an order given by the king about a year before, that no coaches should drive into the inner court of the palace, except those of the royal family. The first persons who were stopped were the senators ladies. The senators were prudent enough not to complain upon their own account, but they prevailed upon the French ambassador to attempt to drive in likewise, and upon his being stopped, to make his complaint to the senate; who upon this resolved, that all persons of a certain rank then specified, should enjoy that *important privilege*.

"other fidelity and merit than obedience to the
"laws, or any other marks of dignity or reward,
"than those which your majesty's justice distri-
"butes among your faithful subjects.

"The general assembly of the states, as well as
"the whole kingdom are convinced, that your
"majesty thoroughly dislikes these proceedings:
"they desire no happier government than what
"your majesty's kind and fatherly disposition
"promises them; but, when things contrary to
"this disposition are transacted so near the throne,
"it cannot but occasion reflections among fo-
"reigners, as well as uneasiness and trouble within
"the realm. Your majesty's wisdom cannot fail
"to observe, that examples thus imprinted upon
"the tender minds of the hereditary princes, who
"instead of acquiring a love for the nation, for a
"free people, and an esteem for fidelity and merit,
"are taught to look upon other men as born to
"be miserable for their pleasure; and as happy or
"unhappy, well or ill intentioned, according to
"the favours or disgraces they meet with at
"court.

"The queen came into this kingdom to be
"your majesty's consort, not to add to the weight
"of government.

"This weight ought the more easily to be borne
"by so gracious and just a king, as your majesty
"possesses the most sovereign power and the
"surest reward in the hearts of your subjects.
"When therefore by-ways are taken by any other
"person, contrary to the engagements your ma-
"jesty has entered into before God and the king-
"dom,

"dom, and consequently against your views and
"intentions, they tend either to make two go-
"vernments in the kingdom, the one with, and the
"other without law; or a king without constitu-
"tional direction, and laws without power.

"But of all that has appeared, nothing was
"more unexpected, than that a declaration should
"be made in writing by her majesty, in which she
"says, that she looks upon the desire of the secret
"committee to review the jewels, as the effects of
"distrust, and concludes with these words: That
"she thinks herself too good to wear them for
"the future.

"It is not customary, nor indeed agreeable to
"our form of government, to take notice of any
"communication or correspondence between the
"queen and the states of the kingdom, concern-
"ing the affairs of the diet. But when the
"states have done nothing to draw upon them-
"selves such expressions from her majesty, and
"a writing falls into their hands, which con-
"tains so public a contempt for the government,
"it does not become their dignity to be silent:
"though what the states shall in this case think fit
"to do, is not to be applied to other occasions,
"or to become a precedent hereafter, as the ge-
"neral assembly of the states hopes, and *will also
"take care*, that what now gives occasion to these
"proceedings, shall never happen again."

After dwelling some time upon their right to make the review in question, their remonstrance concludes thus:

"The states desire no change in your majesty's
"sentiments

" sentiments towards the queen your confort; but
" very much that her majefty fhould change her
" fentiments towards the kingdom.

" They afk nothing more than that your ma-
" jefty may be left quietly to make your fubjects
" happy, and your reign glorious; and therefore
" wifh that a perfon whofe welfare is fo nearly
" connected with your majefty's, might conftantly
" poffefs their moft humble refpect and devo-
" tion.

" With regard to thefe matters, the whole af-
" fembly of the ftates humbly confide in your ma-
" jefty's paternal care, glad not *to ftand in need of*
" *thofe means*, which God and their right have
" otherwife given them.

" Your majefty's engagements with the king-
" dom are your firft and moft important en-
" gagements; from the obfervance of them, a
" whole nation is to expect its welfare; and upon
" that too depends the happinefs of pofterity.

" The conftitution muft be maintained; and
" thus will your majefty be freed from a variety of
" cares; and the country and its inhabitants will
" then fully enjoy the fruits of fo worthy a
" prince's government."

So ferious a remonftrance as this, required on the part of the king, as ferious an apology for what appeared to have given the ftates fo much offence.

He affured them of the fentiments of love and efteem which her majefty entertained for the nation, and endeavoured to foften the harfhnefs of fome of the expreffions fhe had ufed in
her

her letter to the states, by attributing it to their being made in a language she did not sufficiently understand: but he still insisted, that as her majesty had worn the crown jewels for upwards of ten years without such a review as that in question, having ever been thought of by the states during all that time, her majesty could not but consider their conduct on the present occasion, as arising from a distrust, which touched her honour in the most sensible manner. He farther declared, that as to the jewels which had in his name been given to her majesty at Berlin, she could not but look upon them as her own, according to one of the articles of the marriage-agreement.

One would have imagined this wretched affair would have ended here; but upon receiving this answer, the states sent up another remonstrance to prove that the jewels presented to her majesty at Berlin as a marriage-gift, were jewels of the kingdom, and therefore insisted on the review of them. In this second remonstrance was the following curious passage, reflecting on the supposed influence of the queen: " The states beg that " your majesty, without being disturbed, may be " master of your court, and king of your king-" dom; and finally, they beg (with humility) " that all farther correspondence upon this and the " like matter may cease *.

Having

* The secret history of the states making the reviewal of the jewels so serious an affair was this: The ruling party had been informed, that some of the queen's jewels were pledged

at

Having carried this point, so mortifying to the king, the states proceeded to further exertions of power, of a nature still more personally vexatious to him.

His majesty had appointed a sub-governor to the prince royal. He imagined, that with regard to his own family at least, he might be at liberty to chuse the persons that were to be immediately about himself and his children. But this was deemed too important a privilege to be intrusted in the royal hands. The states shortly came to a resolution, that the office of sub-governor to his royal highness, should be abolished. Their letter to his majesty upon this occasion, is sufficiently curious to be inserted here. Nothing can give a more ample idea of the peremptory humility which accompanied their requests to the throne. It was as follows:

"Most mighty and most potent King,

"Having deliberated upon the affair of educa-
" tion, which is of so much importance to your
" majesty and the kingdom, it has appeared to us,
" among other things, that the office of sub-go-
" vernor to his R. H. is unnecessary; the states
" must therefore, with submission, represent, that
" such an establishment is altogether unusual in
" this kingdom, and that what is practised in other

---

at Hamburgh, and their great object in obliging her immediately to redeem them was, to deprive her by that means of the money which they apprehended she might be able to raise for the support of the court party in the Diet.

A young lady about the queen betrayed the secret of the jewels, for which she got a pension from the states.

" countries,

"countries, cannot be applicable to a kingdom
"which has different principles of government
"from those countries.

"In the opinion of the states, as long as the
"governor is in health and vigour to perform what
"is entrusted to his care, the office of sub-gover-
"nor can hardly be productive of any advantage,
"but may very probably of some inconveni-
"ence.

"The states, in all submission, respect the care-
"ful and tender views which have given rise to
"this establishment of your majesty's; but they
"trust that they shew the same respectful and sub-
"missive sentiments in giving their most earnest
"advice, that the above-mentioned office of sub-
"governor, may be entirely suppressed for the
"future.

"Beside which, the states most humbly desire,
"according to the right given them by the form
"of government, that no new establishments may
"be made without their knowledge, in what re-
"lates to the education of the princes; and that
"no persons be changed otherwise than in the in-
"struction to the governor."

The states had no sooner abolished the office of
sub-governor, than an address appeared on their
part to his majesty, containing an order, in the
form of a request, That Mr. Von Dalin should be
dismissed from his office of preceptor to the prince
royal. They laid no particular crime to his charge,
and it ever continued a secret what they had to
alledge against him. But he was notwithstanding
for the future to be refused all manner of inter-
courſe

course with his R. H. and to abstain from going to court till farther orders. Two days after this another remonstrance was made to the king, in consequence of his answer to a former one, on the occasion of the secret committee's having chosen senator Scheffer to be proposed to the states general for the office of governor to the prince royal.

The purport of his majesty's answer was, that though he was no less persuaded than the states, of the good qualities of the senator Scheffer, yet he could not consent, nor declare it to be his pleasure, that the above-mentioned senator should be chosen governor to his son, as the appointing to that office, was a right, which by the third article of the form of government was clearly vested in him.

Nothing can illustrate more fully what I have had occasion to observe concerning this form of government, than the reply of the secret committee.

" The states of the kingdom, (said they) are le-
" gislators, and possess power; two qualifications
" by which they are marked out in the form of
" government.

" But both the legislature and the power would
" be without effect, if obstacles or resistance
" could prevent the execution of them; or if the
" sentiments of the legislators were subject to the
" controul of any one else. His majesty has for
" this reason, obliged himself by a solemn oath,
" always to agree with the states assembled, ac-
" cording to the words of the fifth article of the
" royal

" royal affurances ; fo that their acts are, or ought
" to be, his majefty's pleafure, &c. &c.

This is literally tranflated. It is obfcurely worded, but the meaning of it is fufficiently evident, and I think requires no comment.

Accordingly the ftates proceeded not only to appoint a governor to the prince royal, but likewife to nominate the attendants upon his royal highnefs's perfon. The king was obliged on this occafion, as on every other, to acquiefce.

After thefe inftances of the plenitude of power affumed by the ftates, and of the impotence of the royal authority, it might have feemed unneceffary to lay any frefh reftraints upon an authority already fo confined.

But the object of the next ftep taken by the ftates, feemed to be totally to annihilate the remnants of the few privileges the crown had hitherto been fuffered to poffefs.

Some time after the above-mentioned tranfactions, they prefented an *humble* addrefs to his majefty, containing an *humble* requeft, that upon fome occafions, where the king's fignature had hitherto been requifite to the difpatching of certain affairs; inftead of fuch fignature, a ftamp left in the hands of the fenators, fhould for the future be made ufe of.

This addrefs fet forth, that according to the fixteenth article of the form of government, fhould the king be upon a journey, or fo ill that he could not be troubled with public bufinefs, in that cafe, the fenators ought to fign fuch difpatches as do not admit of any delay. That by the twentieth
article

article of the ordinance of 1723, it was incumbent upon the senators, if the king should defer signing longer than the importance of the business could admit of, to sign themselves, whatever the states general sent to his majesty to be executed by him. That there were *more* causes than *sickness* or *absence* which might prevent the king's signing what was presented to him for that purpose; and that there were other affairs beside those resolved upon by the states general, which were of sufficient importance to require their being speedily dispatched. For these reasons it was the humble opinion of the states, " that for the future, in " *all affairs without exception*, which hitherto re" quired the sign *Manual* of the king, his majesty's " name might be affixed by a stamp, whenever " the signing has not followed the first or the " second request of the senate."

But it should not be forgot, that in one part of this curious address, the states seem fairly to confess, what they conceive to be the chief use of having preserved in their form of government, the kingly office. " The states general (it is there said) " having a scrupulous regard to this consideration, " that the *high name* of the *king*, renders commands and expeditions more effectual." That is to say, that in fact, the bulk of the people were attached to monarchy, and that it would not have been found an easy matter to govern them, unless at least a nominal king appeared to preside in the state.

In this manner did the Hat party, or the friends of France, rob the crown of its constitutional rights,

rights, under the pretext of securing the liberties of the nation. It could little have been imagined at that time, that the chiefs of the same party, should, in a very few years, adopt the opposite system, and overturn the constitution itself, under pretence of procuring a proper degree of power to the king.

It was not however to be expected, that no attempts should be made on the part of the king, or his friends, to resist attacks so fatal to the royal authority. But the success of such attempts must have been very dubious. Force alone could enable his majesty to preserve or recover those rights which the states had thought proper to allow him no legal means of defending. A plot was accordingly set on foot by count Brake, baron Horn, the marshal of the court, and some others; the object of which appears to have been, by means of exciting an insurrection among the people in favour of the king, and by corrupting the soldiers and sailors at Stockholm, to restore his majesty at least to all the power he was possessed of at the first establishment of the form of government.

This conspiracy was discovered at the moment the conspirators were going to carry their designs into execution. In consequence of which count Brake and baron Horn, together with a number of other suspected persons, were arrested by order of the secret committee.

Asiatic despotism could not on a similar occasion have paid less attention even to the appearance of justice, than was conspicuous in the conduct of the ruling party, with respect to the trial of these unfortunate

unfortunate men. This, as it might have been presumed would be the case, was referred to one of those extraordinary courts of judicature, the members of which were chosen by the states from among themselves.

The very title of these extraordinary courts, proves them to have been little better than state inquisitions. They were denominated *secret* high courts of justice, which is a contradiction in terms. Accordingly, no persons except the parties concerned, were allowed to be present at their proceedings. They were bound neither by law, form, or precedent, but their own arbitrary will and pleasure were to be the sole rule by which they were to determine upon the lives and property of their fellow subjects.

Before such a court were count Brake, baron Horn, and their accomplices to appear. The members of it being chosen by the states, amounted in fact to the same thing, as if they had been nominated by the ruling party, from among themselves; and consequently these were composed of the very persons against whom the offence, with which the prisoners were charged, was committed. In any case where the characters of judge and party are united, we must have a better opinion of human nature than experience perhaps will justify, to expect impartiality. But when the violence and heat of faction are superadded to the bias that self-interest gives to the judgment, it were vain to hope even for mercy.

All the confessions made by the persons that were seized upon this occasion, were obtained by torture,

torture, which horrid practice the ordinary courts of justice did not admit.

The chief thing proved against count Brake was, his having made balls and cartridges at his country seat; which the count alledged in his defence, had been done by the king's immediate order, and for his majesty's defence in case of an unexpected attack. However, this unfortunate nobleman, together with baron Horn and six others, were condemned to be beheaded, and were executed accordingly.

The crime for which these men thus forfeited their lives, not only was by no means sufficiently proved against them to justify their condemnation, but it was in itself of a very dubious nature. It never appeared that their design had been to render the king an absolute monarch, but only to reinstate him in his constitutional rights. And, as in a free government, all power that is usurped, whether by the crown or the popular branches of the legislature, may be equally dangerous to liberty; resistance in the one case, may perhaps be as justifiable as it is in the other.

After the repeated vexations the king experienced during the course of this Diet, it may easily be conceived how much this last blow must have affected him.

At the beginning of it he had seen himself insulted by the treatment the queen met with from the ruling party; a treatment as illiberal in the authors of it, as it was humiliating to her majesty. The king next saw his domestic peace and tranquillity

tranquillity broke in upon by the same party; his paternal and royal rights alike invaded; his children delivered into the hands of persons chosen against his will; while those in whom he confided were banished from his presence. His majesty afterwards beheld the states strike at the very root of the small share of power he had as yet retained. He saw them so lost to decency as to render it legal to forge his signature, and to practise the ridiculous farce of issuing ordinances in his name, and to all appearance with his sign Manual annexed, against the execution of which he had probably protested with all his might. Lastly, he beheld his best friends, for having formed a design to rescue him from such a situation, brought to the scaffold.

He beheld this without being able to stretch forth a hand to the assistance of those who had risked every thing to serve him. In vain did he, as well as his royal consort, descend to supplicate in the most humiliating manner, those rigid judges who had passed so severe a sentence, in order to obtain some mitigation of it;—they were harshly refused, and in a style as peremptory as it was disrespectful.

Such was the situation to which the late king was reduced by the French, or Hat party, in the Diet of 1756.

SECTION

SECTION III.

View of the political system of the North, with respect to Sweden; and of the motives which induced England, Russia, and other foreign powers, as well as France, to interfere in the Swedish government, during the three last Diets.

AS the object of the French intrigues at Stockholm, manifestly was to disturb the peace of the North, whenever they thought proper, it was not to be supposed, that the powers situated in that part of Europe, would remain inactive spectators of measures which so highly concerned them.

Russia had often experienced the effects of the influence which the court of Versailles had acquired in the government of Sweden. She had, in consequence of that influence, been engaged in a most unnecessary war with the Swedes*; and though she had no reason to regret the event of it, yet it could not be a matter of indifference to the court of Petersburg, to behold so near a neighbour as Sweden, under the immediate direction of a power, one of whose principal objects ever since Russia emerged from barbarism, seems to have been to check the rise, or oppose the aggrandisement of that empire.

It was upon this principle, that through the mediation of France, Sweden had in 1740, entered

---
* In 1742.

into an alliance with the Porte; an alliance evidently designed to operate against Russia, as it was only in case of a war with the last-mentioned power, that any advantage could result from it, to either of the contracting parties.

The king of Prussia had also, during the late war, felt the consequences of the French influence in the Swedish Diets; and though perhaps the armies of Sweden never made so contemptible a figure as on that occasion, yet the part then taken by the Swedes, must have been sufficient to have made his Prussian majesty see the necessity of overturning the French system in a country, which, possessing in the province of Pomerania a key to the heart of his dominions, was by that means enabled exceedingly to annoy him whenever he should be engaged in a war with other powers.

With regard to Denmark, the interests of that country relative to Sweden, have, in the course of the present century, undergone a total change. Peace between those two nations is now become requisite to both. At variance with each other, they have every thing to apprehend from their powerful neighbours: united; if not formidable, they are at least respectable, and able to maintain their independence.

France has long aimed at bringing about a close alliance between them, in order to oppose their joint strength to the power of Russia, and to render that empire open to an attack on one side, whenever the Turks should engage in a war with it on the other. But an alliance, formed

with

with a view rather to disturb than establish the tranquillity of the North, however it may coincide with the designs of the French cabinet, could not but be productive of the worst consequences both to the Danes and Swedes.

If the natural antipathy, which unfortunately still subsists in some degree between those two nations, could be so far subdued as to allow of their being connected by a close alliance, the object of it should be peace, not war; it should be calculated to preserve the friendship, not awaken the jealousy of Russia.

The interests of the different countries of Europe, are now so interwoven with each other, that no material change can take place in the political system of any one of them, without affecting in some degree many others. Could France therefore have succeeded in her scheme of uniting Sweden and Denmark, with a view of producing a breach between those powers and Russia; whenever this should have happened, it would probably have involved Europe in a general war.

It is by sea only that Denmark and Sweden could receive any effectual assistance from France: the great maritime powers could not possibly suffer a French fleet to give law to the Baltick; consequently either the Danes and Swedes would be deprived of the only succours they could receive from their Southern ally, or France must on their account engage in a war with the maritime powers. In the one case, they would be left at the mercy of Russia; in the other, the ruin of their trade and commerce would necessarily ensue.

While therefore it is the interest of Denmark to live in harmony with Sweden, it likewise highly concerns her to cultivate the friendship of Russia. The object of the Danish policy ought consequently to have been (as previous to the late revolution in Sweden it for some time had been) to endeavour to overturn the French system at Stockholm, which always tended to hostile measures; and at the same time to preserve, if possible, the Swedish form of government *.

That form was by no means calculated to admit of Sweden's making those sudden and violent exertions of her strength, from which the Danes had, on former occasions, so often and so severely suffered: it consequently had proved much more favourable to the repose of the North, than the unlimited authority before possessed by the Swedish monarchs. Accordingly a secret article of a treaty, concluded between the courts of Petersburg and Copenhagen in 1766, expresly says, " Whereas it
" is of great importance to the two crowns, that
" the liberty and present constitution of Sweden,
" should be preserved entire; and whereas of late,
" by means of foreign influence, several changes
" have been brought about in that kingdom; so
" that a war has been declared, and the people
" have been taxed, without the previous consent
" of the three estates of the nation; by which
" changes the fundamental constitution is, from

* The late king of Denmark has been heard to declare, that he would sooner risque the loss of his crown, than suffer any material change to be made in the Swedish form of government.

" one quarter or another, constantly exposed to
" be totally overturned: the two high contracting
" powers shall order their respective ministers
" at the court of Sweden, to act in concert
" and confidence at all future Diets, for the
" purpose of maintaining the fundamental con-
" stitution of that kingdom; and for re-esta-
" blishing it according to the true spirit and true
" sense of the law."

The very active part taken by England in the three last Swedish Diets, remains to be accounted for.

To destroy the French influence in Sweden, was certainly a point of some importance to the British court. It was not however of itself considerable enough to justify the expence which must necessarily have attended it. But there were other objects of the first consequence connected with it. A plan had been formed to make a grand alliance in the North, of which Great Britain and Russia were to be the principal parties; Sweden and Denmark were to follow; and Prussia was finally to be invited into it. This would have ben an alliance capable of ballancing that strict union which then reigned, and still continues among the three great powers of the South.

As the passions and inclinations of individuals always influence public affairs more or less, this project of demolishing the French system in Sweden, though it perfectly coincided with the empress of Russia's general view of increasing her weight in Europe, and particularly in the North; yet perhaps it owed it's origin to the manner in which

which the Court of France had behaved towards herself and some of her ministers. The plan however was a grand one, and admirably calculated to preserve the peace of Europe. The pacific system, with respect to this part of the globe, together with a close connection with Russia, appear to have been ever since his majesty's accession, the two great objects of British policy. It was natural therefore for the English ministry, to enter into a scheme which tended to the obtaining of points, as beneficial to England in particular, as they were advantageous to the general interests of mankind.

There were many causes too which made it necessary for England to take a leading part in this design.

Independent of the view of obtaining some commercial advantages, in a country where the ballance of trade was, and is so exceedingly against her; England was the only power among those who united to destroy the French system in Sweden, against a close connection with which the popular prejudices of the Swedes would not have run exceedingly high. The natural antipathy between Sweden and Russia, is not perhaps inferior to that which subsists between Sweden and Denmark; so that, to prepare the minds of the Swedes for a total change of system, with respect to foreign politics, it was necessary that the engagements preparatory to such a change, should at first be entered into with a power, against which the nation entertained no antipathy of this sort. There might be perhaps other reasons of a more private nature for the part taken by England upon this occasion.

The French party had governed Sweden absolutely, without the assistance of the court; and we have seen, by the summary account given of the transactions of the Diet of 1756, to what a wretched state of insignificancy they had reduced the king. Foreign money had enabled the Hats to carry all their points against the regal power; his Swedish Majesty therefore was justified, in having recourse to the same means, in order to recover those prerogatives which had been wrested from him.

After the enormities committed by the Diet of 1756, the Swedish court requested and obtained some assistance from England. The situation of the king and queen of Sweden was, about that time, placed in a strong light, by a very great personage at Stockholm.

According to the representations of that personage, "all the endeavours of their Swedish ma-
"jesties to promote the true interest of the na-
"tion, had been rendered ineffectual by the pow-
"ers of corruption, which France had furnished
"to the partizans of her political system. That
"she had drawn to her all the factions of the
"nation, who, partly for the sake of the money
"to be distributed, and partly from views of pos-
"sessing the revenues and posts of the kingdom,
"had employed their talents only for the support
"of their party; so that France governed Sweden
"with the same ease that she did one of her own
"provinces. That the public treasury had been
"pillaged,

" pillaged, the appropriation of the revenues
" changed, the defence of the country neglected,
" and every branch of commerce ruined. That
" in consequence of French influence, the states
" had trampled on the rights of their majesties,
" placing themselves above the laws, even the
" fundamental ones.

" That under the same influence, they had en-
" tered into two ruinous wars one after another,
" which brought the kingdom to the brink of de-
" struction; that every attempt of their majesties
" to correct these abuses, produced no other ef-
" fect but to augment them. These attempts
" were set in a bad light; insinuations were
" thrown out that something was meant against
" liberty; innocent persons were brought to the
" scaffold, the unhappy victims of their love of
" their country; and royalty was robbed not only
" of the power which belonged to it, but even
" of the rights and prerogative of majesty."

In this situation it was natural for their Swedish majesties to have recourse to England, and to desire the interposition of Great Britain, to take them out of the trammels in which they had been so long held by France. This was not however a point to be suddenly or easily accomplished. All intercourse between the British court and the ruling powers in Sweden, had been cut off for a number of years; and as the renewal of it must have been fatal to the interest of the French party in that country, it was obvious, that party would oppose with all their might, the admission of an English minister at Stockholm;

an

an opposition, which coming from those who then held the reins of government, could not fail to prove an effectual bar to prevent such a measure from taking place.

For this purpose therefore, it became necessary to wait till some favourable juncture should occur, in which either the Hats should cease to be all-powerful in Sweden; or the friends of the court, and the Cap party, should acquire sufficient influence with the senate, to prevail upon that body, to consent to the admission of a British minister.

In the mean time it was thought proper in England, to preserve a communication with the Swedish court, and with those Swedes who were averse to the French system. This correspondence was managed by Sir John Goodricke at Copenhagen, till after the end of the war; the French party in Sweden having prevailed so far as to refuse the receiving of a minister from Great Britain during the war, under pretence of their strict alliance with the French king, and that of Great Britain with the king of Prussia.

But in the latter end of the year 1763, just as Sir John Goodricke was leaving Copenhagen, by orders from London, on account of the improper behaviour of the Swedish Court, he fell into a negociation with Mr. Faxell, then charged with the Swedish affairs in Denmark, which terminated in an agreement between Great Britain and Sweden, to send reciprocally ministers to each other.

The re-establishment of peace had left the senate

nate of Sweden no excuse for declining any longer to receive a minister from the king of Great Britain. Besides, the very unjustifiable length the Hat party had gone during the Diet of 1756, had considerably shaken the credit they had till then maintained with the nation.

In proportion as the Hats lost the confidence of the public, their antagonists grew into popularity. The bad success of the war against the king of Prussia, into which Sweden had been hurried by the Hat party; the want of money occasioned by the erroneous calculations of the expences of the army; and the failure of France in the payment of the arrears due to Sweden, had in some measure opened the eyes of the nation, with respect to the pernicious consequences of their French connections.

For these reasons, as well as the advantages accruing to them, on account of Sir John Goodricke's residence at Copenhagen, the Swedish court began visibly to gain ground during the Diet held in 1760. The chiefs of the ruling party became more circumspect in their conduct, and a fatal blow might have been then given to the French system, if a great part of the money obtained by the court for that purpose, had not been thrown away in order to gratify private resentment.

Little was done towards accomplishing a change of system in the Diet of 1762; but the affairs of Sweden were then in so critical a situation, that nothing but a change of measures could preserve them from immediate ruin. The arrears of the French subsidies amounted at this time to

between

between ten and eleven million of livres; the payment of which France had constantly evaded, tho' in consequence of the war undertaken at her instigation by the Swedish ministry, they had run so considerably in debt, as not only no longer to be able to carry it on, but even to provide for the current expences of government.

At length a proposal came to them from France*, too unreasonable to be digested even by the most zealous of her partizans.

Instead of satisfying the demands of Sweden, the court of Versailles only offered to enter into a new treaty with that country for ten years; by which they proposed to give a million and a half of livres per annum, on condition that the Swedes should, during that time, allow them the use of six ships of the line and four frigates, all compleatly armed and equipped.

A treaty of this nature highly concerned England, as it tended to put the whole maritime force of Sweden into the hands of France.

In answer to this overture, the court of Sweden replied, that it was impossible for them to hearken to any proposals on the part of France, till she had previously paid at least four millions of livres, of the arrears so long due to them; and so much were they provoked at the delays and chicaneries of the cabinet of Versailles; that it was at the same time given out, that if France did not immediately comply with this demand, the Swedish ministry would give their hearty consent that a British minister should be received at Stockholm.

* A. D. 1763.

The

The anfwer from Paris to the requeft of Sweden not being a fatisfactory one, and the negociation with Mr. Faxell, mentioned above, being happily concluded before the end of 1763; in the month of April 1764, Sir John Goodricke arrived at Stockholm, with the character of his Britannic Majefty's Envoy Extraordinary to that Court.

This was a great point gained towards overturning the French fyftem in Sweden, and preparing the way for the intended grand alliance in the North.

The Britifh minifter had notwithftanding many difficulties to contend with; the tafk impofed upon him was an arduous one; but his abilities were equal to it, and his fuccefs was anfwerable to the indefatigable zeal with which he exerted them.

Hitherto France had been unoppofed in all her manœuvres in Sweden: to deftroy therefore a fyftem which had lafted eight and twenty years; that was built upon the moft folid foundation; fupported by fubfidies, as well as by its being rendered the private intereft of the leading people in the country to preferve it, was evidently an undertaking not eafily to be accomplifhed.

The difordered ftate of the finances in Sweden, which it was impoffible to rectify without the affiftance of French fubfidies, increafed the difficulty of fuch an undertaking; while the apprehenfions that thefe fubfidies would be withdrawn, in cafe Sweden difgufted France by forming an alliance, or entering into too clofe connections with England, feemed to form an infuperable bar to its

being

being accomplished. This was apparently to be done only by an indemnification for the loss Sweden was to sustain by the non-payment of the arrears due to her from France; but both England and Russia were averse to offering any such indemnification to Sweden, which proved the chief obstacle their respective ministers had to surmount.

On the other hand there were, at the time they commenced their operations, some circumstances in their favour. These were principally the inability or disinclination of France at that juncture to pay the arrears due to Sweden; the total want of internal resources in that country, to supply the deficiencies occasioned by the non-payment of so considerable a sum; and the unsettled state of the parties, which were divided among themselves.

The first of these had considerably diminished the partiality the bulk of the nation had hitherto entertained for the French system. The second rendered the calling an extraordinary Diet a measure indispensably necessary. And the last disposed the minds of the people to a reformation of the many abuses in the constitution, of which party violence had been productive.

We may add here, that at this time the court of Sweden gave frequent assurances of their being strongly attached to his Britannic majesty, and the interest of his crown; and that nothing but the last necessity should make them consent to the continuance of the engagements with France. What change was afterwards made in these good dispositions

dispositions towards the court of London, we shall soon see.

Upon the arrival of the English minister, his first object was, in concert with count Osterman, the minister from the court of Petersburgh, who having assisted at the Diet of 1762, had all the experience in Swedish affairs, and all the knowledge of the persons and characters of those who took the lead in the conduct of them which was necessary for the forming of a new system, to procure the convocation of a Diet extraordinary, as previous to this no steps could be taken in the intended changes in the administration. The leading senators of the Hat party did not exert their utmost strength to defeat the endeavours used for this purpose, because they saw that their opposition would be fruitless, and they were not united among themselves; so that a resolution was carried in the senate totally against the interests of those who were devoted to he French system, that a Diet extraordinary should be held in the January following.

The success of the Caps on this occasion, was principally owing to the superior abilities of count Lowenhielm, who was the chief of that party in the senate, and the great promoter of the negociation which brought the English minister to Stockholm.

Thus far matters were in as favourable a train for the views of the Caps as they could wish; but every thing depended upon the success of their elections at the approaching Diet. In these too, notwithstanding the great sums spent by France on the occasion, the English and Russian ministers took their measures so well, that the Cap party appeared to have a considerable majority in the four orders. In consequence of which, when the states assembled in 1765, the marshal of the Diet, and the speakers of the three inferior orders, were all of that party, tho' the French ambassador was supposed, I know not with what truth, to have laid out no less than four hundred thousand livres upon the election of the marshal alone †.

The Cap party being now masters of the Diet, the resolutions upon which they built their plan of future operations were, first, that the subsidy paid by France, far from being useful to Sweden, had been highly detrimental to the kingdom, by engaging her in expences exceeding, at least, three times the amount of it, as well as of the extraordinary additions made to it in the war.

Secondly, that the twelve millions of arrears, which France could never be brought to liquidate, had been reduced by different chicaneries, according to the French accounts, to seven millions.

Thirdly, that those seven millions, which perhaps might not be paid in seven years, were not an object that could be brought in competition

† The office of marshal of the Diet was of the greatest consequence, not only from the distinction he had in all deliberations in the House of Nobles, but likewise from his privilege of entering into and voting in all committees; and above all, because the Secret Committee could not be assembled without him.

This last circumstance proved to be of great consequence at the time of the late revolution.

with

with a new war, or with that of an interruption of the beneficial commerce with England; one or both of which would probably happen, if the French treaty for ships were to take place.

Fourthly, that the kingdom of Sweden had resources within herself sufficient, if properly employed, to extricate her out of her present difficulties, without the assistance of any foreign power whatever, provided that the crown could keep clear of new engagments, or a foreign war for a certain number of years.

With regard to the intended reformation of the abuses which had crept into the constitution, the design of the Cap party, was not in any way to change the form of government of the year 1720, but only to re-establish the royal authority in all its rights and prerogatives, founded in the laws; to regulate the functions and duties of the senate; and to put just limits to the power of the states.

It had been a favourite project with France, to gain a full power to the senate, with regard to foreign affairs. As she was supposed to distribute more in annual pensions to those who serve her in foreign countries, than any other court in Europe, she consequently could always have the majority in a body composed but of sixteen persons.

Other courts, less liberal in pensions to foreigners, and who are supposed only occasionally to employ money in secret service, thought it was their general interest to diminish the authority of the senate in favour of the king and the states. This
point

point therefore, together with that of taking the administration of affairs out of the hands of the French party, were to be the chief objects of the attention of the English and Russian ministers, during the course of the Diet.

But a change in the disposition of the court, which became very shortly visible, rendered it necessary to make an alteration likewise in the first part of this plan.

The friends of the court had hitherto voted with the Caps: they seem however to have done this only to secure the admission of some of their number into the secret committee, for shortly after that was formed, the Caps found they had lost their majority in the house of nobles, which sufficiently proved that the court had changed sides. The explanation of this event furnishes us with a clue to the revolution which happened seven years afterwards.

During the Diet 1762, two years before the arrival of an English minister at Stockholm, the court party finding themselves disappointed in the quantum of the resources they expected, or rather having expended those they had upon unessential points, instead of applying them to capital ones, resolved while their credit was good, and before their opponents found out the weakness of their finances, to enter into a composition, desired at that time by some of the chiefs of the French party, in order to close that Diet upon the best terms they could. Their fears of Russia then running very high, the persons treated with on this occasion, agreed to pay some of her majesty's debts, to repeal an act of the former Diet, which was very offensive both to the king and queen, to restore the credit of the court, by admitting several of those who had been most zealous in that interest to some of the best employments; and lastly, they promised, on the first meeting of a Diet, that they would consent to new interpretations being made of those passages in the fundamental laws, the sense of which had been perverted by former assemblies, to the prejudice of the royal authority.

The particulars of this agreement were only known to a few; but the consequences of it had given disgust to many of the opposers of the French system, who were not pleased to find two of its principal advocates well received at court, and to all appearance in great confidence with the queen.

Their disapprobation of it was afterwards justified by the event. From that time, those of the French party, who by this means had gained access to her majesty, used their utmost endeavours to produce a breach between the court and the Caps; but it was not till after the commencement of the Diet of which we are now treating, that the success of this attempt was publickly known, though before the time that the disaffection of the court became visible, some private informations were given to the leaders of the Caps, that one of the chiefs of the opposite party had engaged the French ambassador in a new treaty with the queen of Sweden, by which

which he was to endeavour to persuade his court, that the only way of effectually breaking the measures of the Caps was, to bestow the sovereign authority on the king of Sweden, upon condition that the French alliance should be preserved.

Here then was at once unravelled the whole mystery of the variations observed in the conduct of the Swedish court: which had now undertaken to protect those persons they had once desired to remove from the helm of government, and to support that system which they had so openly declared against from the beginning of the Prussian war to that time.

Deserted by their Swedish majesties, the English and Russian ministers, with whom the Prussian envoy had about this time received orders to act in concert, found themselves obliged to proceed upon a new plan.

To increase the regal power at the expence of the senate, could form no longer any part of it; and all they had now to do was, to acquire as great an influence in that body as France had formerly possessed there.

For this purpose it was necessary they should try to obtain the dismission of those senators who had ever proved themselves the most strenuous advocates for the French system, and to have their places supplied by such of the Cap party as were well-wishers to the courts of London and Petersburgh.

In the mean time the partizans of France were not idle. In order to stop the clamours of the nation respecting

respecting the delay of the payment of the French arrears, they had prevailed upon the court of Versailles to make a new proposal to that of Sweden, by which they offered to pay twelve millions of livres in eight years, at the rate of one million five hundred thousand per annum *. This proposal the senate thought proper to accept, however short it had fallen of the just demands of Sweden upon France; but the distrest state of the finances of the kingdom, had rendered them eager to grasp at any thing that they thought would extricate them out of their present difficulties.

The Hat party had likewise, by their being united with the friends of the court, a considerable majority in the house of nobles; and the French ambassador spared neither pains nor expence to detach the other orders from the English system.

The secret committee however, in which the Caps had entirely the ascendency, proceeded according to the plan laid down by the leaders of that party. In order to shew the French they had lost their influence in the Diet, and to stop the supplies for the purposes of corruption, which their ambassador at Stockholm expected from Paris, the committee voted it unnecessary to keep an ambassador at the court of France.

Their next resolution was, that no less than seven of the senators had abused the confidence that had been placed in them by the states, and therefore were no longer to be trusted. These

* November 22, 1764.

were the chief supporters of the French system; and their dismission, in order to make room in the senate for the same number of the opposite party, corresponded exactly with the views of the English and Russian ministers.

But a most extraordinary change appeared on this occasion in the disposition of the Diet.

When the house of nobles divided on the question, whether they should approve of the resolution of the secret committee, respecting the dismission of the senators, without farther deliberation or not, it was carried, as might have been expected, against the Caps; but in the order of the clergy, in which the Cap party had hitherto had the most decisive majority, to the great astonishment of the leaders of that party, the votes upon the same question were equal, and it was agreed to resume the debate another time. Among the burghers, where too the Cap party had till then greatly the ascendency, after much disputing, it was carried only by two votes, to approve of the resolution of the committee. As to the peasants, they did not take up the affair at all.

This sudden change among the orders in favour of the Hats, was as alarming to the leaders of the opposite party, as it had been unexpected by them. The whole Diet appeared now to be overturned; and all that the English minister had been labouring to accomplish, seemed to be defeated in a moment. The French party, imagining they had recovered the superiority, immediately declared they would make a new marshal of the Diet, break the secret committee, restore two of the senators who had resigned, from the apprehensions of the Caps, and totally undo all that had been done." This event furnishes a most striking instance of the dreadful corruption which prevailed in the states, as the result of it does how bare-faced that corruption must have been[*].

The fact was, the day before the above-mentioned question was to come on in the plenum, the French ambassador had spent no less a sum than seven thousand pounds, and his emissaries were employed the whole night in distributing more among the different orders. The clergy alone were supposed to have had at least three thousand pounds divided among them.

However the alarm of the Caps and the triumph of their antagonists upon this occasion, were equally short-lived; and the ambassador had the mortification to find that he had been at a great expence without having carried his point.

Measures were so well taken by his opponents, that the clergy were regained the next day; and when the same question came on again before the orders, it was carried in the three inferior ones by no inconsiderable majority, to approve

---

[*] Some time before the meeting of this Diet, it was publickly proposed in a club of burghers, that every man should take what money was offered, but vote according to his own conscience notwithstanding. This was done to frighten the French from corrupting, and it had the desired effect; for the Hat party thought it more safe to make only promises; and the ascendency of the Cap party among the burghers was chiefly owing to this.

of the resolution of the secret committee: so that the dismission of the senators took place.

Shortly after this, count Lowenhielm, chief of the Caps in the senate, was chosen president of the Chancery: and as twelve out of the sixteen senators were now heartily opposite to the French system, little more seemed requisite to be done to complete the destruction of the influence which the court of Versailles had so long maintained in Sweden.

But the English and Russian ministers had still one great difficulty to contend with, before they could effectually erect a system of their own in the room of that they had been able to overturn. A foreign alliance was absolutely requisite to give stability to the new ministry. To form an alliance with Sweden was also the object of England and Russia; yet there was an almost insuperable bar to prevent this measure from taking place: this was the constant refusal of England to give any subsidies. Russia had likewise always declared against them: and indeed it would have been at that time a bold stroke in the Caps to have ventured upon accepting a subsidy from Russia, even had she been disposed to give one, on account of the jealousy which has ever subsisted between the two nations; and the fear the Swedes had of giving the court of Petersburgh any public influence in their government.

Besides, another opinion prevailed among the people, that if the French subsidies were lost, their contributions must on that account be increased: hence an alliance with England, unless productive of a subsidy, could not fail to be an unpopular idea. The senate had therefore great apprehensions with regard to defending their conduct in a future Diet, should they reject so considerable a sum due to them by the old system, without making sure of some assistance by means of the new one; and they esteemed it indispensably necessary for them to obtain some object to present to the nation, which might be considered as a compensation for the loss of the ten millions and a half of livres still due to them from France, and which the French court would not fail to find a pretence for not paying, should any alliance be made between England and Sweden.

In this situation of things the principal leaders of the Cap party judged that nothing would be more expedient than a simple treaty of friendship between the two kingdoms; the general intention of which should be to give no umbrage to France for the present; and yet upon the foundation of this treaty, the secret committee might be able to frame instructions for the conduct of the senate, between the Diets, in a manner that would break the French system entirely. This treaty met with many difficulties in its progress, from the apprehensions entertained by the Swedish ministry of forming any engagements where no subsidy was to be given. The abilities of the negociator however overcame them all, and it was signed the sixth of February 1766. The chief article of it was, that the subjects of each nation were to enjoy reciprocally in their respective kingdoms, ports, and harbours, all the advantages and immunities

which

which the moſt favoured nation did then, or might afterwards enjoy. Inoffenſive as this treaty was, France pretended to be exceedingly diſatisfied with it, as well as ſurprized at its being concluded without having been previouſly communicated to her. She accordingly made uſe of it as a pretext for putting off the payment of a part of the ſubſidies, which had been then ſome time due *. She further threatened, that in caſe Sweden entered into a defenſive alliance with England, that ſhe would deprive the Swediſh ſhips of all the advantage they poſſeſſed in the ports of France. There is ſomething in the French ambaſſador's declaration to the Swediſh miniſtry, on this occaſion, which gives ſo true an idea of the dependence in which Sweden was held by France, that it deſerves a place here.

" The true reaſon, ſays he, of the delay of the
" payment of the ſubſidies is, that his Moſt C. M.
" had made, in conſequence of treaties which he
" religiouſly obſerved, certain political arrange-
" ments relative to his interior affairs; that one
" of theſe arrangements of his majeſty, with re-
" gard to the North was, that Sweden ſhould con-
" clude no treaty without his majeſty's conſent.
" That in contempt of this engagement, the motive

---

* There was an article in a treaty made between Sweden and France in 1738, and renewed in 1758, by which they reſpectively engaged not to enter into or renew any treaty, convention, or alliance, under any name whatever, with any power whatever, but with a common conſent.

France had however adhered to this only when ſhe thought proper.

" of

" of the subsidies of France to the Swedish court,
" Sweden had made a treaty with a foreign
" power, without waiting for the consent of his
" C. M. That Sweden, not attending to this en-
" gagement, had deranged the political views
" of his majesty, as the non-payment of the
" subsidies would derange the œconomical views
" of Sweden."

It is time to take some notice of the conduct of the court. After the affair of the dismission of the senators, they no longer kept any measures with the Caps, or concealed their having entered into the closest connections with the French ambassador.

A treaty of marriage had been some time on foot between the Prince Royal of Sweden, and the Princess of Denmark. This was a point concerning the success of which the Danes were exceedingly anxious, but to which the Swedish court had ever appeared very much averse. They, however, made proposals to the Danish ministers through the French ambassador, insinuating, that if the court of Denmark would give some money, and join intirely with the French party, the court's aversion to the marriage might be removed. This obliged the Caps to make the marriage themselves, in order to keep Denmark firm to her engagements with them; but by so doing, they greatly widened the breach that already subsisted between them and the court-party.

These backed by France appeared, at length, to have come to a resolution to attempt the re-establishment of an absolute government in Sweden.—The plan upon which they proceeded, was, to endeavour to create an open quarrel between the house of nobles and the other orders; to hasten the conclusion of the Diet; and to work immediately upon the means of obtaining another; to decry in all the provinces what had been done by the Caps in that Diet; to insinuate that they were governed by Russia; that Sweden would become a province to that empire; that the Swedish manufacturers would be driven out of the country to oblige England; and finally, that these disorders could only be remedied by desiring the king to interpose his authority.

It was not long before there appeared proofs by no means equivocal of the reality of such a design.

A person named Hoffman, who pretended to act by the king's orders, excited an insurrection in one of the provinces: but, upon his not being able to produce those orders, he was delivered up by the peasants, and brought to Stockholm. Upon his trial it appeared, that this had been a concerted plan; that an insurrection was designed at the same time in three other provinces; and that Hoffman had disconcerted the whole enterprize, as well as ruined himself, by his precipitation in not waiting for the day appointed for its being carried into execution.

It is to be regretted that upon this occasion, the Caps had recourse to one of those odious tribunals, of which an account has been already given.

Its

Its establishment was violently opposed by the Hat party; who, forgetting what they did themselves in 1756, loudly proclaimed it to be an inquisition set up for persecution; and it must be owned the Cap party equally departed from the maxims they then laid down, of having no extraordinary tribunals for the future. Their conduct was, however, very different from that of their opponents in similar circumstances: they carefully avoided carrying their inquiries too far, in order to prevent much effusion of blood: and Hoffman and two others only were condemned to be beheaded.

As the court had kept of late no measures with the Caps, notwithstanding their being all powerful in this Diet; so that party, on the other hand, appeared resolved to observe none with the court.

It was remarked, on a former occasion, that the king's possessing so small a share of power, was not only a great defect in the Swedish constitution, but also a circumstance dangerous to the liberties of the nation.

Hitherto the Caps appeared to have been of this opinion; and we have seen that at the commencement of the Diet, part of their plan was to increase the regal power, and diminish that of the senate.

But when the Swedish court had thought proper to throw themselves entirely into the arms of France, it certainly became a point of some difficulty to determine how the friends of England and of Russia were to act. The offers of France

to

to their Swedish majesties were of such a nature, that the Cap party could hardly flatter themselves they should be able to detach the court from the French interest, by any proposals they could justify themselves in making.

They, therefore, perhaps erroneously, thought it safest, instead of augmenting the regal power as they had at first projected, to lay new restraints upon it. This they accordingly did in a very material article.

The king, as it has been shewn, was allowed by the form of government to take his choice of three persons presented to him by the states, any one of whom he might appoint to the office of senator, whenever a vacancy happened in the senate: and by this means no person exceedingly obnoxious to his majesty could be forced upon him. But the Cap party now came to a resolution, that should a candidate for the senatorial office be three times presented by the states to the king and rejected by him, the states might then, if they thought proper, present him a fourth time alone, in which case his majesty should no longer have it in his power to reject him. This certainly was not the way to reconcile the king to a form of government, the restraints of which upon the royal authority had already exhausted his patience.

To counter-balance, however, this imprudent step, the Cap party caused another resolution to be passed in the diet, in which there appeared much more wisdom than in the preceding one.

This was, that no change should be made in

the fundamental laws, unless it was proposed in one diet and agreed to in another by all the four orders. Nothing could be better calculated to give a degree of stability to the Swedish government, of which it was never before possessed.

Not only all sudden resolutions of the states respecting changes of this nature, frequently the effects of the heat of party or violence of faction, were by this means guarded against; but the nation had a further security for their liberties, in the negative here given to any one order, in all constitutional questions, upon the propositions of the other three.

In consequence of the first of these resolutions, Baron Duben having been three times rejected by the king, when presented for the office of senator, the states appointed him to that office without farther ceremony.

His majesty refused to sign his patent, saying, they might stamp his name to it if they pleased; and it was said the queen would not suffer the new senator to kiss her hand, as was customary on those occasions.

The king shortly afterwards took a still bolder step. Upon three persons being presented to him for the office of secretary of state, he, of his own authority, and contrary to the express words of the form of government, named a fourth to it. This conduct of his majesty sufficiently indicated that he had some secret reliance upon his being powerfully supported in these attempts, and that what had been done in the course of the diet would not be of long duration. In the mean time,

time, the marriage of the Prince Royal with the Princess of Denmark was concluded under the auspices of the Caps*: after which it was determined to put an end to the diet.

During the course of it, the French influence would have been completely overturned, had England or Russia authorized their ministers to offer a subsidy: but, considering the many difficulties their not being allowed to make any such offer threw in their way, the change they effected in the interior of Sweden, as far as related to the administration, the senate, and the disposition of the diet, was infinitely more than in their circumstances there was any reason to expect they could have accomplished.

Count Lowenhielm, at this time a determined opposer of French measures, was now at the head of affairs. Of the sixteen senators, twelve were the fast friends of the English and Russian system; and the instructions framed by the secret committee to regulate the conduct of the senate, were evidently

---

* The states gave many instances on the occasion of this marriage, of that littleness and illiberality of mind, which it must be confessed, too frequently marked their conduct.

They created a variety of disputes concerning the regulation of the most trifling ceremonies. The king had intended after the marriage, to give an entertainment at one of his country-houses, but the secret committee ordered him to give it at Stockholm.

Upon the arrival of the Princess, the states interfered so far as to nominate even the ladies of the bed-chamber. Her Royal Highness requested that she might be allowed to appoint to that office herself. It was at length resolved that this should be left to the king.

calculated

calculated to give a final blow to French influence, and promote a union between Sweden and England.

By thefe the Swedifh miniftry were ordered to declare to the Britifh envoy, that Sweden was at prefent at liberty to liften to the propofals of England for a defenfive treaty.

In cafe an alliance was formed in the North, in confequence of the union of the South, the Swedifh miniftry were to enter into it preferably to any other fyftem; whether by feparate, whether by acceffary treaties, they were to accept of no propofition on the part of France, 'till what was ftipulated by the treaties of 1757 and 1758 was completely fulfilled, and the money due from her to Sweden paid; and even then they were to enter into no engagements with that crown, which could prevent or check the great plan abovementioned.

Laftly, by the final refolution of the committee, the public expences were provided for 'till 1770, without reckoning upon the French fubfidies, which was the principal point relied on by the friends of France, for obliging the fenate to call a new diet.

Such was the refult of the diet concluded the 11th of October 1776.

SECTION

SECTION IV.

Containing a sketch of the transactions preceding the calling of an extraordinary Diet in 1767, and of the changes brought about during that Diet.

IN so fluctuating a government as that of Sweden, where venality and corruption had arisen to a height scarcely credible, and where the total indifference of those entrusted with a share in the legislature to the public good, could be equalled only by their ignorance of the true interests of their country; it could little be expected that the new system of politics, produced by the labours of the English minister, should long resist the attacks that would certainly be made upon it.

No sooner was this Diet dissolved, than the French and court parties set all engines at work, devising to distress the ministry, and compel the senate to convoke another.

The ministry attempted to get a loan from Genoa of a hundred and fifty thousand pounds sterling: had they obtained it, the defensive alliance with England might possibly have been concluded without a subsidy: but France, not content with persisting in her last refusal to pay the ten millions and a half of livres she owed to Sweden, interfered also on this occasion. The duke de Choiseuil told the Genoese minister at Paris in plain terms, that the king his master having reason to be displeased with the conduct of Sweden, and having learnt that the subjects of the republic were going to lend a large sum of money to that country, he had his majesty's orders to write to the regency to forbid any such loan. In consequence of this, the government of Genoa sent an order to the principal person concerned, and to the bank, to put a stop to all farther proceedings, either with regard to the subscription *, or the remittances.

It was shortly made no secret that the court of Versailles projected to give more power to the king of Sweden. France offered the payment of four millions and a half of livres, on condition that Sweden renewed the treaty of 1738: and the French party spread reports all over the provinces among the peasants, that if the money from France was obtained, their contributions would be taken off. This the Hats imagined would occasion such clamours for an extraordinary Diet, as it would be impossible for the senate to resist.

In the mean time persons were appointed by that body, to treat with the English minister on the subject of the defensive alliance. But the negociation went on slowly, as the determination in England, not to give any subsidy, proved an insuperable obstacle to its success. The necessity of doing something to ballance the above-men-

* This prohibition was some months afterwards taken off by the Genoese government, in consequence of the remonstrances of the Swedish minister at Vienna.

tioned

tioned offer of France, in the eyes of the people, was obvious. The Swedish demand upon England was fifty thousand pounds. The senate proposed that this subsidy should not commence till the end of two years, and that it was to be paid only during five, though the treaty was not to expire in less than ten. The British minister, in his answer to this proposal, softened as much as possible the refusal of the subsidy: it was however too evident, that the senate, although perfectly well inclined to it, dared not proceed in the business, without procuring some indemnification for the loss Sweden would sustain of the French arrears, in case she formed any connections with England.

While this affair remained in suspence, the French and court parties continued indefatigable in their endeavours to distress administration.

They at length conceived a project, which they justly imagined could not fail to render an extraordinary Diet absolutely necessary. This was, that the king should declare to the senate he was resolved to abdicate the crown. The court and French party were at the same time to guarantee to his majesty, that the states, when called together, should request of him to resume it.

Agreeable to this project, the king produced a written paper in the senate, which he desired the prince royal to read, and to deliver in order to be inserted in the protocal.

It set forth, "That the king had been called to
" the throne by the free choice of the states.

" That he had laboured for the happiness and

"for the liberty of his people; but that as soon
"as the late king was dead, the states exacted
"from his present majesty an assurance, conceived
"in much stronger terms than that which had
"been given by his immediate predecessor;
"that afterwards the states had abridged his
"rights and prerogatives, so as to render him
"only the first slave in the nation.

"That in the preceding diet, they had again
"made regulations prejudicial to his rights, to
"which he declared he would never give his
"consent; nor to the appointment made by the
"states of Count Posse, to be about the person of
"his son."

Upon this two senators were sent to the king, with a representation concerning the necessity of putting the orders of the states into execution, as well as of his signing the new regulations; but his majesty absolutely refused to do it.

Nothing was in the mean time left undone by the French party, to prepare the minds of the people for the extraordinary step it was intended his majesty should take of abdicating the crown.

The prince royal, in a tour he made through the kingdom, during which his winning address and amiable manners gained him great popularity, collected a variety of complaints, to shew the necessity of calling the states, in order to redress the grievances which occasioned them.

All the governors in the French interest were prevailed upon to draw gloomy pictures of their respective provinces; representing that their manufactures

nufactures were ruined, and the people in the greatest misery.

The merchants likewise, who were for the most part in the same interest, endeavoured to lower the course of exchange, in order to put a stop to the working of the iron forges.

In short, every measure was taken by the Hats that could embarrass administration, however ruinous it might prove to the country.

The senate, in order to defeat the main attack of their opposers, resolved not to call an extraordinary Diet upon any verbal declaration of the king's; but only in case he signed a formal act of abdication, to which they imagined the queen would never give her consent.

It is certain, their agreeing to call another meeting of the states at that juncture, would in fact have been to consent to their own deposition. When the French party was overturned in the preceding Diet, the nation expected that the Caps would have been able to have formed a new system abroad, as well as at home; which should they fail to accomplish, it was impossible for that party to maintain themselves in the administration: they might then be accused indeed with some justice, of having thrown away the subsidies of France, and broke off all connexion with that country, without having gained any new ones to compensate for the loss of the old.

Sometime in February 1768, the king, in pursuance of the plan of the French party, had proposed to the senators to call a new Diet. This proposal

proposal was then rejected by thirteen voices, only one of the senators voting with his majesty. The Hats were however determined to renew the attack on the first favourable opportunity. The death of count Lowenheilm, which happened shortly afterwards; the war which broke out about this time between Russia and the Porte; and the arrival of a new French minister at Stockholm, seemed to have furnished them with as favourable a one as they could have desired.

The death of the count was a fatal blow to the Cap party; whilst the war between the Russians and the Turks gave new life and vigour to the Hats.

It was now therefore determined to carry into execution the long-projected plan of the king's abdication.

His majesty however, having some apprehensions on the occasion, previously sent to five of the chiefs of the French party, and declared to them he thought the measures proposed to him too hazardous, without his having some security that the promise made on their part should be performed. He therefore required a solemn engagement from them, that the rest of the plan of the court of France, and of that formed for the change of government, should be the first business entered upon by the states in the ensuing diet, and finished before any other was undertaken; to which they all agreed.

Encouraged by this, the king on the twelfth of December 1768, having refused to sign an act presented

presented him by the senate, addressed a letter to that body; the purport of which was, "that " when, sometime before, the major part of the " senators objected to the calling of the states, tho' " his majesty had acquiesced in their resolution, " yet it was without the least conviction, as to the " principles on which their objections were " founded. That since that time, the publick " distress had daily increased; for the truth of " which he referred them to the many petitions " presented to his son; to the sudden decay of " the iron works, trade, and manufactures; and " to the neglect even of the cultivation of the " land. That his paternal heart could not but " be afflicted at the thoughts of the weight of " the present taxes, and the unheard of distresses " which the raising of them occasioned. That " by the sudden fall of the course of exchange, " his subjects had been forced to pay a third " more than they had consented to give*; that " he was obliged to take notice of this, as by his " solemn oath he was bound to preserve his " subjects inviolably in the enjoyment of their " rights and privileges. That he did not lay the " fault of this illegal taxation on the senate; but " from whatever cause it had arisen, the nation

---

* There is hardly any specie in Sweden; and though the nominal value of the paper-money in that country continues always the same, the current value of it is perpetually varying. It is by its *nominal* value that the taxes are paid: hence these may be said to increase in proportion as its current value increases, and *vice versâ*.

" had

"had a right to examine whether they would
"grant it or not; that is to say, the states must
"be assembled as soon as possible. If, added he,
"contrary to my expectation, the senate should
"still object to it, I am forced hereby to declare,
"that in that case I do renounce the burthen of
"government, which the tears of so many of my
"distressed subjects, and the decaying state of
"my kingdom render intolerable to me; reserv-
"ing to myself, when my faithful counsellors
"the states are assembled, to declare to them my
"reasons for having till then laid down the go-
"vernment. In the mean time I forbid most
"strictly the use of my name in any of the reso-
"lutions of the senate. Signed,
Adolphus Frederic."

His majesty insisted on having an answer to this in eight and forty hours. The senate however declined giving one until some days after; and in the mean time every thing was done by the British and Russian ministers to keep them firm.

On the fourteenth the king went to the senate, and demanded an immediate answer. They represented the impossibility of examining in so short a time, all the reasons for and against the assembling of an extraordinary Diet; and desired at least, that they might be allowed till the following Monday to consider of it: but as to what his majesty had said with respect to laying down the government, they hoped he would not pursue a measure so contrary to the laws, and to his own gracious assurances.

The

The king replied, that he looked upon this reprefentation as a refufal; declaring, that he would from that hour, have nothing to do with the regency; fo rofe from his chair and left the fenate.

As foon as his majefty returned to his apartment, he fent the prince royal in a coach and fix, attended by feveral of the officers of his royal highnefs's houfhold, to the college of chancery; where he made a formal demand in the king's name, to have the ftamp delivered up to him, with which his majefty's fignature was made.

The college declined complying with this demand; and the prince went thence to all the other colleges, declaring to them, that the king his father had laid down the government, and giving them a printed copy of his majefty's reafons for fo doing.

In the mean time, the fenate continuing affembled, deputed four of their body to wait upon the king, and to befeech him not to abandon the regency. They received for anfwer, that his majefty perfifted in his refolution.

On their return, baron Triefendorf vice-prefident of the chancery, ftood up, and fet forth the great confufion into which the whole country would be thrown, in cafe the fenate pretended to carry on the government for eighteen months (the time before which, in the ordinary courfe of things, a Diet would not be affembled) without the king.

That no idea was lefs popular in Sweden than that of an ariftocracy; he therefore concluded,

that

that two senators should be sent to his majesty, to acquaint him that there was some appearance of the senate's conforming to his majesty's desires, and to entreat him to resume the reins of government.

This proposition was carried by a majority of six to three, nine being the whole number present. The king's answer was; when the Diet is resolved upon, my resignation falls of itself.

The speech made by baron Triesendorf in the senate, discovering that their weak side was fear, encouraged their antagonists to venture to engage the colleges, the magistrates, the clergy, in short, all the executive part of the government that resides at Stockholm, excepting the high court of justice, openly to take part with the king. The day after his majesty's abdication, the senate had issued out a species of proclamation to the following purpose. (The use made of the king's name in it, in direct opposition to his own act and deed, gives it an appearance truly ludicrous.)

" Whereas his majesty in the senate is informed,
" that the prince royal, by particular order, noti-
" fied yesterday to all the colleges, that the king
" would not concern himself any longer in the af-
" fairs of the government, it becomes highly neces-
" sary to remind the colleges how the kingdom is
" to be governed, according to the form of govern-
" ment, which they are sworn to maintain; and
" in consequence of which, no other orders are to
" be valid or obeyed, but those which are given
" out

" out in his majesty's name from the senate, and
" properly counter-signed. *His majesty* having
" that confidence in all those who serve in the se-
" veral offices of the kingdom, that in such pref-
" sing and dangerous circumstances for the nation
" and for liberty, they will conduct themselves
" according to the form of government, so as
" they may answer it to God, the *King*, and the
" states."

The answer of the principal colleges was, that as by the fundamental laws Sweden could not be governed without a king, any more than without a senate, they must remain in inactivity till the states were convoked.

The refusal of those, who had so considerable a share in the executive part of the government, to obey the senate until a meeting of the states, rendered this a measure absolutely necessary.

The senate accordingly were compelled to come to the following resolution. " That whereas se-
" veral of the colleges have declared that they
" would not obey his majesty's orders from the
" senate, till the states were convoked; that the
" exchequer had refused to supply money; and
" that Colonel Ehrenswärd and General Ferfen,
" commanders of the two regiments quartered in
" this city, have declared that they could not an-
" swer for the obedience of the soldiers, the senate
" find themselves obliged to call an assembly of
" the states on the 19th of the ensuing April."

By this step an effectual stop was put to the treaty of alliance with England, as the senate durst

not

not have ventured to take it upon themselves after having convoked the states. These would of course have expected an affair of such importance should have been deferred till the time of their assembling, and consequently the precipitating of this point, would of itself have been in the eye of the states a sufficient cause of complaint against the senate, independent of the light in which they might view the treaty itself.

Thus the French party destroyed at one blow the new system that the friends of England and Russia had erected in Sweden during the last diet. A system which had required great abilities, joined to the most indefatigable zeal in those who introduced it.

The king now returning to the senate, expressed the infinite pleasure he received from the convocation of the states; and declared that he doubted not to be able to shew how innocent his intentions were in all the transactions of the preceding days; adding, that he had the fullest conviction that what he had done would be approved both then and afterwards.

Thus ended the interregnum, and the confusion that had prevailed for some time in public affairs. The measures pursued by the Hats upon this occasion were the boldest ever ventured upon from the time of the commencement of the late form of government. They were consequently a convincing proof that the leaders of that party were secure of being so powerfully supported by France

France at the enfuing diet, as to have nothing to apprehend on account of a conduct, which might otherwife have brought fome of them to the block, and realized the abdication of the king.

The fact was, France had refolved to light up a war in the north. It is well known fhe had a confiderable fhare in promoting that in which Ruffia was then involved with the Porte. It is likewife paft a doubt that her ambaffador at Conftantinople had been very liberal of his promifes to the Turks, that the Swedes would make a diverfion in their favour by attacking Ruffia in the north, while the Ottoman armies purfued their operations in the fouth.

In the preceding Auguft* the Swedifh minifter at the Porte, had an audience of the Reis Effendi, who afked him, if what the French ambaffador at Conftantinople had reported relative to the preparations making in Sweden was true, and how foon they might expect to fee hoftilities begun againft Ruffia. The Reis Effendi put him in mind, at the fame time, of the generofity of the Turks in remitting the debt of Charles the XIIth, and infifted upon a pofitive anfwer.

France, therefore, was apprehenfive of lofing her credit at the Ottoman Porte, if fhe did not engage the Swedes to perform the promifes fhe had made for them to the Turks. For this reafon, fhe refolved to fpare no expence to recover her former influence in Sweden, as well as to carry

* In 1767.

into

into execution, at the approaching diet, the plan she had for some time projected of changing the Swedish government.

The Diet of this year was consequently likely to prove the most critical, with respect to the fate of the form of government, of any since its establishment; and, which was a point of much greater importance, if France was to have remained unopposed during the course of it, she would probably have involved all Europe in a war.

All parties now applied themselves vigorously to pursue their several interests in the elections for the Diet. The French minister at this time had a considerable advantage over his opponents; he was the only one who had eventual orders, none of those of the other courts knowing the sentiments of their respective sovereigns in regard to these extraordinary measures. Reports were also spread, that he should shortly have twelve millions of livres at his disposal to bestow in subsidies, &c. provided Sweden would enter thoroughly into the views of France; and advice was soon afterwards received, that ten millions were actually deposited in four different houses at Amsterdam, to be made use of by the French minister for this purpose. Even Spain, little as she may seem concerned in the affairs of Sweden, began, at the instigation of France, to take a part in the transactions going forward in that country; and in order to detach Denmark from the English and Russian interest, offered the Danes to allow them to transport negroes to the Spanish West Indies. Added to all this,

this, the Swedish merchants entered into a large subscription to support the friends of the French party.

Such formidable preparations seemed to threaten at once, the entire re-establishment of the French system in Sweden, and the total overthrow of the Caps.

These, however, were not idle. Russia was too much interested in the event of the approaching Diet, and too well informed of the machinations of France, not to resolve upon giving that party the warmest support.

With regard to England, her minister at Stockholm was authorized to assist the Caps in obtaining a majority in the Diet; and as to Denmark, she then entered into these measures with as much zeal and vigour as Russia.

But the Hats had considerably got the start of their opponents in canvassing for the elections; and the sum said to have been furnished them by the French minister for this purpose was immense. Accordingly, on the opening of the Diet, the majority among the nobles, clergy, and burghers appeared to be greatly in favour of the French party. Among the peasants indeed, the Caps retained their superiority. The elections of the speakers of all the four orders were likewise carried against the Cap party *. General Ferfen, one of the most zealous and able partizans of France, was elected marshal of

---

* The night before the day of electing the speaker of the peasants, a report was propagated among them that the Caps intend-

of the Diet; and the French party having the secret committee entirely at their devotion, as not a single Cap had been chosen into it, they immediately became possessed of the whole government; and could, if they had thought proper, have pursued every part of the plan laid down by the court of Versailles.

Fortunately for the Caps the friends of France were divided into two parties; one of which entered into all the projects of the court for rendering the government absolute; while the object of the other was, only to turn out the present ministry, and put themselves in their places; but they declared, that they were, at the same time, equally averse with the Caps to any material change in the constitution. The former were more particularly stiled the court-party, and the latter the old Hats. At the head of these last was colonel Pecklin, a man of the first abilities, as well as of the greatest influence in the Diets; and who, may with justice be said, to have belonged to no party, any farther than that party adhered to principles from which he never swerved himself.

The first business entered upon in the secret committee, was, as might have been expected, the deposing of such members of the senate as had been introduced into that body through English and Russian influence. In this point all the Hats were agreed, and indeed they had not scrupled for

intended to depose the king, which was the cause of their losing the majority in that election.

some

some time before to tell those senators openly that they would be immediately deposed, to make room for another administration attached to the French alliance. Nothing could be more frivolous or worse grounded than the charges brought against them, and brought, it must be presumed, only for the sake of form, as at all events they must have been dismissed by a Diet, of which the Hats were masters.

Accordingly their deposition took place immediately on the meeting of the states; who came to a resolution to restore all the senators removed by the preceding Diet, and to make Count Eckebladt again president of the chancery.

It was resolved likewise in the house of nobles, to present an address to his majesty, to thank him for his great goodness and love of his people, in having determined to abdicate his crown, if the senate could not have been prevailed upon to assemble the states; and that the king should in his turn thank the colleges for the resolution they had taken not to proceed in any business, in case of such abdication.

The foreign ministers, who supported the Cap party, were convinced of the little utility of opposing at this juncture the deposition of the senate, or change of the administration, and therefore did not attempt it; reserving their whole strength for the intended attacks upon the constitution.

In the mean time the French minister used his utmost endeavours to convince the Swedes of the necessity of their entering into the closest connections with his most Christian Majesty. The language

guage held by the Hats, was, that Sweden wanted subsidies of all sorts both publick and private; that France would give them, England would not; that a thirty years friendship had subsisted between Sweden and France, who had now made offers to the Swedes, highly advantageous to their commerce in the Mediterranean*. That England was their rival in shipping and manufactures; that she spoke openly of supplying herself with iron from her own colonies, and already took a great quantity from Russia, in order to have nothing more to do with Sweden.

These arguments might have had some weight, had they been backed by the immediate payment of a part of the French arrears; but this was not to be done, unless the project of France with regard to the constitution succeeded. The Cap party did not fail to take advantage of the delays of France with respect to this point, to foment the discontents occasioned by them among the people. They asserted, and with great justice, that France only wanted to involve them in a war with Russia; that they had already sufficiently suffered from the two last wars, in which they had been engaged by the artifices of the court of Versailles; that the subsidies granted them by that court were not only altogether unequal to the expences which French

---

* The offer of France on this occasion was, that having made a conquest of the island of Corsica, she was determined it should be a free port; that if Sweden would enter into a strict alliance with his most Christian Majesty, he would grant such privileges to the Swedes, as would make that island a magazine for all sorts of Swedish merchandize.

connexions

connexions had ever led them into, but that small as these were, they had been so irregularly paid, and so much remained due, that they had brought the country into the most serious distress: finally that at the present juncture, the finances, the military establishments, and the marine of Sweden, were not in a condition to take any vigorous measures, so that without injuring Russia, they might ruin themselves.

The arguments of the Cap party were too well founded not to have their due weight with the nation, which, together with the division among the Hats, enabled the friends of England and Russia to oppose the views of France during the remainder of the Diet, with a success they could scarcely have hoped for, from the aspect of affairs at its commencement.

After the deposition of the senators in the Cap interest, and placing the administration in the hands of the Hats, there still remained three points to be accomplished by the French party; without which all the expence France had before been at, would have proved of little or no advantage to her.

These were, to effect a change in the Swedish constitution, to engage Sweden in a French alliance, and to involve her in a war with Russia. With regard to the first, the object of the court of Versailles, was principally to give to the king and the senate a power to expedite all affairs between the Diets, of whatsoever nature they might be; and to form alliances, or even make war without assembling the states. This would have
rendered

rendered France miſtreſs of the whole military force of Sweden, and conſequently have enabled her to purſue her favourite deſign of attacking Ruſſia, in order to make a diverſion in favour of the Turks.

The leaders of the French party did not however ſucceed in their firſt trial on this occaſion, in the manner they expected. Having ſounded their friends upon the queſtion of giving the diſpoſition of the military employments as far as a lieutenant-colonel incluſive, abſolutely to the king, without any preſentation, it did not appear to be at all reliſhed by them. And when the affair was brought before the Diet, the propoſed changes in the conſtitution, were in three of the orders rejected with great warmth and indignation, by a conſiderable majority; the clergy alone decided in their favour.

The French party having failed in this point, the intended treaty of alliance between the courts of Stockholm and Verſailles met with no better ſucceſs. By one of the articles of it, Sweden was to conclude no treaty with England, or with any other power, without the participation of France. She was likewiſe to obtain the recall of the Engliſh miniſter then at Stockholm, and to have no other for the future from the court of Great Britain, after this alliance ſhould be concluded. By another of the articles, Sweden was to keep fifteen thouſand men in Finland, ready to march on the ſhorteſt warning; ſo that it is obvious a war between Sweden and Ruſſia would have been the conſequence, if France had ſucceeded in her
deſign

designd uring the Diet. Upon the whole she had gained nothing in the course of it, from all her expence and trouble but a change of the administration; and even this proved of but little advantage to her, on account of her partizans having failed in their attempt to give a power to the king and senate, to carry on a defensive war, without assembling the states; as well as because the senate were forbid to transport any troops from Sweden to Finland, before the next meeting of the Diet.

The instructions however of the secret committee, which were to regulate the conduct of the senate after the separation of the states, were pretty nearly the reverse of those formed only two years before, by the secret committee of the preceding Diet.

The substance of these was, that though the senate was to maintain a good understanding with all the neighbouring courts, it would not be prudent to enter into any defensive alliance with any of them for the present; but particularly not into the northern league, which had been for some time in agitation. They declared that France and the Ottoman Porte were the natural allies of Sweden. Spain and Austria, as being in an intimate union with France, were likewise recommended as her natural friends.

They observed that the object of England was, to acquire the empire of the sea, and to augment her commerce at the expence of other nations: she could not therefore be looked upon as a well-wisher to the prosperity of Sweden; particularly as she had so lately an opportunity of entering into a close connection with Sweden, of which she did not chuse to avail herself by granting a subsidy. The senate were therefore to form no engagements with the British court.

It was at the same time insinuated to the French ministry, that notwithstanding their friends at Stockholm had found it impossible during this Diet to satisfy the court of France, according to former promises, yet every means should be used to put the kingdom in a proper state of defence, and to prevent any extraordinary Diet for the future. That the miscarriage of the affair of the constitution should not impede the execution of the plan of operations formerly settled, nor diminish the disposition of the Swedish ministry to go through with it; provided the French arrears were paid, in order to furnish money for the preparations, which should go on as soon as the Diet was finished.

It was likewise intimated to the Porte, that the state of affairs in Sweden, would not allow of her making any immediate diversion in favour of the Turks; but that it was notwithstanding her intentions to embrace the first opportunity which should offer for this purpose; and in the mean time every necessary preparation should be continued, that the Swedes might hold themselves in readiness.

This was all that occurred worthy notice, in the Diet concluded the thirtieth of January 1770.

SECTION

SECTION V.

Containing an Account of the Revolution, and of the Steps which immediately led to it.

IN the preceding sections, I have endeavoured to give a succinct view of the state of affairs in Sweden, during the two Diets immediately antecedent to that in which the late Revolution was accomplished.

The designs of the court, the nature of the parties, the intrigues of the foreign ministers, and the different objects of the powers who employed them, were all points with which it was necessary the reader should be made acquainted, in order to enable him to see into the true sources of the great event which followed.

It may not be requisite to recapitulate these, only let it be remembered, that the intention of France had now for some time been to overturn the Constitution of Sweden; that of England and Russia, to preserve it.

It did not, however, appear that the court of Versailles had as yet determined in what manner this revolution was to be brought about.

During the preceding Diet the French party had been foiled in all their attempts to effect such a change by means of the states themselves. A method, which from being the most secure, was the most agreeable to the disposition of the late king.

king. Those people who thought the members of the Diet sufficiently corrupt to have been bribed into any measures, did not attribute to their virtue the preservation of their form of government; but imagined they had been as well paid for doing their duty, as they could have been for betraying their trust.

Defeated in her expectation of being able to accomplish her point by means of corruption alone, it became necessary for France to make use of some other mode more likely to be attended with success. That of effecting a revolution by force, appeared, from the temper of the Swedes, by no means impracticable. But the gentle pacific disposition of Adolphus Frederick was ill adapted to an undertaking of this sort. He was besides a foreigner; the nation would not consequently have had that confidence in him, which they might have placed in a prince born and bred among them.

Possessed of every virtue which adorns private life, but unacquainted with that ambition which thirsts after power, he was devoid of the spirit of enterprize, which usually accompanies it. Formed for domestick happiness, his paternal feelings would not have suffered him to take any step, which, if unsuccessful, might involve his family in ruin. It was only after much solicitation that some time before the last Diet he had ventured upon that of abdicating the crown; and as he advanced in years, he seemed anxious only for tranquillity and repose.

During

During the life, therefore, of Adolphus Frederick, the court of Verſailles could have little expectation of being allowed to attempt by force any change in the conſtitution of Sweden.

In the mean time a ſhew of military preparations was carried on there, in order to fulfil the aſſurances given by the Swediſh miniſter at the Ottoman Porte, and to deceive the Turks into an idea of Sweden's making a diverſion in their favour; by which it was preſumed they would be induced to prolong the war with Ruſſia.

The delay at this time of the Daniſh court in ſending back their miniſter who had been abſent nine months, gave the French party in Sweden room to flatter themſelves with the hopes of a change of ſyſtem in Denmark, which might bring about the old French project, mentioned on a former occaſion, of an alliance between the Swedes and the Danes againſt Ruſſia, under the direction and ſupport of France.

Great expectations were likewiſe formed by them from the event of the Prince Royal's journey to Paris, which he had at this period undertaken. A viſit that was then ſuppoſed to be made at the expreſs deſire of the duke de Choiſeuil, in order that the young prince might confer with that miniſter, upon means of changing the Swediſh government into a more abſolute one, as well as to eſtabliſh a French ſyſtem there upon a more ſolid foundation.

On the other hand, the Caps having defeated the chief objects of their antagoniſts during the preceding Diet, were no wise alarmed either at the present situation of things, or at the schemes which the French party appeared to be meditating for the future.

They were sensible the disposition of the late king would, during his life at least, secure the constitution from being overturned by violence; and though the Hats had put themselves in possession of the administration, and of all the principal posts of the kingdom, yet the sense of the nation was evidently against them.

This was owing to two causes. First, Because the people were fully convinced of their own inability to support a war with Russia, which they perceived the leading party, out of compliment to France, aimed at producing: Secondly, Because they had been highly disgusted with the last mentioned power, on account of the chicaneries and delays which the court of Versailles had so often put in practice, with respect to the payment of the arrears.

The English and Russian ministers did not fail to lay down a proper plan to improve this disposition in the nation, and to secure the most decisive majority in the next Diet that should be assembled.

They observed that France seemed startled at the expence with which the contest was likely to be attended. And they judged it very probable that if her party was not more successful at a future Diet, than they had hitherto been with respect to the points she was desirous of obtaining, she would altogether withdraw her support from that party,

party, and watch for some opportunity when she might effect by force, what she was unable to accomplish in a less hazardous way.

The designs of France against the constitution were well known, for they had been in some measure avowed. This had awakened the jealousy of such of the Hat party as were desirous to preserve the form of government entire, however they might otherwise be attached to the French system; and it confirmed the Caps in the opinion, that they had no other way of securing their constitution from the dangers with which it was threatened, than that of throwing themselves into the arms of England and Russia.

It was expected that wrought upon by their fears, the Cap party might be induced at the ensuing Diet, to accede to the alliance proposed to them by the English and Russian ministers, without insisting upon the point of the subsidy, which hitherto proved the only obstacle to prevent that alliance from taking place.

England and Russia were in that case to guarantee to Sweden her form of government; and the grand northern league, the formation of which was the undoubted interest of Great Britain, would probably have been the consequence of the union of these three powers.

Such was the situation of things in Sweden when the death of the late king* gave a new face to the affairs of that country.

---

* In February, 1771.

This event threatened to prove as fatal to the views of the Cap party, as it appeared favourable to those of the friends of France. It removed the chief obstacle which had hitherto prevented the cabinet of Versailles from pursuing the object of effecting by force a change in the Swedish constitution, and consequently deprived the friends of England and Russia of their principal security, that no such attempt would be made before they were sufficiently guarded against it.

The prince royal was at Paris at the time of his father's death, where he was endeavouring to obtain certain points from that court, concerning which the Swedish administration had hitherto remonstrated in vain. The acquisition of the regal dignity, by giving a new consequence to the royal negociator, gave an unexpected success to the negociation itself.

The French court agreed to pay Sweden a million and a half of livres annually, and it was no longer a question whether she would furnish money to support her friends at the ensuing Diet.*

According

---

* Lieutenant General Count Scheffer, who on this occasion was dispatched by the senate to compliment his majesty on his accession, by a piece of address obtained from the French court a considerable part of the arrears so long due to Sweden.

It was night when the count arrived at Versailles, to acquaint the late king of France with the death of Frederic Adolphus; and as his majesty had retired to his bedchamber, it was with some difficulty the count gained admittance to him:

According to the new form of government, a new Diet was to be convoked within thirty days from the death of the king; but on account of the prince's absence, and in order to enable him to compleat whatever might remain unsettled between him and the court of France, the senate did not appoint an assembly of the states till the June following.

This delay was fortunate for the Caps, as it gave the British and Russian ministers time to exert themselves during the absence of the young king, in order to procure a majority at the approaching Diet.

It was then obvious this diet was to determine the fate of the Swedish form of government, and that if the friends of France obtained an ascendency in it, the partizans of England and Russia would never again be able to make a stand against the French interest, since the change the court of Versailles designed to make in the

him: he then abruptly informed his majesty of the death of the king of Sweden. By the unexpectedness of the visit at so unusual an hour, the old king was taken by surprize, before he could have any previous consultation with his ministers; and the nature of the intelligence appeared highly to affect him. Count Scheffer seized upon that moment to paint to his majesty the deplorable situation of the finances of Sweden, and the distresses consequent upon it, to which that country had been reduced; adroitly insinuating that this was altogether owing to the non-payment of the French arrears. In the situation of mind into which the king had been thrown, the eloquence of the count could not fail to have due weight; and accordingly his majesty gave him his word he would next day order his ministers to satisfy the Swedish demands.

Swedish constitution, would infallibly deprive them of the means of opposing that interest for the future.

Accordingly the Caps were so strenuous in their efforts on this occasion, and so powerfully supported by the British and Russian ministers, that after the elections had taken place, there appeared among the three inferior orders a considerable majority of that party.

In the mean time the young king wrote in the most gracious terms to the senate, approving of all the steps they had taken, and repeatedly assuring them that he designed to govern according to the laws.

The language held by the French party, was also that no attempt would be made upon the constitution; that they only meant to procure the payment of the arrears due to them from France; but that they would do nothing to obtain them which could justly offend any other power.

This was calculated wholly to abate the opposition made to them, and to keep themselves in the administration till they had ruined the other party, which would have set them at liberty to act afterwards according to the suggestions of France.

His Swedish majesty in his way from Paris paid a visit to his uncle the king of Prussia, and gave him the strongest assurances of his pacific intentions, and of his desire to govern according to the laws of his country, without aiming in the least at any augmentation of his authority. His Prussian

Prussian majesty expressed the highest satisfaction at these declarations, and strongly recommended it to his nephew to persevere in those intentions:[*] immediately afterwards the king set off for Stockholm, where he arrived about the end of May.

Since the establishment of the late form of government in the year 1720, the Swedes had hitherto beheld only foreigners on the throne, Frederic the First, and Frederic Adolphus; princes who neither of them had any hereditary claim to the crown, and who both were consequently indebted for the dignity they enjoyed to the free election of the people they governed: who therefore could not conceive they possessed

---

[*] It has been a generally received opinion that the king of Prussia had no inconsiderable share in bringing about the late revolution. But the reverse of this is the truth.

When the king of Sweden arrived at Brunswick, on his road to Stockholm, he wrote a letter to the king of Prussia, in which he acquainted him, that he had come so far in the intention of paying his court at Berlin; but that affairs were so pressing for his return to Sweden, that it would be impossible for him to have that satisfaction. As soon as the king of Prussia received this letter, he sent to prince Henry, telling him, that he supposed his nephew was diverted from seeing him by the insinuations of France; that it must appear extraordinary in the eyes of all Europe, that he should have been twice at Brunswick without going to Berlin; and therefore he recommended it to the prince, who knew the young king's character better than he did, to write a proper letter upon the occasion, which should be delivered into his Swedish majesty's own hand.

This was accordingly done, and on the receipt of the prince's letter the king set out for Potsdam.

any right to a greater share of power than that people had allotted to them; and who unexpectedly finding a scepter placed in their hands, must naturally have considered the external honours paid to royalty as an acquisition of no small importance; an acquisition sufficiently dazzling to those not accustomed from their childhood to look forwards to it, to make them forget in the splendor of a crown, how little real power that of Sweden conferred upon the wearer.

It was to these circumstances perhaps that the Swedish constitution partly owed its safety during the reigns of the above-mentioned monarchs; but from the temper and dispositions of those princes it likewise derived security.

The character of Frederic Adolphus has been already given; and that of Frederic the First so far bore a resemblance to it, that he was equally incapable of any enterprize which required a spirit of intrigue to carry it into execution; and equally averse to disturb the tranquillity of his reign, by any violent attempts to increase his authority.

It was perhaps only under two such monarchs as these, that the Swedish form of government, defective and corrupted as it was, could possibly have subsisted so long.—But in his present majesty of Sweden, the son and successor of Frederic Adolphus, his subjects beheld a prince of a very different genius.

Gustavus the Third was about five and twenty when he was proclaimed king of Sweden.

From his mother, the present queen dowager,

sister

sister to the king of Prussia, he seems to inherit the spirit and abilities of his uncle; from his father, that benevolence of heart, which still renders the memory of Frederic Adolphus dear to the Swedes.

Born with talents that would have reflected lustre on any rank, but peculiarly suited to the exalted one he was destined to hold; his natural endowments were cultivated to the highest pitch, by an education the most finished, and most nicely adapted to a situation, which would probably one day require their fullest exertion.

By a graceful and commanding oratory, the most captivating manner and insinuating address, he caught the hearts of those who beheld him only in public; by an extent of knowledge and depth of judgment, he excited the admiration of such as had an opportunity of being nearer his person. But neither of these could as yet suspect him of that genius for intrigue, of that bold and enterprizing spirit which have since distinguished him; neither could hope that such a genius, whilst it was exerted to promote the particular interests of the prince who possessed it, should yet never lose sight of the happiness of the people; that such a spirit should be under the direction of prudence, and in its course be marked by a moderation as amiable as it is rare.

Neglectful of pleasures, yet not averse to them, without being dissipated, he tasted the amusements of a court; and in the midst of the closest application to study, retained all that graceful ease which qualifies to shine in a circle. He cultivated with

S   equal

equal succeſs the arts of governing, and of pleaſing; and knew alike how to gain the reſpect, and win upon the affections of his future ſubjects.

Under the appearance of the moſt diſintereſted patriotiſm, an ambition great as his talents, lay concealed: and covered by a zeal for the welfare of his ſubjects, his deſigns upon their liberties might have eſcaped the penetration of the moſt ſagacious.

Such were the talents, ſuch the ambition of a prince deſtined to wield a ſceptre, that could afford no ſcope for the one, no gratification to the other. Who, maſter of every popular art, was in a popular government, to ſubmit to the caprice of a ſenate, or the dictates of a foreign miniſter: who, fully equal to the taſk of governing others, was to be himſelf allowed no will of his own; and who, poſſeſſed of the hearts of his people, was to be their king only in name; was to content himſelf with the gaudy trappings of royalty, which he deſpiſed; and was to refrain from graſping at that power which formed the firſt object of his wiſhes.

Nothing could exceed the demonſtrations of joy teſtified by the people at the arrival of the king at Stockholm, but the amiable affability with which he received all who approached him. No conduct could be better calculated to extend his popularity to the remoteſt parts of his dominions, than that which he adopted.

Three times a week he regularly gave audience to all who preſented themſelves. It required

neither

neither rank, fortune, or interest to obtain access to him; it was sufficient to have been injured, and to have a legal cause of complaint to lay before him. He listened to the meanest of his subjects with the dignity of a sovereign indeed, but at the same time with the tenderness of a parent. He entered into the minutest details that concerned them; he informed himself of their private affairs; and seemed to take all that interest in their happiness which is so grateful to the unfortunate, and so rarely to be met with in persons, whose elevated station place them in a manner beyond the reach, or even the knowledge of the sufferings of the lower classes of mankind.

When a sovereign condescended to cares like these, he could not fail to be considered as the father of his people. In the warmth of their gratitude, they forgot that motives of ambition might have had some share in forming a conduct which to them appeared to proceed wholly from the purest benevolence; a conduct, in which the tenor of his majesty's actions has indeed proved he consulted his feelings, but which has likewise been since proved by the event, to have been the wisest he could have chosen for the purpose of carrying the design he meditated into execution.

If his Swedish majesty aimed thus successfully at popularity, he likewise endeavoured to persuade the leading men of the kingdom into an opinion of his sincere and inviolable attachment to the constitution of his country; of his being perfectly satisfied

satisfied with the share of power that constitution had allotted to him; and took every opportunity to declare that he considered it as his greatest glory to be the first citizen of a free people.

He seemed intent only on banishing corruption, and promoting union; he declared he would be of no party but that of the nation; and that he would ever pay the most implicit obedience to whatever the Diet should enact.

These professions created suspicions among a few, but they lulled the many into a fatal security. Those however who possessed a greater share of penetration, thought his majesty promised too much to be in earnest; and notwithstanding he maintained an outward appearance of impartiality, they could not help observing that all his favourites were of the French party, as well as that the whole administration was at the beck of the court of Versailles.

It was evident to the friends of England and Russia, that they had in Gustavus a more formidable opponent to contend with than they had as yet encountered, since those powers first interfered in the interior policy of Sweden.

Shortly after the king's arrival at Stockholm, the court of France, which had lately employed only ministers of the second order in Sweden, now sent an ambassador* thither, which was a sufficient proof of the importance of the commis-

---

* Mr. de Vergennes who just before had been Ambassador at Constantinople, a worthy and respectable man. He is now minister for the department of foreign affairs at Paris.

sion

fion with which he was charged. A minister from Spain soon after made his appearance there: this seemed to threaten the opening of a new source of assistance from Madrid, to support the cause and friends of France in the approaching Diet.

In the mean time the English and Russian ministers were indefatigable in their endeavours to guard against those designs of the Swedish court, which they had long known were in agitation, and which from such formidable preparations appeared to be hastening to maturity.

It was impossible to oppose these with effect, but by a speedy conclusion of the treaty of alliance between England, Russia, and Sweden, which was to form the basis of the projected northern league. As long as an administration devoted to France, and warmly supported by the king of Sweden continued in power, no negociation for this purpose could be renewed.

The first step therefore that it was necessary for them to take, was to procure the dismission of a majority of the senators, who were all in the French interest, and to place the administration in the hands of those who had proved themselves the staunch friends of the English and Russian system.

This being accomplished, they might leave the remainder of their plan to be compleated by the apprehensions which the gradual disclosing of the intentions of his Swedish majesty could not fail to excite, not only among the Caps, but even such of the Hats as were not disposed, however otherwise attached to France, to purchase a connection with that power at the expence of their constitution.

On the other hand, the king easily penetrated into the views of his opponents, and by the most artful policy endeavoured to defeat them.

On the opening of the Diet the Caps appeared to have the most decisive majority in the three inferior orders. In the house of nobles it is true the Hats had the superiority, and of course the marshal of the Diet was of that party, which afterwards proved a point of great consequence to the king. But in the secret committee, all the members taken from the order of Burghers were of the Cap party; and there were only four Hats among those chosen by the clergy.

That committee, as was observed on a former occasion, possessed absolute power in what related to foreign affairs, and in a great degree directed all the operations of the states. Their resolutions generally became the acts of the Diet; and consequently the English and Russian interest having the ascendency in that body, the king must have soon perceived that his influence in it would be proportionably small.

This situation was certainly truly critical. Should the Caps become masters of the Diet, an event he had every reason to apprehend, the dismission of all his friends and partizans from every office of trust and power, would be the infallible consequence. This would probably be immediately followed by the completion of that treaty with Russia and England, by which his hopes of subverting the constitution would be cut off for ever,

ever, as the contracting parties were to be guarantees for its safety.

The Hats indeed had a great majority in the house of nobles, but even that party was by no means at his Majesty's devotion. On the contrary, instead of having any reliance upon their supporting *him*, he appeared to derive his principal consequence from his adhering to *them*.

Their leaders had too long fed on the bounties of France, to be easily prevailed upon to yield up their title to them, by consenting to any material change in the constitution. It was only in virtue of the power which that constitution had vested in them, that they possessed any claim to the favours of the court of Versailles. The subversion of it would therefore destroy all their hopes of obtaining future emoluments from the same quarter.

Only a few friends personally attached to the king, were ready to co-operate with him in whatever he should undertake; but their number was so small, they could hardly be denominated a third party in the Diet; neither did they assume the appearance of one, by acting in any manner from themselves.

Hardly seated on the throne, the affections of his subjects as yet untried, ignorant of the disposition of the soldiery, and some parts of his plan not ripe for execution, his majesty was obliged to act with all the caution and deliberation that the delicacy of his situation required.

It was not sufficient for his purpose that the bulk of the nation had for some time viewed the conduct of their governors with a silent and sullen discontent. It was necessary to have their indignation sufficiently kindled to make them take an active part in favour of their sovereign, in case his first attempt should prove abortive. In their affections only he might ground his future security, should the blow he meditated to strike miss it's aim; but it was by rousing their courage and calling their zeal into action, that he could alone hope to be furnished with the means of repeating it afterwards with more success.

Patience and submission have been long the characteristics of the lower class of the Swedes. They are not consequently easily moved to resistance; and though it was probable they would not oppose a change in their constitution, it was not to be expected they would contribute to it, unless their minds had been previously prepared for the purpose which would require both management and time to effect.

Hence the king perceived, on the one hand, the hazard he ran, should he precipitate the execution of his schemes; on the other, the ascendency the friends of England and Russia had acquired in the Diet, seemed to render delay equally dangerous.

Thus circumstanced, he pursued the conduct which might have been expected from his prudence, his judgment, and his penetration. A conduct which deceived all parties, and imperceptibly promoted his own ends, as much as it was calculated to defeat theirs.

As the deposition of the senate would be one of the first objects of the Caps, it became necessary fary for the king to endeavour to protract, if he could not prevent their fate. On this account it was requisite that the Diet should be rendered as inactive as possible, by throwing difficulties in the way of every transaction, which in the usual course of business was to precede that measure.

One of the first points gone into by the states after their meeting was, that of regulating the assurances which were to be signed by his majesty previous to his coronation.

This created a dispute between the house of nobles and the other orders. A coolness had for some time before subsisted between them, owing to a very imprudent step taken by the senate the preceding summer.

Upon a particular occasion they had laid it down as a maxim, that all the great offices of the state were to be filled by the nobility only. The inferior order asserted that this was directly contrary to the fundamental laws of the constitution, and that every man of merit of whatsoever rank, was eligible to the highest offices; and they were even much disposed to decide that a burgher might be a senator.

Contentions of this sort in a free state, have been ever fatal to liberty; and one great defect in the Swedish form of government was, that in its own nature it was peculiarly liable to them.

To widen this breach between the house of nobles and the other orders, became evidently the interest of the court party, from its tendency to create that inactivity in the Diet, which was so favourable to the views of the King.

Notwithstanding that it is to be presumed his majesty secretly fomented this disunion among the states, he had the art however at once to reap every advantage he could derive from it, and at the same time to acquire in the eyes of the nation all the merit of endeavouring to heal divisions so prejudicial to the state.

With a paternal care he appeared solicitous only to reconcile the different parties to each other, whom he amused by repeated proposals for an accommodation between them, which he well knew could not, nor never in reality wished should take place: yet his discourses wore such an air of sincerity, he seemed animated by so warm a zeal for the happiness of his people, appeared so indifferent to his own interests, and so indefatigable in using every means which could in any shape promote union among the members of the Diet, that it was hardly possible to penetrate into his real intentions.

"If," said he in the conclusion of one of his speeches, " my intentions were less pure, less in-
" nocent, less sincere; if my heart was not filled
" with the most tender love for my country; for
" its independence, its liberty, its glory, and its
" happiness; I might quietly have watched my
" opportunity, and after the example of other
" kings, my predecessors, have seized the occa-
" sion to take advantage of their divisions, at
" the expence of their liberty and their laws."

Such

Such was the language held by the king. He even went a step farther. He sent to the English and Russian ministers, to know whether by their means a union of the parties could not be brought about.

His majesty likewise set many negociations on foot for this purpose, which could answer no other end than to expose the conduct of the states to the nation, and place his own in the most amiable point of view. By the one, he was sure to add to his popularity; by the other, he hoped to create among the people a dislike to their form of government.

The point in dispute between the house of nobles and the other orders, was, whether any addition should be made to the assurances which had been signed by the late king in 1751.

The latter asserted that as many new laws had taken place since that period, it was necessary some notice should be taken of them in the assurances his present majesty was to give. The former insisted that those should remain as they were. Both parties adhered pertinaciously to their opinion, and the consequence was that a stop was, in a great measure, put to the proceedings of the Diet.

The lower orders had certainly on this occasion just grounds for complaint, and perhaps to suspect the sincerity of the king. What had been resolved upon by three of the orders, could not, according to the form of government, any longer be considered as a matter in dispute, but ought immediately to have passed into a law. This the

nobles

nobles had evaded by endeavouring to render the present case, one of those in which the unanimous consent of the four orders was requisite.

They asserted that their privilege would be attacked by some of the additions which the inferior orders proposed to make to the king's assurances. His majesty therefore by taking advantage of this evasion, and refusing to sign the assurances without the concurrence of the nobles, rendered it tolerably evident, that he was not altogether so anxious to see union established among the states, as he endeavoured to have his subjects imagine.

There was another reason still stronger for their entertaining this opinion. The Caps had even in the house of nobles a very considerable party. The king's friends in that house could have turned the majority in favour of the Cap party by abandoning the Hats. Consequently it was in his Majesty's power at any time to have had the concurrence of that house to the assurances which he declared himself so ready to sign, if such concurrence could be obtained.

In this manner was the Diet rendered inactive, and its operations suspended; so that though the states had been assembled in June, it was not till the February following, that is, till eight months after, that the assurances were finally regulated and signed by his Majesty.

The obstinacy of the lower orders not to suffer any alteration to be made in them, together with the inability of the leaders of the Caps to gain a majority in the house of nobles had even then rendered this a point of the utmost difficulty; and

its

its being at length accomplished was altogether owing to the prudence and moderation of a few of the chiefs of the Hat party, who became apprehensive of some material breach in the constitutution, should the confusion in public affairs continue much longer. They therefore assisted the Caps on this occasion in carrying the assurances through the house of nobles.

But this confusion had already lasted sufficiently long to make an impression on the people; to expose the defects of the form of government; to shew the influence that foreign powers had acquired in the Diet, and to display the wisdom, the disinterestedness, and patriotism of the king, who had so often, though in vain, offered his mediation to accommodate the disputes which agitated the Diet. It had been of sufficient duration to enable his majesty, secretly to take many of those steps which were preparatory to the blow he intended to strike.

No methods had been in the mean time left untried to foment the jealousies which subsisted between the different orders, and if possible to bring them to an open breach. There were emissaries likewise planted in every part of the kingdom, for the purpose of sowing discontent among the inhabitants; of rendering them disaffected to the established government, and of exciting them to an insurrection.

The affair of the assurances being thus determined, the next point gone into by the states, was, an enquiry into the conduct of the senate since the last Diet. The secret deputation appointed for

this

this purpose did not finish their examination till the end of March; the result of which was, that the senators had forfeited the confidence of the states, and the three inferior orders came to a resolution, to depose them all.

This was a resolution equally violent, impolitic, and unjust; and was entered into by the Cap party, in direct opposition to the advice of the wisest of their own leaders, as well as that of the foreign ministers who supported them. In common prudence they should have observed some measures with the Hats, and have dismissed such a number of them only from the senate; as would be sufficient to secure to themselves a majority in that body. It was certainly the height of folly in them to render the other party desperate, at a time they knew a design was formed against their constitution, and to make the Hats indifferent to its fate by leaving them no interest in its preservation. Had indeed this step been taken at the commencement of the Diet, the consequences of exasperating that party, might not then have been equally fatal. But after a delay of ten months, chiefly occasioned by the obstinacy of the three lower orders; a delay of which the king had taken every advantage to prepare for the execution of his plan, which he had now nearly brought to maturity; it was perhaps impossible for the Caps to have made choice of a conduct better calculated to accelerate the revolution they intended to guard against. This, therefore, may be considered as one of the principal causes of the extraordinary facility with which that Revolution was brought about.

The fact was, that the lower orders of the Cap party, finding themselves completely masters of the Diet, became intoxicated with their success. They were no longer to be governed by the councils which the abilities of the British envoy and count Osterman had hitherto dictated to them, and to which they were chiefly indebted for the superiority they had obtained over their opponents.

Transported by their animosity towards the adverse party, by their greediness of emolument and thirst for power, they set no bounds to their desires, no limits to their demands. Nothing less would satisfy them than the total exclusion of the Hats from every office of profit, trust, or dignity. In the violence of these pursuits they forgot there was one point at least in which many of that party coincided with them in opinion; namely, that the constitution should be preserved. They forgot the dangers with which that was threatened, and how much they would stand in need of the assistance of the opposite party to enable them to avert the stroke by which it was likely to fall.

The king, whose sagacity nothing could escape, whose vigilance never failed to seize upon every circumstance which could promote his ends, instantly saw the folly of the Caps, and lost not a moment to take advantage of it.

At that moment it furnished matter of surprize, that the resolution of the three inferior orders relative to the deposition of the senators, should be immediately agreed to by the house of nobles. It was

was expected that this measure would have been most violently opposed by the court party, and the success of the Caps on this occasion in all the four orders, was considered as a final overthrow of the French and Hat interest. But it should rather have been attributed to that refined policy which directed the conduct of his Swedish majesty.

The preservation of a senate in the Hat interest was now no longer an object with the king, whatever it might have been at the commencement of the Diet. It had been only necessary for him to prevent for a time the establishment of a Cap administration. In this he had succeeded. The more violent the Caps afterwards became in their measures against the other party, the less likely were his majesty's designs to meet with the opposition he might otherwise have apprehended, from such of the Hats as had hitherto declared themselves warm friends to the constitution. To see them stript of their offices, deprived of their power, and in a manner proscribed by their antagonists, was what, perhaps, at the present juncture, he would secretly have wished. It could not fail to render the Hats, in some degrees, dependent upon himself, and teach them to look up to him alone for support.

Some steps had indeed been already made apparently with this view. In the preceding December it had been notified to the Hat party, that all pecuniary assistance was from that time to cease. This naturally created great dissatisfaction among them, as many of them had no other resource to
enable

enable them to attend the Diet, but what they derived from money given them by their leaders. However, all possible pains were taken to pacify them, by promises of favour and advancement from the king.

The Hats then not only perceived themselves on the point of being deprived of all their power and influence for the present, but that every future expectation of their being restored to either would infallibly be destroyed, should the plan of the British and Russian ministers take place. They foresaw that this would be the consequence of their being supplanted by a Cap administration. They knew that unsupported by France they would be then left at the mercy of that party which they had so often oppressed; the leaders of which they had on a former occasion brought to the scaffold: and of whose animosity against them they had now such convincing proofs. In short they beheld their rivals rising upon their ruin, and ready to adopt a plan, calculated to exclude them for ever, from any share in the government.

Thus circumstanced the fears of the Hats for the safety of the constitution must naturally have yielded to their apprehensions for their own. Accordingly many of them became secretly inclined to co-operate with the king in whatever he should undertake; and such of them as had always declared themselves averse to any measures which directly tended to overturn the constitution, retired from Stockholm to their country seats; there quietly to wait the event.

T Among

Among these was field marshal count Ferson, who was one of the ablest of the leaders of the Hat party, and who, though a zealous partizan of the court of France, had been ever considered as warmly attached to the established form of government.

The absence of the count, who was likewise colonel of the guards, was a circumstance as favourable to the views of his majesty, as the most sanguine of his adherents could have wished.

After the deposition of the senate had been resolved on by the states, they proceeded to the choice of the persons who were to form the new administration; but from the mode prescribed by the form of government on those occasions, it was in the power of the court party to create such a delay, as the state of his majesty's affairs might still render necessary; by which means, together with the business of the coronation, the operations of the Diet were suspended as long as they judged proper.

In the mean time, the king had assembled a corps of about one hundred and fifty officers, commanded by lieutenant colonel Springporten, under pretence of exercising them in military manœuvres; but in fact to found their dispositions, and to attach them to his person. These constantly attended him; by his amiable affability he soon won upon their affections, and inspired them with a zeal to support his cause.

The abilities of this prince knew how to render the most casual circumstances instrumental in promoting his designs.

There

There was at that juncture an accidental dearth of corn in the kingdom, which had reduced the inhabitants to the greatest diftrefs. The court party took infinite pains to propagate an opinion among the people, that the fcarcity was intirely owing to the negligence of the ftates, in not having provided againft it, by encouraging the importation of foreign corn. This was certainly a groundlefs charge. The fact was, the ftates had ufed their utmoft endeavours to relieve the people, and had for that purpofe fent no inconfiderable quantity of corn to the governors of the different provinces to be difpofed of among the inhabitants of their refpective diftricts. But the king's party in order to foment the difcontents which reigned in the nation, had the art to prevail upon fuch of the governors as were devoted to his intereft, to withhold from thofe over whom they prefided, the fupply which the Diet had provided for them; and thus by creating an artificial want, to add to the diftreffes, which the failure of the preceding crops had already created. No meafure could have been better calculated to irritate the people againft the government, and it was attended with a fuccefs equal to the policy by which it was dictated. Complaints were echoed from every quarter of the kingdom, and nothing but the fubmiffive temper of the Swedes could have prevented an open infurrection.

They became, however, by this means not only prepared, but anxious for a change of their mafters; and no means were left untried by the king's friends,

friends, which could tend to excite them to a revolt.

Persons were employed in every province, to exhort the people to repair to Stockholm, and lay their grievances before the throne; similar attempts were practised even in the capital. And if it was found difficult to prevail upon them, to have recourse to violence, they were taught, however, to behold without concern the subversion of their constitution.

While his majesty, and those who had his confidence, were thus occupied, an administration was at length formed, composed of the friends of England and Russia. The former negociation relative to a treaty between Sweden and Great Britain was immediately renewed; and a new one set on foot to lay the foundation of another between Sweden and Russia. It might have been expected that at the present crisis these treaties would have been concluded with that expedition which the critical state of affairs seemed to render so necessary. The same difficulties which had formerly prevented their being carried into execution were, however, again started; the loss of the million and a half of livres received annually from France, and the necessity of obtaining a subsidy in lieu of them, were still insisted upon as strongly as ever. The new administration appeared much more solicitous to deprive the Hats of every share of power, than to adopt the only measure that could give stability to their own.

They were without doubt fully convinced of the

the neceffity of that meafure; and their true motives for throwing obftacles in its way were by no means fo juftifiable as the oftenfible reafons they gave for their conduct.

They had early in July received intimations from different authorities concerning the reality of the king's defigns againft the conftitution, but the mode by which thofe defigns were to be carried into execution was not known to them, and divers conjectures were formed upon that fubject. Some on this account affected to difbelieve it; others confidered the different plans they had heard of, as impracticable; and the greater part imagined, that admitting any of them to be attempted, they could with eafe defeat them.

Such was, at leaft, the various language held upon the occafion. But in fact, fome of the members of the Diet were become fo deplorably corrupt, that their confent could not be obtained to the points neceffary even to their own falvation.

The lower orders alfo triumphed too much in their power of carrying points againft the houfe of nobles; and their appetite for fhewing this power, which, by the conftitution, belonged to the majority of three orders againft one, difgufted the nobility, and was of great prejudice.

It was feen in the affair of depofing the fenators, that they had loft all fenfe of their danger, when they refufed to comply with the earneft and repeated defires of the minifters of thofe powers who fupported them: It was alfo feen in the delay of forming an alliance, on which their very exiftence depended. They trufted their fafety to the

the solicitude those powers had testified, to see such an alliance concluded; called loudly for means to continue the Diet, while they neglected to take the steps necessary to preserve that form of government, by which it was established and upheld.

A month had thus elapsed in fruitless endeavours on the part of the ministers of Great Britain and Russia to carry the affair of the treaties through the different orders; and the moment drew nigh which was to decide the fate of the constitution.

The apprehensions of the ruling party were at length roused by an incident, which corroborated too fully the intimations they had already received of designs against the constitution, to allow them any longer to remain inactive.

Hitherto the king's adherents had used some caution and secresy in their endeavours to foment the discontents of the people. A libel was now found stuck up in the most public parts of Stockholm, exciting the inhabitants to an insurrection. The leaders of the Caps immediately took the alarm; they assembled and resolved to bring this matter before the secret committee, when some measures of defence should be proposed to guard against surprize.

But the marshal of the Diet, who was entirely devoted to the king, refused to let the committee meet upon that day, and thus delayed a step which could not have been made with too much expedition.

However when the committee did assemble, they

they ordered a battalion of the regiment of Upland to hold itself in readiness to march. Colonel Springporten, of whom they had many reasons to entertain the strongest suspicions, and of whose continuance at Stockholm, they were very apprehensive, received likewise orders to repair to Finland; nominally for the purpose of preventing a tumult there, but in reality to keep him at a distance. General Rudbeck, grand governor of Stockholm, upon whom the committee had a thorough reliance, and who was likewise one of the most popular men in the kingdom, was dispatched into Scania, to Gottenbourg and Carlserona, to quiet the minds of the inhabitants, and counteract the manoeuvres of the emissaries of the court; and general Pecklin the ablest and boldest of the leaders of the Caps, was charged with the direction of such measures, as might be necessary for the tranquillity of the city during the governor's absence.

The commission appointing the general to this trust, was sent the same day to the king, who was at one of his country houses, for his signature; which his majesty did not then think proper to comply with, nor to take any notice of it afterwards in the senate: by which means the general was prevented from entering into his office, till the king judged it would be too late for him to provide effectually against the attack it was now daily expected his majesty would make upon the states.

The chief disadvantage the administration lay under upon this occasion, was, that no measures could

could be taken in the senate without the king's knowledge, nor any carried into execution without the approbation of the secret committee; this rendered every scheme of defence proposed by the ruling party in a great degree dependent on the will of the marshal of the Diet; without whose consent that committee could not be assembled, and who, as we have already seen, was strongly attached to the interest of his majesty.

The royalists, however, seemed highly alarmed at the precautions that were taken against them. The king alone appeared unconcerned, and never betrayed in his countenance or discourse the slightest agitation of mind.

He still continued to disguise his intentions in a manner that deceived even those who had been most cautioned against them.

At this very time he desired an interview with the Russian minister; he informed him of his intentions of visiting the empress of Russia, immediately after the conclusion of the Diet: adding, that he would the following day declare his resolution to the senate; and obtain for this purpose the consent of that committee, which he so shortly intended should have no power either to grant or refuse him any request.

The Caps now began to lament that the treaty with Great Britain and Russia was in no greater forwardness, and to be thoroughly inclined to accede to the proposals of those two powers. But this change of disposition came too late. Some time must necessarily elapse before such a measure could be accomplished, and his majesty was too

wise

wife not to take advantage of the delay. The king now judged himself secure of the major part of the officers of those regiments which were quartered at Stockholm. But he likewise conceived it would be necessary for him to have no inconsiderable party among the provincial troops.

This was a point not easily to be accomplished. The Swedish army consists of a militia, which is embodied only at certain times of the year. It was impossible to assemble them out of the usual course without some ostensible reason; and if the states should be before-hand with his majesty, in giving orders for this purpose, and appoint generals in the Cap interest to command them, the king foresaw there would be an insurmountable obstacle to his design. To prevail upon this militia to rise of their own accord in order to promote his views; at once to shake off long habits of obedience, and turn their arms against those from whom they were accustomed to receive commands, was a measure evidently impracticable.

The king's brothers, prince Charles and prince Frederic, were at this juncture in the province of Scania, and Ostrogothia, where they had resided some time upon different pretences.

Their real object was to ingratiate themselves with the officers, the soldiers, and the people. They practised there the same arts the king had employed at Stockholm for similar purposes, and with nearly equal success. But still a pretext was wanting to assemble the provincial troops. The princes had no legal authority over them; many of the officers were of the Cap party, and it was not to be expected they would pay obedience to orders given by those who had no right to command them. Such obedience indeed would, according to the form of government, have been construed into treason. It became necessary therefore to create a case, the exigency of which might justify the officers in departing from the strict line of their duty, should they be induced to assemble their respective corps at the simple request of the king's brother, without waiting for formal orders from the secret committee.

A plan had been some time formed for this purpose. Among the inferior officers with whom the king had an opportunity of conversing, there was a captain named Hellichius, who had attracted his notice. Hellichius was possessed of that bold and daring spirit, which, when accompanied by ambition, prompts to the most hazardous undertakings. He had long aspired after the honours of nobility, and was impatient for an opportunity to distinguish himself. The king saw into his character, and resolved to make him one of his principal instruments in accomplishing his designs.

Hellichius was accordingly trusted with the secret of the intended revolution, and instructed in the part he was to perform in it. Being commandant of the fortress of Christianstadt, one of the most important in Sweden, it was fixed, that on an appointed day he should publish a manifesto against the states, in which he should dwell upon the distresses of the people, the un-

heard

heard of dearness of every necessary of life; and attribute the whole to foreign influence, and the corruption which reigned in the Diet.

He was immediately afterwards to excite the troops under his command to revolt, to shut the gates of the fortress, and prepare for its defence. At the same time he was to dispatch an officer to prince Charles, who, under pretence of having made his escape, was to acquaint the prince with what had happened, and by that means enable him to prevail upon the officers of the neighbouring regiments to assemble their men, and put themselves under his command, for the ostensible purpose of suppressing the growing rebellion. No plan could have been better conceived, none could have been more successfully executed.

Hellichius fulfilled his instructions to the minutest article, and the prince almost immediately appeared at the head of five regiments.

As these troops had thus voluntarily put themselves under the command of prince Charles, were altogether unacquainted with his real intentions, and ignorant of what was going forward at Stockholm, it was no difficult matter for him to create among them such a disposition as would be favourable to his designs. Reports were spread in this army, that the constitution was indeed in danger, but not from the quarter whence danger was in reality to be apprehended. It was, on the contrary, whispered that a design was formed against the king, which perhaps aimed at more than depriving him of his crown; that it was intended to establish an aristocratic form of government,
under

under the direction of Ruffia; againft which country the Swedes had entertained an ancient antipathy. Such reports, at that time out of the reach of contradiction, could not fail to make impreffion. And had the king's attempt at Stockholm proved unfuccefsful, the meafures which the ftates might in confequence of it have legally purfued, would have been confidered as corroborating proofs of the truth of thofe reports.

Had the fenate then arrefted his majefty, it would have been attributed, not to the neceffity he had himfelf laid them under of taking that violent ftep, but to a premeditated defign, correfponding with that of which they had been accufed.

Thefe troops therefore thus prepared, and headed by the brother of their fovereign, would not have hefitated in fuch a cafe to have marched to his relief.

Thus his majefty, though engaged in an enterprize in which fecrecy was fo requifite, that there were not perhaps half a dozen perfons in the kingdom privy to it, contrived to guard againft every contingency which might happen.

Happily for the king, the event proved he had no need of any other fupport than what he derived from his talents and his popularity.

On the fixteenth of Auguft, general Rudbeck, who in his tour through Scania, had attempted to vifit the fortrefs of Chriftianftadt, and had therefore become acquainted with what was going forward there, returned fuddenly to Stockholm late at night; and the secret committee being

affembled

aſſembled next morning, he informed them of the revolt of Hellichius.

Upon this report the committee immediately reſolved, that a battalion of the regiment of Upland, and another of that of Sudermania, ſhould be ordered into the city of Stockholm; and that the cavalry of the burghers ſhould patrole the ſtreets every night.

They likewiſe reſolved that two regiments of cavalry ſhould immediately inveſt the fortreſs of Chriſtianſtadt; and a deputation was ſent to the ſenate to communicate to them the reſolutions that had been taken, and to have them carried into execution.

The ſenate at the ſame time deſired the king to remain in town, and diſpatched two couriers to the princes his brothers, to order them to return immediately.

Even now that the firſt ſtep towards the revolution had in fact been taken, it would have been ſtill impoſſible, from his majeſty's conduct and deportment, to have penetrated into his deſigns, had there been no other grounds for ſuſpecting him.

The ſurprize he was able to affect at the news of the revolt; the concern he ſo well counterfeited on the occaſion; and his apparent readineſs to concur with the ſenate in every meaſure they thought requiſite, not only in order to ſuppreſs the rebellion, but to provide likewiſe for their own ſecurity, aſtoniſhed the few who were not the dupes of his behaviour, as much as it deceived the many who were.

When

When general Rudbeck firſt communicated this intelligence to the king, his majeſty embraced him, called him his beſt friend, and ſo warmly expreſſed his obligations to him, that the good old general, although one of the chiefs of the Cap party, left his majeſty's preſence firmly perſuaded, not only that he had not been privy to the revolt in Scania, but that it was impoſſible the reports could be true concerning the king's deſigns upon the conſtitution.

This was the more extraordinary, as the general had certainly a long time before ſuſpected thoſe deſigns.

It is probable the king now deferred giving the final blow to the power of the ſtates, only till he had received from prince Charles the news of his having ſucceeded in aſſembling and putting himſelf at the head of a conſiderable body of the provincial troops. In the mean time however he gave a new proof of his ability in gaining over to his intereſt all he had an opportunity of converſing with.

The cavalry of burghers, who had been ordered to patrole the ſtreets, were accompanied by his majeſty in their rounds. The ſenate could find no pretext to object to this, as it certainly had the appearance of nothing more than a laudable zeal in his majeſty to preſerve the tranquillity of the city. But the king knew how to make another uſe of it. In the courſe of two nights only, thoſe very perſons whom the ſtates had armed for their defence, were, by the almoſt faſcinating power his majeſty poſſeſſed, converted into zealous well-

wiſhers

wishers of his cause; and they were afterwards among the foremost to declare themselves in his favour.

When the king had received prince Charles's letter, with the account of his being at the head of five regiments, he immediately sent it to the senate, who laid it before the secret committee. In this letter the prince expressed a strong desire to be continued in the command of the troops he had assembled, taking an opportunity at the same time to declare his inviolable attachment to liberty. The senate however refused, as might have been expected, to comply with his request, and appointed one of their own body to command in the room of the prince.

The critical moment was now come, when delay far from being any longer necessary to the king's designs, must, on the contrary, prove fatal to them.

Only two days had elapsed since the revolt in Scania was known at Stockholm. We have seen how the king employed part of that time in gaining the cavalry of the burghers; during the remainder of it his emissaries were busy in every quarter of the town, talking and treating with the soldiers of the guards, and the *artillery. His

---

* A private soldier gave on this occasion an instance of fidelity which deserves to be recorded. The night preceding the revolution, the king being desirous of visiting the arsenal, went thither, and ordered the sentinel to admit him. The latter refused. Do you know who you are speaking to? cried the king. Yes, answered the soldier, but I likewise know my duty.

majesty

majesty likewise assembled all the officers who were devoted to him; and attended by them paraded through the streets, not only for the purpose of shewing himself to the people, but even for that of conversing with all who approached him. The senators and others, who were most concerned in their consequences, were advertised of these motions; but some trusted to the precautions already resolved upon, and on the point of being carried into execution; while others, and much the greater part, intimidated by the king's popularity, and the attachment the officers testified to his person, were persuaded, that if any steps were taken towards confining his majesty to his palace, or any open declarations were made of the states distrusting him, that it would accelerate the revolution, and bring it on before the regiments they had ordered into town for their safety, and which were then within a day's march, could arrive.

But the same reasons which prevented the senate from adopting any violent measure, previous to the arrival of those regiments, rendered it incumbent in his majesty to hasten with all possible expedition the execution of his plan.

Should we now give a glance back at the state of affairs in Sweden from the time when England and Russia first jointly opposed the influence France had acquired there, we must perceive that every defect and vice in the government had, during that period, arrived at full maturity. The principles of corruption, interwoven in the original frame of the constitution, cultivated and protected

protected by the policy of France, had before gradually expanded themselves. But when other powers adopted the same policy, venality of a sudden rose to its utmost height among the Swedes.

Among the higher ranks of people, their attachment to the constitution, or even to their country was abated by the violence of parties, and diverted by the eagerness of gain. Among the lower ranks, the spirit and character of the nation were degraded by servility and an abject submission, as well as the traffic carried on in the Diets. The contagion of corruption had spread itself from the capital to the most distant provinces. That constitution designed to establish liberty, became, in the hands of those whom it intrusted with any share of power, only the instrument of their obtaining foreign gold. For the last nine years the government had continually shifted backwards and forwards into the hands of two different sets of men, of opposite interests, pursuing opposite systems, supported by powers inimical to each other; by turns persecuting or persecuted; who, as each happened to gain the superiority over their antagonists, became solicitous to revenge former injuries, or guard against future resentments.

It was not surprising if a government so conducted had lost the respect and confidence of the people.

Should we next consider the policy with which the king had turned all these circumstances to his own advantage; with how much address he had fomented the discontents which had at length begun to prevail among the people; with how much ability he had prepared their minds for the change he meditated; how well he had succeeded in exposing the venality and corruption of the states, by a conduct which had at the same time gained him the love of his subjects; and lastly, when we reflect that no nation in Europe entertain a higher veneration for the regal dignity than the lower ranks of the Swedes have at all times testified: after taking this view, I say, of the state of affairs in Sweden at the juncture we are treating of, it might appear that the king ran little or no risque in endeavouring to overturn at one blow, a fabric defective in all its parts; the foundation of which had been long sapped; and which, by the depravity of those whose interest it was to defend it, was left destitute of support.

The fact was however otherwise. The circumstances I have enumerated, did indeed operate greatly in his favour: but it is likewise to be considered on the other hand, that the king was certain of meeting with opposition from a party which had compleatly got the possession of the reins of government; that he himself had no share of the executive power, and could not, unknown to the senate, give orders to a single company of his own guards without a breach of the constitution; that the senate were apprised of his intentions against them, had taken proper precautions, and that troops commanded by officers warmly attached to the ruling party, were within a few hours march of Stockholm.

Secure of the affections of the people, his majesty

jesty might perhaps have relied upon their not opposing him; but their submissive temper likewise precluded him from any expectation of their taking an active part in his favour. The whole therefore turned upon this single point, viz. the impression his first harangue should make upon the soldiers. Should they even hesitate to embrace his cause, the tragical catastrophe of the year 1756, in consequence of an undertaking similar to that in which he was embarked, immediately presented itself to his view.

Thus circumstanced his Swedish majesty, in the morning of the nineteenth of August, determined to throw off the mask, and seize by force upon that power which the states had so long abused, or perish in the attempt.

As he was preparing to quit his apartment, some agitation appeared in his countenance: but it did not seem to proceed from any apprehensions for his own fate. Great as this prince's ambition is, his humanity is not inferior to it. He dreaded lest the blood of some of his subjects might be spilt in consequence of an enterprize, which he could not flatter himself to succeed in without having recourse to violence.

His whole conduct during that day, as well as after the revolution had taken place, justifies this conjecture.

A considerable number of officers, as well as other persons, known to be attached to the royal cause, had been summoned to attend his majesty on that morning. Before ten he was on horseback and visited the regiment of artillery. As he passed

passed through the streets he was more than usually courteous to all he met, bowing familiarly to the lowest of the people. On the king's return to his palace, the detachment which was to mount guard that day being drawn up together with that which was to be relieved, his majesty retired with the officers into the guard-room. He then addressed them with all that eloquence of which he is so perfect a master; and after insinuating to them that his life was in danger, he exposed to them in the strongest colours, the wretched state of the kingdom; the shackles in which it was held by means of foreign gold; and the dissensions and troubles arising from the same cause, which had distracted the Diet during the course of fourteen months. He assured them that his only design was to put an end to these disorders; to banish corruption, restore true liberty, and revive the ancient lustre of the Swedish name, which had been long tarnished by a venality as notorious as it was disgraceful. Then assuring them in the strongest terms that he disclaimed for ever all absolute power, or what the Swedes call sovereignty, he concluded with these words; " I am obliged to " defend my own liberty, and that of the king- " dom, against the aristocracy which reigns. " Will you be faithful to me as your forefathers " were to Gustavus Vasa, and Gustavus Adol- " phus? I will then risk my life for your wel- " fare, and that of my country."

The officers, most of them young men, of whose attachment the king had been long secure, who did not thoroughly perhaps see into the nature of the requeſt his majeſty made them, and were allowed no time to reflect upon it, immediately conſented to every thing, and took an oath of fidelity to him.

Three only refuſed. One of theſe, Frederic Cederſtrom, captain of a company of the guards, alledged he had already and very lately taken an oath to be faithful to the ſtates, and conſequently could not take that which his majeſty then exacted of him. The king, looking at him ſternly, anſwered, "think of what you are doing." "I "do," replied Cederſtrom, "and what I think to-"day I ſhall think to morrow; and were I ca-"pable of breaking the oath by which I am al-"ready bound to the ſtates, I ſhould be likewiſe "capable of breaking that your majeſty now re-"queſts me to take."

The king then ordered Cederſtrom to deliver up his ſword, and put him in arreſt.

His majeſty however, apprehenſive of the impreſſion which the proper and reſolute conduct of Cederſtrom might make upon the minds of the other officers, ſhortly afterwards ſoftened his tone of voice, and again addreſſing himſelf to Cederſtrom, told him, that as a proof of the opinion he entertained of him, and the confidence he placed in him, he would return him his ſword without inſiſting upon his taking the oath, and would only deſire his attendance that day. Cederſtrom continued firm; he anſwered, that his majeſty could place no confidence in him that day, and that he begged to be excuſed from the ſervice.

While the king was ſhut up with the officers,

senator Ralling, to whom the command of the troops in the town had been given two days before, came to the door of the guard-room, and was told that he could not be admitted. The senator insisted upon being present at the distribution of the orders, and sent into the king to desire it; but was answered, he must go to the senate, where his majesty would speak to him.

The officers then received their orders from the king; the first of which was, that the two regiments of guards and of artillery should be immediately assembled, and that a detachment of thirty-six grenadiers should be posted at the door of the council chamber, to prevent any of the senators from coming out.

But before these orders could be carried into execution, it was necessary that the king should take another step; a step upon which the whole success of his enterprize was to depend. This was to address himself to the soldiers; men wholly unacquainted with his designs, and accustomed to pay obedience only to the orders of the senate, whom they had been taught to hold in the highest reverence.

As his majesty followed by the officers, was advancing from the guard-room to the parade for this purpose, some of them more cautious, or perhaps more timid than the rest, became, on a short reflection, apprehensive of the consequences of the measure in which they were engaged: they began to express their fears to the king, that unless some persons of greater weight and influence than themselves were to take a part in the same cause,

cause, he could hardly hope to succeed in his enterprize. The king stopped a while, and appeared to hesitate—The fate of the revolution hung upon that moment. A serjeant of the guards overheard their discourse, and cried aloud—" It shall succeed—long live Gustavus." His majesty immediately said, " then I will venture"—and stepping forward to the soldiers, he addressed them in terms nearly similar to those he had made use of to the officers, and with the same success. They answered him with loud acclamations; one voice only said, no; but it was not attended to.

In the mean time some of the king's emissaries had spread a report about the town that the king was arrested. This drew the populace to the palace in great numbers, where they arrived as his majesty had concluded his harangue to the guards. They testified by reiterated shouts their joy at seeing him safe; a joy which promised the happiest conclusion to the business of the day.

The senators were now immediately secured. They had from the windows of the council-chamber beheld what was going forward on the parade before the palace; and at a loss to know the meaning of the shouts they heard, were coming down to enquire into the cause of them, when thirty grenadiers with their bayonets fixed, informed them it was his majesty's pleasure they should continue where they were. They began to talk in a high tone, but were answered only by having the door shut and locked upon them.

The moment the secret committee heard that

the senate was arrested, they separated of themselves, each individual providing for his own safety. The king then mounting his horse, followed by his officers with their swords drawn, a large body of soldiers, and numbers of the populace, went to the other quarters of the town where the soldiers he had ordered to be assembled were posted. He found them all equally willing to support his cause, and take an oath of fidelity to him. As he passed through the streets, he declared to the people, that he only meant to defend them, and save his country; and that if they would not confide in him, he would lay down his sceptre, and surrender up his kingdom. So much was the king beloved, that the people (some of whom even fell down upon their knees) with tears in their eyes implored his majesty not to abandon them.

The king proceeded in his course, and in less than an hour made himself master of all the military force in Stockholm.

Powder and ball were distributed to the soldiers; several pieces of cannon were drawn from the arsenal, and planted at the palace, the bridges, and other parts of the town, but particularly at all the avenues leading to it. Soldiers stood over these with matches ready lighted; all communication with the country was cut off, no one without a passport from the king being allowed to leave the city.

A paper intitled the king's declaration to his faithful subjects was then stuck up in every street; which was to the following purpose; " that his
" majesty

"majesty thereby exhorted all his faithful sub-
"jects and the inhabitants of this capital city, to
"remain quiet and respectful spectators of the
"steps and measures which must be taken for the
"preservation of the public security, the inde-
"pendency of the kingdom, and its true liberty;
"since his majesty has been obliged to make use
"of the power that still remained to him, to free
"himself and the kingdom from the aristocratic
"government which had now an intention more
"than ever to oppress all his faithful subjects.

"His majesty orders also, graciously and ear-
"nestly, his faithful subjects and the inhabitants
"of this city, to remain in their houses, and to
"keep their doors shut to prevent disorders;
"being assured that any one high or low who
"should oppose his lawfully crowned king, or
"should transgress his oath or duty as a subject,
"will be punished instantly, or according to the
"circumstances; therefore nobody is to obey any
"other orders than those which will be given by
"his majesty, on pain of such consequences as
"would follow upon their disloyalty."

An officer was likewise dispatched with orders to the regiments of Upland and Sudermania, which were within a few hours march of Stockholm, to return to their quarters; and that the commanding officer, who was a violent Cap, should instantly repair to Stockholm. This was executed without the smallest difficulty. The precaution the king had taken not to suffer any person whatsoever to quit Stockholm, had necessarily left these troops in the dark respecting the

transac-

transactions going forward there. The orders used on this occasion were in the usual form, and countersigned by the secretary of state; so that it was impossible for the commanding officer to know whether they had been issued by the secret committee or not; consequently the most prudent step he could take was to pay an implicit obedience to them.

An officer, however, who was sent after general Pecklin, had not the same success. The general had his passport and orders signed by the king the day before, to assemble his own regiment and two others. With these he left Stockholm before twelve o'clock. Other orders were given the same day to follow him and bring him back. The officer who was charged with them, found him setting out from Suder Zelia about twenty English miles from Stockholm; he acquainted the general with his errand, who asked him if he had any orders in writing; and upon his answering, no; the general said his own orders were in writing, and he was not obliged to believe every one that came to tell him a story. The officer had no force to stop him, and thus he got away for the present.

Beside the senators who were confined in separate apartments in the palace, general Rudbeck, and all the leaders of the Caps, with many others of inferior note, were put under arrest. No one attempted to resist, to expostulate, or to escape; and the king, who that morning rose from his bed the most limited prince in Europe, in the space of two hours rendered himself no less absolute at
Stock-

Stockholm, than the French monarch is at Versailles, or the Grand Seignior at Constantinople.

The Hat party, in the satisfaction they felt at the downfall of the Caps, seemed to forget that what had overthrown their antagonists, had at the same time destroyed the constitution. They beheld with a foolish exultation, power snatched from the hands of their rivals, without reflecting that they would themselves be no gainers by the event, but that the king alone was to reap the advantage of it.

The Caps too distrusting each other, the major part of them being ignorant of the full extent of the king's designs, as well as how far the whole Hat party might have entered into them, obeyed without murmuring his majesty's orders. Many of them, indeed, appeared solicitous to vie with the Hats in paying their court to the king, and expressing their satisfaction at what had happened; and they seemed for the most part, less concerned at having lost their liberty, than anxious to obtain in lieu of it, a portion of the royal favour. The lower rank of people, who were too insignificant to be of any party rejoiced at the destruction of a government in which they had no share, and from which they derived no advantages. They beheld with the highest satisfaction the power of an aristocracy, from which they had experienced only insolence and oppression, transferred into the hands of a monarch, who was already master of their affections.

Thus without a drop of blood being spilt, a
blow

blow struck, or even the slightest appearance of tumult or disorder, the inhabitants of Stockholm surrendered that constitution, which their forefathers had bequeathed to them after the death of Charles the XIIth, as a bulwark against the future despotism of their future monarchs.

At the commencement of the revolution, the king sent to the foreign ministers to request their attendance at the palace. When they arrived there, he addressed them in these words: "It is "for your own safety, gentlemen, that I desired "your attendance here. I should have been "highly concerned if any thing disagreeable had "happened to you, and the criticalness of the "present moment, did not allow me to answer "for the event. I shall say nothing to you con- "cerning what is going forward; you must "have foreseen it long since. I have been com- "pelled to it, and shall be justified by the cir- "cumstances. But I would not have you remain "in a moment's ignorance of one thing, which I "desire you will immediately communicate to "your respective courts, that what has happened "does not in any shape change my pacific incli- "nations, and that I shall carefully cultivate "friendship and harmony with my neighbours "and allies."

The remainder of the day his majesty employed in visiting different quarters of the town, to receive the oaths of the magistrates, of the colleges, and of the city militia.

His suite increased every moment; the officers of

of both parties uniting to follow him. They all tied round their left arm a white handkerchief, in imitation of his majesty, who at the commencement of his enterprize had done so himself, and desired his friends to distinguish themselves by that token, from those who might not be wellwishers to his cause.

The king likewise passed the whole night in going the rounds through the city, during which time the troops also continued under arms.

His majesty, not content with receiving the oaths of all the civil and military officers, was resolved if possible, to administer an oath of fidelity to the whole body of the people. A measure, which, considering the religious disposition of the lower classes of the Swedes, would by no means be without its utility. A report of the king's intention having been spread over the town, several thousands of the populace assembled on the 20th, in a large square. When the king arrived there, a dead silence prevailed. His majesty on horseback, with his sword drawn, advanced some paces before his attendants. He then made to the people a long and pathetic discourse, in a voice so clear and distinct, that his auditory lost not a syllable that fell from him. He concluded his harangue by declaring that his only intention was to restore tranquillity to his native country; by suppressing licentiousness, overturning the aristocratic form of government, reviving the old Swedish liberty, and restoring the ancient laws of Sweden such as they were before 1680.—" I re-
" nounce

"nounce now (added he) as I have already done all idea of the abhorred abſolute power, or what is called *ſovereignty*, eſteeming it now, as before, my greateſt glory to be the firſt citizen among a truly free people."

The populace, who had not heard their ſovereign ſpeak Swediſh ſince the reign of Charles the XIIth, liſtened to the king with all that admiration which ſo unuſual an addreſs would naturally excite in them. They frequently interrupted him with the loudeſt acclamations, and many of them even ſhed tears of joy. The king then read the oath he took to the people, and had that likewiſe read which the people were to take to him.

In the mean time the heralds went through the different quarters of the town, to proclaim an aſſembly of the ſtates for the following day. This proclamation contained a threat that if any member of the Diet ſhould dare to abſent himſelf, he ſhould be both conſidered and puniſhed as a traitor to his country.

While his majeſty was ſo effectually accompliſhing his point at Stockholm, he neglected nothing that could inſure equal ſucceſs to his enterprize in the provinces. The regiments which were in full march for the city, had, as was before mentioned, returned quietly into their quarters. The king's brothers were each of them at the head of large bodies of troops; Hellichius had ſurrendered Chriſtianſtadt into the hands of Prince Charles; prince Frederick had ſeized upon general Pecklin, who was confined in the caſtle of Gripſholm on account of a manifeſto he had drawn up, up, of which his majesty had got a copy; and all the orders to the governors of the fortresses and provinces, running exactly in the form prescribed by the constitution, those orders met with an implicit obedience from every quarter; so that all things were conducted in the country with as little tumult and opposition, as had been met with at Stockholm.

It is true the soldiers and people in the provinces were in a great measure ignorant of what had been transacted in the city; and the king very prudently resolved that their first authentic intelligence relative to it, should not be till after the states, assembled in Diet, had ratified in the most solemn manner, the change he had introduced.

For this reason the king had by proclamation appointed an assembly of the states on the twenty-first, when the old form of government was to be abolished by the states themselves, and a new one was to be produced by his majesty, to which care would be taken that they should scarcely venture to refuse their assent.

A report was for this purpose industriously propagated, that a large body of troops, which the king had ordered from Finland, were actually at the gates of the city, and quarters were marked out for them in the town, as if this had been absolutely the fact. This could not fail to intimidate the states, and the more so, as from the circumstance that no one could pass through the barriers of the town without a passport from the king,

king, it was impossible for them to be satisfied as to the truth or falshood of this report.

But his majesty did not stop here. In the morning of the twenty-first, a large detachment of guards was ordered to take possession of the square, where the house of nobles stands. The palace was invested on all sides with troops, and cannon were planted in the court facing the hall where the states were to be assembled. These were not only charged, but soldiers stood over them with matches ready lighted in their hands.

The several orders of the state were not on this occasion allowed to assemble themselves in their respective halls, and march from thence in a body, preceded by their speakers, as was customary; but every individual was to make the best of his way to the palace, where they all entered without observing any form or ceremony, each being solicitous only to avoid the punishment held out to those who should absent themselves. It was remarked also, that the marshal of the Diet entered the hall of the states without the staff, which was the mark of his office.

The king being seated on his throne, surrounded by his guards and a numerous band of officers, addressed the states in an harangue, wherein he painted the excesses, the disorders and misfortunes into which party divisions had plunged the nation, in the most glaring colours. He reminded them of all the pains he had taken to heal those divisions, and the ingratitude he had met with in return. He glanced at the infamy they had incurred

red from their avowed venality, and the baseness of their having been influenced by foreign gold, to betray the first interests of their country. Then stopping short in the middle of his discourse—he cried out, " if there be any one among you who " can deny what I have advanced, let him rise " and speak."

Circumstanced as the assembly then was, it cannot appear extraordinary that no member of it ventured to reply to the king. There was however so much truth in what he said, that perhaps shame did not operate less powerfully than fear, in producing the silence they observed on the occasion.

When his majesty had concluded, he ordered a secretary to read the new form of government, which he proposed to the states for their acceptance. Though it consisted of fifty-seven articles, it will be necessary only to take notice of four of them, to give a compleat idea of the plenitude of his Swedish majesty's powers at this day. By one of these, his majesty was to assemble and separate the states whenever he pleased. By another, he was to have the sole disposal of the army, the navy, finances, and all employments civil and military. By a third, though his majesty did not openly claim a power of imposing taxes on all occasions, yet such as already subsisted were to be perpetual, and in case of invasion or *pressing necessity*, the king might impose some taxes *till* the states could be assembled. But his majesty was to be the judge of this necessity, and we have seen that the meeting of the states depended wholly on

X. his

his will and pleasure. By a fourth, when these were assembled, they were to deliberate upon nothing but what the king thought proper to lay before them.

These articles require no comment.

After the form of government had been read, the king demanded of the states whether they approved of it. They made a virtue of necessity, and answered him only by a loud acclamation. It was proposed indeed by one member of the order of nobles, to limit the contributions to a certain number of years: but the marshal of the Diet refused to put the question without the consent of the king; who expressed his wishes that the nobles might have the same confidence in his paternal care, as had been testified by the other orders, where no such limitation had been proposed.

After this had passed, the marshal of the Diet and the speakers of the other orders, signed the form of government; and the states took the oath to the king, which his majesty dictated to them himself. The whole of this extraordinary scene was then concluded in an equally extraordinary manner. The king drew a book of psalms from his pocket, and taking off his crown, began singing *te deum*, in which he was most devoutly joined by the whole assembly. This at first sight may appear to border on the farcical; but his majesty certainly did not mean to impose upon the states themselves by an affected devotion; it was obviously upon the people, who are in Sweden of a very religious turn, that the

king

king designed by this ceremony to make an impression.

The revolution was now completed. The princes Charles and Frederic had been regularly informed of what passed at Stockholm, as soon as the change in the government had received the sanction of the states. These princes assembled the officers of the troops under their command, and reading the king's letters to them, commanded them to take upon the spot the oath of fidelity to his majesty. No one hesitated to comply with the princes orders, when apparently backed by the authority of the states; and it is to be presumed that these officers were not informed with exactness of the manner in which the consent of the states had been obtained on this occasion; or of the true nature of the change the king had brought about.

The princes next hastened with an expedition equal to their zeal, into every town of consequence in the provinces; where they received in the name of the king, the oath of fidelity to his majesty, from the inhabitants and the troops. So that the revolution which had been effected in Stockholm in the space of a few hours, was in the course of a few days, without opposition or murmuring, subscribed to throughout the whole kingdom.

The senators and all those who had been arrested, excepting general Pecklin and another general officer* in Finland, were now, upon taking the

* These officers were likewise set at liberty some months afterwards.

oath, set at liberty; and the most profound tranquillity and perfect unanimity appeared to prevail among the inhabitants of a country, which but a week before was a prey to civil dissension, and all the violence of party animosities. The calm which on a sudden succeeded to scenes of trouble and confusion; the clemency, the wisdom, the impartiality displayed by the king on the occasion; the love the major part of his subjects bore him, and the admiration in which he was held even by such as had been most inclined to oppose him; all contributed to render the change he had effected acceptable to the bulk of the Swedes; and to convince the few who lost by it, how unequal they were to the task of stemming the popular current which ran so much in favour of their monarch.

Thus all acquiesced, and the majority of the nation viewed with pleasure, nay, even gratitude, the conduct of the king. A conduct which reflected equal honour on his spirit, his abilities, and his humanity. Even on the nineteenth instant, in the midst of the possibly dangerous, and certainly critical and weighty business in which he was engaged, he furnished the most striking proofs of that benevolence which peculiarly marks his character. Nothing could be more amiable than his attention to those, even during the hurry and bustle of the day, who were under any apprehensions for the fate of their friends, whom his majesty had caused to be arrested. He sent particular messages to the wives and relations of these, beseeching them to quiet their alarms, and assuring them that every one who was confined should in a short time have his liberty restored to him. General Rudbeck, who was among the number of these, sent to the king a letter he had written to his wife, requesting his majesty's permission to send it to her. The king with his own hand added several lines to it, couched in the most gracious terms, and intreating her to be under no uneasiness for her husband, to whom nothing would happen but a confinement of a few days. He even sent a message to the children of a poor curate, who had been laid under arrest, to assure them their father would be restored to them in a short time, and that they were to be under no uneasiness on his account. Attentions like these, at the moment when it might have been expected that his majesty's thoughts would have been entirely absorbed by other matters of such high importance to him, were the strongest indications of the goodness of his heart: and indeed, during the whole of this transaction, the king appeared less anxious concerning the success of his enterprize, than solicitous to prevent any, even the meanest of his subjects, from suffering the slightest injury.

Though the treatment the royal family had met with at the hands of some of the leading men under the late form of government, might possibly have justified some degree of retaliation, after the king had compleatly possessed himself of the supreme power; yet his majesty then seemed to have no resentment to gratify, nor even partialities to bias him. He appeared to have acquired

absolute

absolute power only to dispense favours and rewards, not to make his subjects feel the weight of his authority. Those who had been particularly instrumental in promoting his designs, were recompensed with a generosity that exceeded their most sanguine expectations; but with regard to others, of whatever party, they all shared the royal favour alike. Many of the Caps were continued in offices of the highest trust and emolument; to which were likewise advanced even some of those very persons who had in the Diet of 1756 trampled with so much indecency upon the rights of the crown, and who had with so much injustice brought to the scaffold the friends of the late king. By a conduct so impartial, so noble, he conciliated the minds of all, as much as he had before gained the affections of the major part of his subjects.

One of his first acts was to abolish the horrid practice of putting criminals to the torture; of which we have seen that the extraordinary courts of justice used frequently to furnish instances. The king likewise issued a proclamation to forbid the use of those names which distinguished the different parties, into which the Swedes had been so long divided, and which had brought so many misfortunes on their country; a prohibition the more likely to be productive of beneficial effects, as the king himself first set the example of shewing that he considered such distinctions as now at an end.

Shortly after the states had consented to the establishment of the new form of government, they were

were again affembled; when they refolved to addrefs the king, to thank him for having rifked the fafety of his perfon in order to deliver the kingdom from anarchy and confufion. The houfe of nobles ordered a medal to be ftruck in commemoration of the event, to the expence of which the three other orders requefted they might be allowed to contribute. On the 9th of September following, the Diet was clofed; when his majefty acquainted the ftates he fhould call a meeting of them in fix years.

The difmiffion of the ftates was all that was wanting to put the finifhing ftroke to the bufinefs he had fo happily atchieved.

The marfhal of the Diet and the fpeakers of other orders, in their harangues on this occafion, were not content with beftowing the higheft encomiums on the king, but condemned themfelves in a manner which rendered them truly ridiculous.

Nor could there be a more ample juftification of the king's conduct than what was publifhed by the ftates themfelves, in an act called, *the reces of the Diet*. They there declare, that " an ancient
" divifion in the nation had broken thofe ties
" which fhould unite fellow-fubjects in confidence
" and mutual love. Often did his majefty in his
" gracious harangues endeavour to reconcile the
" divifions which fubfifted among his fubjects,
" and to reftore union, concord, and a patriotic
" zeal, the foundation of the happinefs and the
" ftrength of free nations: but our generous
" monarch, who perceived with regret, that his

" benevolent

" benevolent endeavour muſt prove abortive, as
" long as the laws were not fixed, as long as there
" was no balance of power in the government, and
" that liberty was daily abuſed; at length created
" in the midſt of the tempeſt a moment of calm,
" to give us time to reflect more maturely upon
" our ſituation, and upon that of our country.

" It would be unneceſſary to repeat here the
" change which took place in the government of
" the kingdom, when the Swedes conſidered the
" royal power as too dangerous, and that we ra-
" ther feared than loved him who reigned. A
" long and painful experience has convinced us,
" that the fundamental laws have often undergone
" changes, forced conſtructions, and improper re-
" ſtrictions ; that uſurpations have been made up-
" on the royal power, the reſult of which was, in-
" numerable diſorders. That the execution of the
" laws was often entruſted to thoſe very perſons who
" were the authors of them. That the corruption of
" morals being become general, the laws had loſt
" the reſpect, and the judges the obedience which
" were due to them. That foreign views influenced
" the national deliberations. That the ſeeds of diſ-
" cord were carefully cultivated in a ſoil already
" prepared to produce an abundant crop. That ha-
" tred and vengeance appeared in public perſecu-
" tions. That ambition and envy had cauſed
" diſcontents, troubles, and even the ſhedding of
" blood. That an amendment of the conſtitution
" was indiſpenſably neceſſary to ſupport a tottering
" edifice. That the public ſafety rendered new
" laws neceſſary; in ſhort, that the yoke of fel-
" low-

" low-citizens, at all times infupportable, had
" weighed down a people who ought to have ap-
" plied themfelves wholly to regain their ancient
" ftrength and fplendour, by the recovery of true
" liberty, under a king who made the laws the
" rule of his conduct.

" This was referved to be the work of our
" dear king, the magnanimous *Guftavus* the IIId.
" And it will be his immortal glory, that with
" the affiftance of Providence, by his own intre-
" pidity, and the courage and patriotic love of
" their royal highneffes the princes Charles and
" Frederick, he has faved the kingdom, which
" was on the brink of deftruction. We acknow-
" ledge and revere the intrepidity and clemency
" of our king. We blefs the great work accom-
" plifhed by a king obedient to the laws, who
" without being compelled to it, has abjured def-
" potifm, by a new oath, and a new affurance.
" We perceive the ancient liberty and fafety of the
" Swedes confirmed in a new form of government,
" which we for ourfelves, as well as for our de-
" fcendents have accepted, approved of, and con-
" firmed by oath the twenty-firft of Auguft of this
" year; and which we ultimately accept, approve
" of, and confirm, as if it was inferted here word
" for word. By this means Sweden has obtained
" a true king to fill her throne, and all the inha-
" bitants of the ftate may at prefent without
" anxiety leave the adminiftration in the hands of a
" king, to whom it belongs to govern and to pre-
" ferve it; who is king not for his own private
" advantage, but for that of his fubjects; and
" who

"who places his greatest glory, in reigning over an independent people, and in being the first citizen of a free society."

Such was the language now held by the states, who but a few weeks before, were accustomed to set, without ceremony, the king's signature to resolutions, passed in direct opposition to his will. And such was the final conclusion of a revolution, by which on the one hand, the king restored the crown of Sweden to its ancient rights; and by which, on the other, he banished from the kingdom foreign corruption, foreign influence, and party dissentions.

I have endeavoured in the former part of this work, by giving a succinct view of such parts of the Swedish history as tended to illustrate the national character and genius of the Swedes, to shew " how far they were capable of being a free people. I have also endeavoured to point out the defects of the late Swedish form of government, and the absurd and corrupt conduct of those who administered it. In the first, we perceive the foundation of those revolutions to which Sweden has at all times been subject, as well as of that, which so lately happened. In the latter, we are enabled to trace out the particular causes of the extraordinary facility with which the present king of Sweden accomplished the destruction of the constitution he has abolished. It were, perhaps, unnecessary therefore to add here any comments upon the transaction I have described. My object was to enable the reader to make them for himself.

I shall only observe that this revolution furnishes

nishes us with a striking, and I may add a useful, instance, of the fatal effects of corruption; for even in Great Britain corruption has had its advocates. It shews, that to restrain too much the power of the crown, or to deny to the lower orders of the people a due share of the advantages to be derived from a free constitution, are equally dangerous to liberty. It proves, that to disgust the nation with the popular branches of the legislature, and to create in them a distrust of their representatives, is to undermine the government. And lastly, the suddenness and facility with which this revolution was accomplished, should teach a free people never to trust too much to the opinion they may have been accustomed to entertain, respecting the security of their liberties, nor to indulge themselves in the idea that no danger is near, because no danger is apparent.

With regard to the king of Sweden, I shall only remark, that if it were ever justifiable in a monarch to overturn the constitution of his country, it was so in the present instance.

In fact, he only deprived his subjects of a form of government, in its own nature incapable of being well administered, to give them another, which may, and as long as he reigns, certainly will be so. Not to mention the allurements of power to a young and ambitious mind; allurements that operated the more on account of the irksomeness of the situation in which the mistaken policy of the Swedes had placed their sovereigns; the influence foreign powers had acquired in the government; the vices and defects of that; and

the

the abandoned venality of those who held the reins of it, perhaps justified as much his majesty's attempt on the one hand, as the use he has since made of his power, has, on the other, proved him worthy of the success which attended him.

If he destroyed the constitution, he preserved the independence of his country. A constitution which had long answered no other purpose, but that of rendering Sweden subservient to the views of its ambitious neighbours, or pretended friends.

In short, should his Swedish majesty continue to reign as he has hitherto done, we shall see the wish of my lord Bolingbroke accomplished. "We shall behold a king, the most popular man "in his country; and a patriot king at the head "of a united people."

APPENDIX.

The Speeches of the prefent King of Sweden,

From the Time of his Acceffion to the Throne, till the clofing of the Diet 1772.

With fome other Pieces relative to the Revolution.

The KING's SPEECH at the opening of the Diet on the 25th of June, 1771.

EVERY thing at this moment, even the place I fill, recalls to me, as well as you, our great and common lofs. When the ftates of the kingdom clofed their laft affembly, they beheld here a tender and beloved father, a refpected and merciful king, furrounded by affectionate fubjects; and his three fons, who contended with each other for the advantage of giving him the ftrongeft proofs of their veneration and love. You now behold, inftead of that pleafingly affecting fight, three orphans overcome with grief, who mix their tears with yours, and whofe wounds bleed afrefh at the fight of thofe that pierce your hearts.

The nobleft reward of a good king, is the love of his fubjects. The tears you fhed are the moft glorious monument that can be raifed to his memory. To me, they are an incentive to virtue, an encouragement to deferve, after the

example

example of a father so sincerely lamented, your love and confidence, by clemency and goodness.

I need not here mention to you the changes that have happened in the government since your last assembly. You will be sufficiently informed of them by the papers that will be laid before you. My absence prevented me from effecting any thing for the good of the public. However, if we now enjoy the happiness of seeing peace flourish at home and abroad, a good understanding preserved, and confidence well established with our neighbours, and the ancient allies of the kingdom, they are the fruits of the prudence and wisdom of those who have had the care of the administration, and to whom I now wish to give this public testimony of my gratitude. I need say nothing respecting the object you now meet upon. You know what the great change which has happened in the state requires of you. You are apprized of your rights, and it is that you might assert them that you are here assembled. To that purpose I wish you the blessing of the Almighty, that peace and unanimity may preside over your counsels, and prepare a happy issue to them.

Born and educated among you, I learned from my early youth to love my country; to consider it as my greatest happiness that I was a Swede; as my greatest glory, that I was the first citizen of a free people. All my wishes will be accomplished if the resolutions that you are about to take, contribute to secure the welfare, the glory, and independence of the kingdom. To see this nation happy is my first object; to govern a free

and

and independent people, the height of my ambition. Do not suppose these are vain words, contradicted perhaps by the secret sentiments of my mind. They are the true picture of a heart glowing with the most ardent love for glory, and for my country. A heart, too honest to dictate what it does not feel, too proud ever to recede from an engagement. I have seen various countries, and I have endeavoured to acquaint myself with their manners, their government, the advantages and disadvantages attending the situation of the people.

I have observed, that it is neither absolute power, luxury, magnificence, or treasures amassed by too scrupulous œconomy, which make the subjects happy; but unanimity, and the love of their country. It is then in your own power to be the happiest nation on the globe. May this Diet be ever distinguished in our annals for having sacrificed every private view, all personal jealousies and animosities, to the great interest of the public! On my part, I shall contribute in whatever depends on me, to reconcile your divided opinions, to re-unite your hearts, alienated now from one another, so that this assembly may, with the blessing of the Almighty, be the æra of the felicity of this kingdom.

The KING's ANSWER to the Deputies of the Nobility, the 20th of June 1771.

THE sorrow expressed by the nobility opens a wound in my bosom, that time can never perfectly heal. The tears with which the people have bathed the tomb of so good a king, encourage me to follow his example. The welfare of the king is so closely connected with that of the country and of the nobility, that you ought to be assured I shall neglect nothing which may contribute to your happiness. My first attention shall be to support the laws and liberties of my people; to prepare to strengthen and augment their union. Descended from a Swedish gentleman, who merited the crown for having extinguished the fire of discord, and delivered his country from foreign chains, I think I cannot hold his sceptre by a nobler tenure, nor give stronger proofs of the rectitude of my intentions, than by following his steps.

The KING's ADDRESS to the senate assembled the 28th of November 1771.

THE melancholy prospect now before us, which threatens an unhappy division in the state, cannot, gentlemen, have escaped your penetration and zealous attention to serve me and your country. Experience shews to what a height hatred and civil discord may be carried, particularly in a free country; and of what fatal consequences they are to the kingdom. Strongly impressed with these considerations, I declared to the states at the opening of the Diet, that my first care should be to re-unite their hearts, and subdue those animosities which had so long disturbed the kingdom, under my two august predecessors. My conscience is the surest warrant of the truth of my sentiments, and what has passed in the course of this Diet, and is known to all Sweden, will bear an unequivocal testimony that my actions have been conformable to what I then promised.

But the more pains I have taken to obtain this salutary point, the more am I concerned to perceive that the divisions of the two parties have changed into a more dangerous dissension; I mean, a division among the orders themselves. I can no longer doubt it; I cannot even be supposed ignorant of it, since an authentic memorial, with the sanction of the orders of the state, has informed the kingdom of their disagreement. But without seeking for remote causes, I need only

only confult my heart, which fufficiently tells me the dangers of my country, and I confult it at this moment. If my birth and duty had not indiffolubly connected my happinefs with that of the ftate, if I did not confider it as the higheft honour to reign over a free and independent people, I fhould remain a quiet fpectator of the event, or fecure to myfelf in future, a more fplendid fituation, at the expence of your liberty. My heart is not fufceptible of fuch fentiments. I voluntarily promifed my people to be the guardian of their liberties; and as long as providence allows me to hold this fceptre, I will be fo; it is in confequence of this intention, gentlemen, that I find myfelf obliged to make you the depofitaries of my uneafinefs. I do not wifh to interfere with the deliberations of the ftates, but I think it as much your duty as mine to prevent the confequences that the turbulence of inflamed fpirits may occafion on all fides, which may have fatal effects, and prove deftructive to the liberty of the ftate. I have refolved to fend for the four orators of the ftates, to reprefent to them the dangers of our prefent fituation: the bufinefs of the Diet almoft at a ftand; my affurances poftponed; the time of my coronation, which I had fixed for the 24th of laft September, ftill undetermined. How many feeds of diffenfion hourly fhoot up, and what uneafinefs muft the kingdom feel in contemplating thefe events! Nothing can be more interefting to us all. Our country ftands in need of a fpeedy fuccour, which it can receive only from me and the ftates. All I mean to say

say will, I hope, be conducive to their well-being, and the support of the laws. I am their king, a child of the state; who in consideration either of my rights or my duty, do not belong more to one order than another; and consequently am attached to all with the same degree of tenderness. Such, gentlemen, is the resolution I wished to communicate to you, conformably to the laws of the kingdom. But I am still more induced to it, by the opinion I have of your abilities, and your concern for your country's good.

The KING's SPEECH to the marshal of the Diet, and the speakers of the different orders, the 28th of November, 1771.

IT is now almost three months since I informed the states, by an extract from the registers of the senate, of my wish to have the ceremony of my consecration performed, in order to lay at the feet of the Eternal, the crown of my ancestors, which he has been pleased to place on my head. I have ever since expected in silence an answer from the states; but the most unexpected events have since happened, whose fatal consequences give me the greatest uneasiness. I should not think I fulfilled properly not only the duties of a king, but even those of a citizen, the strongest and most sacred I ever contracted since my birth, if I calmly beheld the present situation of public affairs.

From the moment in which, by the will of providence, I found myself unexpectedly placed on the throne, by the most melancholy and unexpected event; my constant care has been to restore harmony to my divided kingdom. My actions are known to all, and by them you may judge of the rectitude of my intentions. With these intentions I received the states at the opening of the Diet. I said I would endeavour all in my power to conciliate their differences, and re-unite their hearts alienated from each other. I certainly did not expect to find before the close of the Diet, the spirit of party break out in altercations, the most destructive to liberty and the nation.

I consider the states too highly, and have too much respect for the laws, to interfere in their deliberations. Far be such a thought from my mind. But when the danger is evident and pressing, to remain a passive spectator of it, would be criminal. It would be but a bad proof of attachment to my country, or love for my fellow-citizens, to look on with indifference at events that may lead them to the edge of a precipice. Penetrated with these sentiments, I thought it my duty to send to you the marshal of the Diet, and the three other speakers, to impart to you my uneasiness at the unhappy differences that now subsist among the four orders, which jointly compose the states of the kingdom. I can no longer be ignorant of these differences, since they have appeared properly authenticated in print; which has excited attention as much abroad, as in the interior parts of the kingdom.

If

If my intentions were less pure, less upright, less innocent; if my heart was not impressed with the strongest love for my country, for its prosperity, its independence, liberty, glory, and happiness, I might have calmly waited for events; and after the example of other kings my predecessors, seized an opportunity of profiting by their divisions, at the expence of the laws and liberty. But when I first saluted the states as their king, I contracted an engagement with them, the more sacred as it was a free one; an engagement too solemn to permit me ever to forget the duty which my honour, and still more, my feelings require of me. I know that kings of this country have been unfortunate enough not to have been always considered as tender fathers formed to unite the hearts of their children, but as foreign powers with whom they were to capitulate. But I feel myself actuated by so sincere a zeal for my country, so disengaged from all personal interest, or any views relative to my personal interest, that I hope to establish that reciprocal confidence between the king and his subjects, which past times have too much contributed to destroy.

It is with those intentions which I this morning communicated to the senate, that I have requested your attendance, in order to represent to the states in the strongest manner, the fatal consequences they, as well as the kingdom in general, have to fear, if they do not in time prevent them; and if they do not put a stop to those shocking disagreements, at this time most particularly so, when a general want of money renders the continuation

nuation of a Diet very burthenfome; when a bad harveft gives us caufe to fear famine, the plague, or fome contagious diforder. All thefe calamities which threaten us at once, require fpeedy remedies, mature deliberations, animated and vigorous refolutions.

Happy in being able to contribute my fhare, I offer myfelf as a bond of concord between the ftates, my dear fellow-citizens, and fubjects. I leave it to them to determine how and in what manner they chufe to make ufe of my good intentions. They may with fo much the more confidence intruft to me that falutary work, as I have already declared to them, and I declare it again in prefence of their orators, that, fatisfied with the claims they allow me, I afk nothing for myfelf. I am the only perfon in the kingdom who, born a child of the ftate, do not belong in particular to any one order; who love them all equally, and whofe fate being ftrongly connected with the true intereft of the ftate, am confequently the only impartial perfon in this delicate bufinefs. I wifh to lay all thefe confiderations before the ftates, to whom I requeft the marfhal of the Diet, and the other orators, may give an account of this declaration.

The

The KING's ADDRESS to the States assembled the 21st of August, 1772.

PEnetrated with the most lively grief at the sight of the situation in which I now behold my country, I find myself obliged to expose the truth in the strongest light. The kingdom being now on the verge of ruin, you ought not to be surprized if I do not receive you at present with the same expressions of joy, as my heart used to dictate when you approached the throne. I cannot reproach myself with having concealed any thing from you. I twice addressed you with all the truth my situation required, with all the frankness honour inspires. The same frankness will now direct my words in the necessary retrospect of past, in order to remedy present evils.

It is a mournful, but generally acknowledged truth, that hatred and civil discord have distracted the kingdom.

For a long time the nation has been a prey to the dissentions that have in a manner divided it into two distinct sets of people, united only in injuring their country. You know that this division has produced hatred; hatred, revenge; revenge, persecution; and persecution, new revolutions.

Those agitations occasioned by a few ambitious men have shook the kingdom. Both parties have shed rivers of blood, and the people have been the unfortunate victims of their disagreement; in which

which they were no otherwife interefted, than in being the firft to feel the unhappy confequences of it. The only intention of their leaders, was, to ftrengthen their own power. Every thing was made fubfervient to that point, often at the expence of the citizens, and always to the injury of the kingdom.

When the fpirit of the law has been evident, they have forced the letter of it to their own purpofes; when it abfolutely condemned their proceedings, it was broke through. Nothing was held facred by a multitude urged on by hatred and revenge. In fhort, confufion was pufhed fo far, that it became a generally received opinion that plurality of voices was above law, and they acknowledged no other rule of conduct but thefe arbitrary proceedings.

Thus it was that liberty, the nobleft right of humanity, was transformed into a defpotic ariftocracy in the hands of the ruling party; which was itfelf overborne in its turn, and governed by a few. The approach of a new Diet occafioned a general confternation. Far from confidering the means of conducting properly the affairs of the kingdom, they were folely employed in getting over numbers to their party, in order to preferve themfelves from the culpable audacity and violence of the other. If the internal fituation of the kingdom was perilous, how humiliating muft it have been abroad? I am afhamed to fpeak of it. Born a Swede, and King of Sweden, it was almoft impoffible for me to fuppofe that foreign views fhould govern Swedifh men; much

lefs

less that such an influence should be obtained, by the vilest and basest means; means odious to every Swedish citizen. You understand what I mean, though my delicacy wishes to throw a veil over the ignominy into which your dissentions have plunged the state.

Such was the situation in which I found Sweden, when by the decrees of Providence I received the Swedish sceptre. You yourselves know that I spared no pains to bring about a reconciliation. When I addressed you from the throne as well on this as on other occasions, I always recommended unanimity, and obedience to the laws. I have sacrificed both my private interest, and that of my station; I have refused no engagement, no step however painful, that might produce so salutary an effect, for the national good. Whoever can contradict this truth let him boldly do it.

I expected my endeavours would have freed you from the chains, that foreign gold, mutual hatred and licentiousness had forged for you; and that the example of other nations would be a terrifying warning to you. All has been in vain. You have been seduced partly by your chiefs, partly by your private animosities. All restraints have been thrown aside, all agreements broken through.

Licentiousness has overleapt all bounds, and has been the more ungovernable as it had been for a time repress'd. The most virtuous, worthy and distinguished citizens have been sacrificed; venerable ministers, degraded; whose zeal and

fidelity

fidelity have been at all times acknowledged. Whole bodies of magistrates depoſed. Yes, the whole people has been cruſhed; the popular voice ſilenced; their complaints conſidered as ſeditious; in ſhort their liberty bowed down under the ariſtocratic yoke. The Almighty has manifeſted his anger at the injuſtice of thoſe who had uſurped dominion. The earth has cloſed her womb and refuſes her gifts. Want, miſery, calamities of all ſorts have oppreſſed the country. Far from ſeeking a remedy when I firſt urged you to it, you then appeared more particularly determined to gratify your private feelings, than to relieve your conſtituents. When neceſſity drove you at laſt to take the means of relieving the ſinking nation, the remedy came almoſt too late.

In this manner has a year paſſed, during a moſt expenſive diet, in which nothing has been done for the kingdom. All my remonſtrances having been uſeleſs, and my care without effect; penetrated with grief for the fate of my dear country, I have waited in ſilence to ſee what the nation would think of the conduct of their deputies towards them and me. One part of the nation bore the yoke with ſighs and murmuring, but with ſubmiſſion, not knowing how to obtain redreſs, nor how to ſave their country. In another part of the kingdom they were reduced to deſpair. They took arms. In this ſituation the ſtate, true liberty, and public ſafety being in the moſt imminent danger (not to mention that which threatened my own life) I had no other reſource than to adopt, with the aſſiſtance of the Almighty, thoſe means

that

that have delivered other brave nations, and latterly Sweden herself under the banners of Guſtavus Vaſa. God has bleſt my undertaking; my people have been once more animated with ſuch a zeal for the good of their country, as once filled the hearts of Engelbrecght and Guſtavus Ericſon. All has ſucceeded to my wiſh, and I have ſaved myſelf and the kingdom, without any of the citizens having ſuſtained the leaſt injury.

You are deceived if you ſuppoſe I intend any thing prejudicial to your laws and liberties. I promiſed to govern a free people. A promiſe the more ſacred as it was voluntary. What I am now about will not make me break a reſolution, which was not founded on neceſſity, but my internal conviction. I am far from wiſhing to deſtroy liberty. I mean only to aboliſh licentiouſneſs; to ſubſtitute for the lawleſs and arbitrary proceedings which have for ſome time tyrannized over the kingdom, a wiſe and well regulated form of government; ſuch as the ancient Swediſh laws preſcribe, and to govern as my great predeceſſors have governed it.

The only end I have propoſed to myſelf in all I have done, is to eſtabliſh true liberty; it is this alone, my dear ſubjects, which can render you happy. I ſhall eſtabliſh it by your ſafety under the laws; by the ſecurity of your property, by the encouragement of induſtry; by the preſervation of good order in the town and country; by the moſt attentive care to augment general opulence, and to enable you to enjoy it in peace and tranquillity;

lity; and finally by promoting true piety without hypocrisy, and without superstition.

All this cannot be accomplished, if the kingdom be not governed by an invariable law, the letter of which cannot be forced: by a law which binds not only the king, but the states; which can neither be abolished nor changed without the free consent of both; which allows a king, zealous for the good of his country, to consult with the states, without their considering him as an object of terror; and which lastly unites the king and states in one common interest, the good of the kingdom.

The law which is to bind me, as well as you, is that which is now going to be read to you.

You will easily perceive by what I have said to you, that far from having any private views, my whole object is, the good of the kingdom. If I have been forced to shew you the truth in its strongest light, I have not done it from motives of resentment, but wholly from a regard for your true welfare. I nowise doubt but that you will receive this with gratitude; and that you will concur with me in placing upon a solid and invariable foundation the edifice of public happiness, and of true liberty.

Illustrious and immortal kings have borne the sceptre which I hold in my hands. It would be more than presumption in me to compare myself to them. But I emulate them all in zeal and love for my people.

If you have the same regard for your country, I hope the Swedish name will recover the consequence

quence and glory which it had acquired in the days of our anceſtors.

The Almighty, from whom no ſecrets are hidden, ſees at this inſtant the ſentiments of my heart: may he deign to grant his grace and bleſſing to your councils and to your deciſions!

The KING's SPEECH to the States on the 25th of Auguſt 1772.

IT is with the utmoſt gratitude towards the Almighty, that I addreſs you this day with that ancient confidence and Swediſh candour, practiſed in the time of my anceſtors.

After ſo many troubles, after having been ſo divided in ſentiment, we have at length but one object, the good of the kingdom. It is now time to put an end to a Diet which has already laſted fourteen months. On this account I have brought the propoſitions I have to make to you into as narrow a compaſs as poſſible.

The wants of the ſtate are conſiderable. On my part, œconomy ſhall not be wanting. What you ſhall grant to me ſhall be employed only to your own advantage.

The KING's SPEECH to the States on closing the Diet the 9th of September 1772.

IN terminating this assembly of the states of the kingdom, which will certainly be one of the most memorable of any that have distinguished our annals, I feel myself penetrated with the most lively gratitude towards the Almighty, who has deigned to protect our country, and dissipate a storm which threatened destruction, not only to the liberty of the inhabitants, but to themselves.

This Diet began, in mourning for the loss of a good king and a beloved father. Your deliberations were interrupted by discord and party hatred. It should seem that Providence had designedly suffered the misfortunes which oppressed our ancestors, to arrive at their utmost height, in order the better to evince the strength of his hand in the remarkable change which has just taken place.

This happy revolution has, under the direction of providence, applied an immediate remedy to all the evils, which have harrassed the kingdom for upwards of a century. A nation before torn by dissentions, it has rendered a united, free, powerful, and independent people, zealous for their country's good. It is thus circumstanced that the government of the kingdom passes from your hands into mine. Liberty is confirmed; the laws are fixed; concord is restored.

You can easily conceive the tender sentiments with which I behold you this day assembled before the throne.

The

The few days that have passed since this great change has taken place, have furnished me with the surest proofs of your affection, and of your entire confidence in me. I have seen those virtues, those great qualities, by which your ancestors honoured the age in which they lived, spring forth anew in your hearts, and shew themselves in your actions. They had only lain dormant in your hearts; the present conjunction has called them forth.

That courage, that attachment towards their king and country, which once distinguished the Swedish nobles, have been revived, and have supported me by the most vigorous exertions. The submission of the clergy to the decrees of providence, their zeal for the glory of God, their obedience to superiors, their love of concord, and of the public good, have re-appeared. Be attentive to inspire your absent brethren with the same sentiments. The zeal of the order of burghers for the commerce of the kingdom, has been manifested, since they have acquired a just sense of their true interest and real prosperity. The respect of the order of peasants for God and the government, has shewn itself fully, as from the time they were left to themselves, they have consulted only that love for their country, which has at all times characterized the Swedish people.

I separate myself therefore from you at this day, with a heart filled with gratitude and joy, after you have concurred with me to re-establish upon the most solid foundations the ancient Swedish liberty; after you have regulated a form of government

vernment which favours it; after being united to me by the strongest ties, you may hope for times more fortunate.

I assure you I shall set no bounds to my cares, and attention to merit the confidence you place in me. And if by mutual union, by œconomy and moderation, you second my labours for the welfare of the kingdom, its aggrandizement will be certain; and I shall see my hopes fulfilled of receiving you after six years, as a faithful, happy, united, free, and independent people.

The SPEECH of the MARSHAL of the DIET, on the same occasion.

IT was with the purest joy, and most profound veneration, that on the opening of the Diet, the nobles testified to your majesty in this place, their submission, their zeal, and their everlasting fidelity. It is with a satisfaction as pure and inexpressible, that at the foot of the throne, they this day reiterate to your majesty an assurance of those sentiments which they have ever testified, and shall ever preserve towards the sacred person of so honoured and so beloved a king.

During this Diet the nobles have given the strongest proofs of the regard they pay to your majesty's rights, well knowing that the Swedish nobility, if separated from the interests of the throne, might likewise bring themselves to forget their duty to their country, what they owed to
their

their own body, and to their posterity. They have therefore concurred with your majesty in every means which your patriotism and enlightened zeal had pointed out as proper to be adopted in order to relieve the nation and to establish its independence.

It only remains for us, at the conclusion of this assembly, to form the most ardent vows for the preservation of your majesty; that the happiness of your subjects may continue as long as your precious life; and that the nobles may contribute hereafter to the strength and glory of this fortunate reign.

SPEAKER of the CLERGY's SPEECH.

WHEN, in obedience to your majesty's orders, the representatives of the clergy assembled themselves before the throne, for the last time during this Diet, their hearts are filled with such sentiments of veneration, of zeal, and of gratitude, as no mortal tongue, much less mine, can adequately express.

If this Diet forms an epocha the most memorable of any in the Swedish history, every thinking being must perceive in it the hand of the Almighty, and contemplate with holy veneration the great designs of Providence.

Every government is marked by the stamp of human weakness, that of being imperfect, inconstant, and variable; they have their beginning, their growth, and their end.

In the same manner that an individual by an irregular life, may himself abridge his days; a people may also, by abusing their freedom, contribute to its destruction.

Happy the people who in such a change can preserve liberty, the soul of civil society!—Happy the Swedish people, who can behold your majesty as the instrument in the hands of the Lord, to deliver the liberty of Sweden from what had debased and degraded it! Happy the states of Sweden, which, notwithstanding such a change, may with the same security and freedom take leave of a king, as gracious as when they first beheld him!

Ever memorable assembly! during which the states converted the tears that a just grief caused them to shed over the tomb of a much regretted monarch, into tears of joy, flowing at the foot of the throne of a king born among us; who has fulfilled much sooner than could have been expected, the great hopes which his country had formed of him, from the moment of his birth.

The states do not now separate without seeing the crown recover upon his head its ancient splendour; after the clouds that had been collected by the vicissitudes of time to darken its lustre, had been so wisely dispersed by your majesty, not with the violence of a storm, but by the gentlest rays of bounty, sparkling from their celestial source.

The clergy deem themselves happy in having been witnesses to so extraordinary an event; the
accomplishment

accomplishment of which providence had reserved for your majesty; and by which the Almighty has resolved to pour his grace and mercy upon this afflicted kingdom, by making your majesty instrumental in bringing a remedy to those great evils it laboured under, before they had had time entirely to corrupt and destroy it.

Blessed be your majesty, who so often endeavoured to restore peace, tranquillity, and union, to minds so agitated and divided!

May God grant that Discord be by this means so totally vanquished, that she shall never again dare to appear in Sweden, and draw upon us deserved punishments from God!

Blessed may your majesty be in all you still meditate, in order to complete the great work began in the name of the Lord, that of restoring tranquillity to the kingdom, of delivering and exalting it; so that your majesty shall not sacrifice yourself in vain, for a people whose love and fidelity are fallen to you as an inheritance along with the crown.

The deputies of the clergy separate from each other this day, rejoicing at what they have seen accomplished by the Lord. They will hasten to spread among their brethren and their congregations, the praises of God and of the king. They will proclaim it in the kingdom, that your majesty has not only offered, but in reality exposed your sacred person in order to be the blessed bond of union among your subjects.

They will encourage the citizen, bending beneath the weight of misery, with the gentle hope of better times. A hope which has never been so well founded as at present, when the great Gustavus has added to the list of his royal titles, that of first citizen of a free people. They will be continually at the feet of the heavenly father, offering the most ardent prayers for your majesty, that you may never want that strength which God inspires, to enable you to wear for a length of years that crown which your majesty, by your extreme love for your country, has rendered more weighty than when you first received it. Yes, with the grace of God, they will take every care to contribute to your majesty's satisfaction in the execution of their functions; knowing that by so doing they fulfil the will of their heavenly master, and promote the good of his church.

SPEECH of the SPEAKER of the BURGHERS.

THE order of burghers lay at the foot of your majesty's throne, their veneration and gratitude, at the close of a Diet so happily concluded.

During this assembly of the states, the moment has arrived, from which the happiness and independence of the kingdom of Sweden, may date a new epocha.

From the time of your majesty's accession to the crown, you have continually strengthened the foundations of government.

Your regard for the welfare of your subjects, your ardent desire to contribute to the happiness of your kingdom, and to follow without obstacle the glorious example of your ancestors, have, together with wisdom, guided the steps of your majesty in the road to glory; and the love of your subjects secures as much as their oath and their duty, your majesty's power and authority.

Your great qualities, your approved virtues, and your signal love for your country, would render all form of government unnecessary. But your majesty has wisely considered times to come, and the kingdom expects, under the scepter of Vasa, the height of felicity.

May the Almighty render your majesty's reign long and happy; may we reap the fruits of peace; and may liberty, that most precious right of mankind, be assisted and protected by the laws, under your majesty's scepter. May licentiousness be for ever buried, and virtue regain her empire. May union and mutual concord, point to the true interests of the kingdom, and sustain its dignity and ancient splendour. May discord be for ever banished from the hearts of the Swedes; obedience contribute to the objects of good laws; industry and diligence render the subjects happy; their prosperity become the first pleasure of your majesty; and the welfare of the kingdom your greatest glory!

SPEECH of the SPEAKER of the ORDER of PEASANTS.

AT the close of this Diet, as long in its duration, as happy in its conclusion, when the order of peasants approach the throne, they recollect with the highest veneration, that it is by the tender and zealous cares of your majesty, that the kingdom has been saved, when even on the brink of destruction; that a ballance of power, which has been hitherto wanting to the form of government has been established, and that the ancient Swedish liberty and independence have been restored. Events which surpassed the hopes of the Swedes, as much as they have astonished Europe.

I want words to express the very humble veneration and the zealous attachment towards your majesty, which the order of peasants, and their absent brethren entertain.

The peasants believe they fulfil the desires of the absent, in humbly laying at the foot of the throne, sincere Swedish hearts, as a possession to which your majesty from a love of your country, has acquired the justest title.

The chains which galled free citizens, having been broken; the rights and ancient security of the Swedes re-established; and the foundation of the strength of the kingdom laid in such a manner, that Sweden may hereafter recover her ancient glory and splendour; a new epocha
commences

commences from this day, which will animate the industrious, though hitherto oppressed mechanic; which will render prosperous manufactures, before fallen into decay; and which will incline every subject to respect the government, to love his country, and obey the laws.

MANIFESTO of CAPTAIN HELLI-CHIUS, Commandant in the City of Christianstadt.

IN order to inform you of the intention of the measures which have been taken, to put this town and fortress into a state of defence, and to establish a sufficient guard in them, this manifesto is to declare that it is only on account of certain persons having by violence and stratagem, at the expence of the laws and citizens, dared to take upon themselves most unjustifiably the name of "States of the kingdom of Sweden;" that they have exercised the most absolute authority, have deviated from the laws and limits of justice, and have banished integrity from all their actions, and favoured foreign views. All which plainly evinces that they have taken no precautions to prevent the want of corn, and the misery that oppresses and afflicts the greatest part of the kingdom, nor have they thought of any remedy, or any means or resource for the security of commerce, and the circulation of money. All our bulwarks are neglected. The ruin of the kingdom must soon have followed. Public and private

vate safety were so far lost, that the reputation, honour, and property, of the citizens, had no defence. The most violent attempts have been made against the just and ligitimate power of the king; all obedience, indeed, to his majesty has been laid aside, on all occasions.

From these considerations it was, that the military power of this town and fortress, supposed that such a mode of governing tended to unlimited power; which each of you by virtue of your oaths and engagements, are bound to reject and prevent. On this account the garrison refuse deference and obedience to the pretended states, and consider and declare all they have done to be null and void: and as the most efficacious remedy to the general disorder, they are resolved to persist with firmness in the resolution they have taken, not to lay down their arms till their views are fully answered.

The work, my brave Swedes, is at last begun. Remember what you owe your king and country: shew your zeal in your several stations: let us have but one interest. It is the only way to save the kingdom from a shameful downfall, and perhaps a foreign yoke; which if not yet quite certain, we have the strongest reason to apprehend. We protest before God, in the face of the world, that our intentions are pure, and free from any hidden design. They only tend to the good of the country, and are to answer no other purpose, than to give to God, what belongs to God; and to the king, what belongs to the king.

At Christianstadt this 1st of August, 1772.

The

The KING's ORDINANCE relating to the Factions that have troubled his Dominions.

OUR cares for your general union, having had, by the powerful protection and blessing of God, such happy success, that the states of the kingdom have unanimously received, and confirmed by oath, a new form of government, by which the safety of the subject is established in the most solemn manner, and which has at the same time put an end to all causes of discord and division; we have room to hope, with good foundation, that from this moment the ancient spirit of party, which had divided and torn the nation, has intirely disappeared; and we shall no longer behold the father opposed to the son, the brother to the brother, and every family a prey to the most fatal divisions, disgracing themselves by such actions, contrary to all the laws and ordinances of God, as afflicted all good people, who could hardly conceive that such corrupt morals could prevail in a christian country.

To accomplish with the greater expedition our designs and hopes, we think ourselves obliged to give warning and order, that no reproach shall be inserted in any writing, that might give offence to the different parties that have heretofore prevailed; and that the contemptuous names which have served till now to distinguish them, be never again employed in the odious sense in which they were accustomed to be used.

The

The confidence with which the fidelity of our subjects inspires us, gives us hopes that what has been said and ordered with respect to those writings, and public discourses, will out of zeal and love for the quiet and tranquillity of their country, be equally observed in private conversations; so that the laws and manners may equally coincide to the same purpose, and render the Swedish people a nation happily united in their veneration for God, their obedience and love for their country, and in the practice of all the social virtues.

Given at the castle of Stockholm, the 24th of August, 1772.

GUSTAVUS.

JEAN DE HELAND.

The KING's LETTER to Prince CHARLES.

GUSTAVUS by the Grace of God, King of Sweden, &c. to the Serene Prince our well-beloved and dear Brother Charles, Hereditary Prince of Sweden, greeting;

SERENE PRINCE, our well-beloved and dear Brother;

WE are informed by your royal highness's letter of the 24th of this month, of what we already had foreseen, that captain Hellichius had, upon the first summons of your royal highness, given up the fortress of Christianstadt, of which he had for some time been possessed. It has been proved to the public that he has not been seditious, that this brave officer revolted only against licentiousness and party rage, but not in any sort against us, or against the country.

We name only him, as he was at the head of the enterprize. We shall, however, always tenderly remember those who assisted him, either such as belonged to the garrison, or any others. They all risk'd their lives, uncertain of success; they did not fear even tortures or the most ignominious punishments. True glory braves them all. God knew their hearts, that they were for us, and for their country. Their vows were accomplished. True liberty is once more established. Oppression, persecution, and all foreign views, have disappeared; and we have recovered the royal authority, under which the kingdom might date its most glorious times. The more providential this revolution, the more are we inclined to declare to captain Hellichius, and to those who have assisted him, or obeyed his orders, our gracious acknowledgements, and the pleasure that their courage, firmness, and loyal conduct, gave us. No one can testify it to them in a more honourable way than your royal highness; whose striking example of love for us, and our country, is the subject of their veneration. On which account it is we give this commission to your royal highness; assuring you at the same time of our royal favour, and brotherly affection, and recommending you to the holy care of the Almighty.

From the castle of Stockholm, the 28th of August, 1772.

GUSTAVUS.

CHARLES CARLSKIOLD.

FINIS.

www.ingramcontent.com/pod-product-compliance
Lightning Source LLC
Chambersburg PA
CBHW032353230426
43672CB00007B/681